DISCARDED

THE BACK BLOCKS OF CHINA

PORTRAIT GROUP OF OFFICIALS AND PARTY.

PLATE I.

THE
BACK BLOCKS OF CHINA

A Narrative of Experiences among the Chinese, Sifans, Lolos, Tibetans, Shans and Kachins, between Shanghai and the Irrawadi

BY

R. LOGAN JACK, F.G.S.
Hon. LL.D., Glasgow

GREENWOOD PRESS, PUBLISHERS
NEW YORK

Originally published in 1904
by Edward Arnold, London

First Greenwood Reprinting 1969

Library of Congress Catalogue Card Number 68-55197

SBN 8371-1650-3

PRINTED IN UNITED STATES OF AMERICA

TO

MY WIFE

INTRODUCTION

WHILE the 'open door' is an expression still in use, the experiences of a party of British travellers who were forced to escape from China by the back-door may be of some interest. The following pages give an account of the condition of things which existed in the western interior at the time of the outbreak of the Boxer rising—an anti-foreign movement which there is good reason to believe was fomented by the ruling powers, and which was accompanied by atrocities painful enough to arouse the indignation of the civilized world.

European readers are doubtless familiar with the events which distracted Eastern and Northern China in the year 1900—naturally much more familiar than the Writer, who was cut off during the eventful months from newspapers and all other reliable sources of information; but an unbiassed and dispassionate account of contemporaneous events in the West, however imperfect, may possess some historical value

Three members of the party, representing Mr. W. Pritchard Morgan, M.P. (who subsequently transferred his interests to the Eastern Pioneer Company), had been at work, chiefly in the province of Szechuan, since the beginning of the year 1900, examining mining properties. They were joined towards the end of June by a fourth, representing the Upper Yangtse Syndicate. After camping for some time at Maha, in the valley of the Ya Lung, west of the city of Ning Yuan, they left together for Burma on August 10, in deference to the urgent request of the British Consul at Chung King, and arrived at Bhamo on October 21.

The party traversed a good deal of country previously untrodden by Europeans, and it has been considered desirable to take the opportunity of recording whatever is new to topography. Map No. II. lays down the route and connects it with the observations of previous travellers. It is based primarily on the admirable maps attached to Count Béla Széchenyi's 'Reise in Ost-Asien,' and has been corrected in a few places where it was found necessary to do so, but the Count's maps stood better than most the severe test of being travelled by. What is new has been filled in, and the new matter, such as it is, has been found to 'tie' remarkably well with

INTRODUCTION

authentic topography. Map No. I., which is new, is designed to illustrate the travels of the party to and around the capital of Szechuan.

The majority of the photographs were taken by Mr. R. Lockhart Jack. Unfortunately, his films had been exhausted before we commenced the 'flight' to Burma, and I am indebted for photographs which supply the illustrations of some of the most interesting portions of the journey to the Chairman of the Yünnan Company (Plates XIV. to XVI.) and Mr. J. Davidson, of the Friends' Mission, Chung King (Plates VII., VIII., IX.*a*, and X.*a*). For permission to reproduce Plate V.*a*, which has already appeared in the *Graphic*, I am indebted to the proprietors.

I have, further, to acknowledge my obligation to the Council of the Royal Geographical Society for permission to reproduce Map No. II., which originally appeared in the Journal of the Society for March, 1902. I must at the same time offer them an apology for altering the spelling of proper names.

In the matter of proper names I have followed the system of Professor Giles, which I believe to be better adapted to the wants of English readers than the 'Germanized' orthography favoured by the Royal Geographical Society. Professor Giles adopts, however, the German 'ü' to represent a sound which does not occur in the English language, and in this I follow him. On the other hand, I see no reason for pushing any system so far as to alter spelling which has been sanctioned by usage; for example, it would be absurd at this date to write *Lee* Hung Chang instead of *Li* Hung Chang, or to spell Shanghai otherwise than it is spelt by the post-office authorities.

R. L. J.

February 1, 1904.

CONTENTS

CHAPTER I

THE START UP THE YANGTSE KIANG

PAGES

The mouth of the river—Shanghai—*Personnel* of the expedition—Interpreter—Chinese family names—Signatures and seals—Servants - - - - - - 1—4

CHAPTER II

NAN KING TO I-CHANG

Treaty port of Wu Hu—N'gan Kai—Orphan Rock—Han Kow—Gold washings—I-Chang—Yangtse Lifeboat Service—The Admiral—Chinese ceremonial—A breach of etiquette - - - - - - 5—9

CHAPTER III

THE YANGTSE GORGES AND RAPIDS

The house-boat—Crew and trackers—Chevalier's charts—Tracking—Magnificent scenery—Rapids—Wreck of the *Sui Hsiang* - - - - - - - 9—14

CHAPTER IV

SIN TAN TO WU-SHAN

The (Lower) Sin Tan, or New Rapid—Wrecks—Mi-T'sang Gorge—I Tan Rapid—Coal and limestone—Unburied dead—Tow-line breaks—Wu-Shan Hsien—Taoist temple—Privileges of a grandfather - - - 15—19

CONTENTS

CHAPTER V
WU-SHAN TO KWEI-CHOW

Fossils—Copper ore—Bellows Gorge—Great tracking-road—Kwei-Chow—Salt-works in bed of river—Measure of rise of water — Reception by the Prefect — Finger-nails — British and Chinese gunboats—Mining men—Wrecks—Presents - - - - - - 20—24

CHAPTER VI
KWEI-CHOW TO THE UPPER SIN TAN

Yeh Tan Rapid—Wrecks—N'gan Pin—Curiosity and hostility—The worst rapid, the (Upper) Sin Tan—Great landslip—Perils of the downward voyage—250 trackers — Our ship afire—Diving—Gold washings - - 24—30

CHAPTER VII
WAN HSIEN CITY, SHI-PAO SHIH MONASTERY, AND FU CHOW

Wan Hsien—A pretty bridge—A sleepy telegraph master—New Year festivities—Shi-Pao Shih—The monastery—Its legend—Its Chamber of Horrors—Wrecks—Fung-Tu Hsien—Fu Chow—Coal and iron - - 31—36

CHAPTER VIII
FU CHOW TO CHUNG KING

Ning Shih—Bridges—'Stoned'—Our passenger intervenes—Chang-Chow Hsien—River-gods—A Chinese hospital—Rise of the river—Coal—Arrival of Mr. Bush—Iron smelting—Arrival at Chung King—Steam navigation 36—42

CHAPTER IX
CHUNG KING AND THE JOURNEY TO CHENGTU

Chung King—Foreign residents—Coal—A Mantzü document—Arrangements for overland travel—The 'Red Basin'—Departure for Chengtu—Honours for the cook—Dysentery—Yung Chang—Transport by river—Nei Kiang—Lung Chang—Cave-dwellings—Gill's 'best inn in China'—A geological puzzle—Bamboo irrigation wheels—Robbers' heads—Kien Chow Plain—Poppy cultivation—Memorial arches—Brine wells—Valleys without outlets—Arrival at Chengtu - - - - 43—54

CONTENTS

CHAPTER X

CHENGTU PLAIN AND THE CAPITAL OF SZECHUAN

Intense cultivation—Irrigation works—Seven crops per annum—Opium cultivation—Bridges—Sin-Fan—Pen Hsien—The escort—Sin-Tu Hsien—Shih-Foong Hsien—Mien-Chu Hsien—Chiung Chow—Chengtu city—Bellamy's ideal—Arsenal—Reception by the Viceroy—Chinese officials—Foreign residents—Arrangements for our protection by the Viceroy—A Proclamation - - - 54—68

CHAPTER XI

AN EXCURSION TO THE NORTH OF CHENGTU

Departure for Tung-Ling Tse—Kwan Kow—Irrigation works—Bamboo suspension-bridge—Fine scenery—Alluvial gold—Waterfalls—Monastery of Tung-Ling Tse—Difficult roads—How a magistrate travels—Never taught to walk—Copper smelting—Turbines—An attempted suicide—Medicinal virtue of mustard - - - 68—72

CHAPTER XII

JOURNEY TO LUNG-AN

Departure from Chengtu—An Appian Way—The White Cloud Range—Killing devils—Bamboo water-wheels—Alluvial Gold—An Hsien—The Cantonese club-house—Execution of robbers—The new broom—Missionaries—Fishing with cormorants—Chu Shan—Shih Chuen—Bamboo suspension-bridge—Single-rope bridges—We empty a theatre—Wool from Tibet—Coal—Tung Kow—Kiang-Yu Hsien—Confusion of place-names—Rafting timber—Chiu Chow—Pontoon-bridge—Iron bridge—Lung-An—Temple—Praying by machinery - - - - - 73—79

CHAPTER XIII

HSUEH SHAN RANGE, SUNG PAN, AND RETURN TO CHENGTU

Valley of the Fu—Fortifications against the Mantzü—Suspension-bridges—Alluvial gold—Mining by fire-setting—Primitive milling—'Bits' for artists—The Hsueh Shan Pass—Mountain sickness—Death of a soldier—In the Mantzü country—Sung Pan city—Chinese road kept open through Mantzü territory—Death of Captain Watts-Jones and Mr. J. G. Birch—We bully the Ting—Privileges of travelling officials—Valley of the Min—Mantzü villages

CONTENTS

—Mantzü fortifications and Chinese garrison towns—Mantzü people—Alluvial gold—Goitre—Mao Chow—'Drive out the foreign devils'—Yen-Hung Ping—Lapidaries—Imitation jade—Coal—Sui Chang—Dragon festival—Return to Chengtu - - - - 80—89

CHAPTER XIV

FAREWELL TO CHENGTU

Boxer rumours—Joined by Mr. Way—The start—Extra precautions for our safety—Arms of the escort—The Wai-Yuan and his court—'Not guilty, but don't do it again'—Pei-Chung Cheng—Count Béla Széchenyi's maps—Ya-Chow—Missionaries—Broken telegraph line—Captain Ryder—Yung-King Hsien—Leprosy—Bridges—Cyclopean masonry—Kwang-Ni Pu—Iron smelting and founding—Artistic castings—Ching-Chai Hsien—Peculiar tombs—Fu-Lin—A French missionary—Ping-Yi Pu—Small-pox in the camp- - - - - - 89—96

CHAPTER XV

PING-YI PU TO SHAA BA

Boxer news—Arrival and detention of s.s. *Pioneer* at Chung King—Yueh-Sui—Alleged famine—Prayers against rain—Lolos capture and enslave Chinese—Lolo customs—Richthofen's tracks—A blood-red river—Lu Ku—Iron foundry—French missionaries—A *feu de joie*—Shaa Ba 96—99

CHAPTER XVI

SHAA BA TO MAHA

Bad news from Pekin, Ning-Yuan, and Chung King—Lolos—A mountain pass—Chinese gold-reduction works—Maha gold-mine—Tong Sing Kow—Transport of machinery—Orders to leave China—Preparations—The currency—A new interpreter—Pidgin English—A bid for fortune
100—107

CHAPTER XVII

THE FLIGHT TO BURMA BEGINS

Preparations—Descent to Moo-Li Chang—The Ya-Lung River—A mule slips—Lolo village of Lo-Ko Ti—A much-married man—On Bonin's tracks - - - 107—111

CONTENTS

CHAPTER XVIII
LO-KO TI TO SHU-PA PU-DZA

A road in the bed of a torrent—Practical engineering—Wet skins and dry throats—Goitre—Irate coolies—Sifan hamlet of Shu-Pa Pu-Dza—Flight of the natives—Friendly relations established - - - - 111—115

CHAPTER XIX
SHU-PA PU-DZA TO KAI-JA PU-DZA

Marble mountains—A dry valley—Lolo cave-dwellings—Village of Ta Pu-dza—Valley of Mai-Tsu Ping—Lolo villages—Intervillage warfare—An old grudge—Kai-Ja Pu-dza—Capons—Feminine curiosity—Prisoners - - 115—120

CHAPTER XX
KAI-JA TO KWA PIT—KWA PIT—A PEEP INTO THE MIDDLE AGES

A lake—A gold-mine—Divide between Ya-Lung and Upper Yangtse—Kwa Pit—A hearty welcome—Interior of a mediæval castle—The Toussa's family history—A Lolo court of justice - - - - - 121—125

CHAPTER XXI
KWA PIT TO YEN CHING

Alterations in the charting of the Ya-Lung River—Hay-Lü Tsu—Lolo escort—Valley without outlet—Were we invaders?—Ka-La Ba—A Lolo tribal dwelling—Wheel traffic—The Kwa Pit Toussa's wars—Pei-Sui Ho—Among Chinese again—Chinese hotels—Yen Ching—Brine wells and evaporation works - - - - - 126—135

CHAPTER XXII
YEN CHING TO TAI-YE FANG

Ho-Show Pu—Lignite quarries—Hoang Shaa Ba—The Toussa of Toong-Su—The Pei-Sui Ho—Yen Tang—Brine wells and evaporation works—Into the province of Yünnan—Tai-Ye Fang—The Pei-Sui Ho and the Wu Liang - 135—140

CHAPTER XXIII
TAI-YE FANG TO YA-SHOW PING

Prince Henri's route to Assam—Large limestone sink on mountain—Sifan villages of Peh-Yang Tsung and Ya-Show Ping—Degenerate pear-trees - - 140—143

CONTENTS

CHAPTER XXIV
YA-SHOW PING TO SHOW PING

Sifan village of Po-Lo—A trial for life—Conditional sentence
—A dance—Show Ping   -   -   -   - 143—146

CHAPTER XXV
SHOW PING TO YUNG-PEH TING

A dissertation on Chinese roads—Architectural peculiarities of
Northern Yünnan—Yung Peh   -   -   - 147—150

CHAPTER XXVI
YUNG-PEH TO TUI-NA KO

Alluvial plain—Villages of Toong-Choo Kai-ja and Ching Kwan—Egrets—Ta Whan—Camp in a farmhouse—A brawling woman in a crowded house—Crossing the Yangtse—A stiff ascent—Tui-Na Ko—Copious springs
150—154

CHAPTER XXVII
TUI-NA KO TO LI KIANG FU

Li Kiang plain and city—Chinese men and Sifan women—Protecting missionaries—Discussion of routes with the officials—Our credentials—The Wai-Yuan's letter—A disturbance   -   -   -   -   -   - 154—158

CHAPTER XXVIII
LI KIANG TO SHI KU AND MOO-CHI TI

Return of the guides—A lake—Llamaserai of La-Sü Ba—Foreign trade—Snowy mountains—Shi Ku—Up the Yangtse—Moo-Chi Ti   -   -   -   - 158—162

CHAPTER XXIX
MOO-CHI TI TO KU-TU WAH

Villages of San-Shien Ku,'Kwo-Tu, Kai-Tsa, Tsu-Kwo Tang, and Ta Tang—Coffins in bedrooms—Foreign trade—Birthday of the moon—Villages of Chow Tang, Chu-Kwo Lia, Pay-Fin Chang, Wu-Lu T'ien, and Wu-Lu Pu—Gold-washing—Chi T'ien destroyed in Mahommedan rebellion—Ku-Tu Wah   -   -   -   -   -   - 162—164

CONTENTS

CHAPTER XXX

KU-TU WAH TO WEI-SI

Villages of La-P'si Ku and Ta-P'ien Ta—Sifans—Goitre—Crossbows—Llamaserai of Lu T'ien—The Llama—A consecration and its cost—Om Mani Pami Hum—The divide between the Yangtse and the Mekong—Wei-Si - 164—168

CHAPTER XXXI

WEI-SI

Cooper's troubles—Discontent in our camp—A missionary besieged—Flint and steel - - - - 168—170

CHAPTER XXXII

WEI-SI TO HSIAO WEI-SI

Villages of Pu Ah and Ka Ga—Camping in a hen-roost—Village of Toong-Show Ah—A gorge—The Mekong River—Villages of Pay-Chi Sui, Chin Shan, Lo Kwo, Zing King, Lo-Chi Pu and Hsiao Wei-Si—Bamboo rope bridges—The Abbé Tintet—Exchanging news—Prince Henri's journey—Manifold and Davies at Hsiao Wei-Si - - 170—174

CHAPTER XXXIII

HSIAO WEI-SI TO SHI KU

Shall we abandon everything?—No; try the Bhamo road—Return to Wei-Si—Pediculi—Loss of a mule—Crossing the Mekong-Yangtse divide—Military exercises—Robbers with poisoned arrows—Snowy mountains—Ku-Tu Wah—Ta Tang—Single-rope bridges—Cantilever bridges—The Yangtse near Li Kiang—Shi Ku - - 174—180

CHAPTER XXXIV

SHI KU TO KIEN-CH'UAN CHOW

Divide between Yangtse and Mekong—Snowy peaks north of Li Kiang—Loong-Sui valley—Pay Han-Chang lake—Kwan Shan—Loong-Yu Tsun—Tu Ho—Kwo Tung—Kwo Tsi—May-Tse Sha—Hay-Tzu Show—Kien Ch'uan—Opportune orders from Viceroy of Yünnan—Magistrate issues a proclamation—Telegrams sent from Tali Fu - - 180—184

CONTENTS

CHAPTER XXXV
KIEN-CH'UAN TO CHOW HO

How Chang—Sa-Chi plain and villages—Smoked out—A lesson in good manners—How to ask for the best hotel—Chow Ho—Brine and rock-salt—News from Tali   184—189

CHAPTER XXXVI
CHOW HO TO YANG-PI

Cooper at Lan Chow—La-Tzu Yi—Evidences of depopulation—Lien-Ti—Market day—Foreign trade—Kwa Chow—San-Cha Tung—Ku-Ah Tse—No purchase in money—Cartridges in request—Ku-Ah Tsin—Ah-Lung—May-To—Ma-Ti plain—The worst road in China—Yang-Pi -   189—194

CHAPTER XXXVII
YANG-PI TO CHÜ TANG

A telegraph survey—Tai-Ping Pu—Ta-Niu P'ien—Swan-Pi Chow—Hoang-Lien Pu—Trade in cotton—Pei-To Po—Telegraphic communication under difficulties—Tien-Ching Pu—Sa-Sung Sae—May-Hwa Pu—A blood-red river—Chü Tang—Goose-breeding—Yung Ping   194—197

CHAPTER XXXVIII
CHÜ TANG TO YUNG-CHANG FU

Tia Tang—Hwa Chai—T'ien-Ching Pu—Sha Yang—Pack bullocks—Crossing the Mekong River—P'yin Pu—Sui Chai—Ta-Li Chow—Divide between Mekong and Salwen—The Yung-Chang plain—Po-Lo Ti—Pan Chiao—Cotton weaving and dyeing—A new fashion in tombs—Yung-Chang—Foreign trade—Foot-binding—Where is Sin Kai? - - - - - - 198—203

CHAPTER XXXIX
YUNG-CHANG FU

Missionaries, runaways, or bad characters?—The Hsien satisfied—A 'crier' sent ahead—The Carriers' Union—Drastic measures—How not to do it—The Li Kiang muleteer to the rescue—The Fever Valley—Corporal Lion-in-the-Path—The foreigner's inside—Opening for an insurance agent—Passages in the history of Yung-Chang - - 203—208

CONTENTS

CHAPTER XL
YUNG-CHANG TO HUNG-MA SHU

Ta-Shu O—Nay-Sui Ching—Loong-Sui Ching—Po-Paio—Fang-Ma Chang—Foreign trade—Ta-Ban Tsu—An early start—The magic pill—The Fever Valley—Bridge over the Salwen River—Plague—Ma-Ma Chih—Hung-Mu Shu 209—213

CHAPTER XLI
HUNG-MU SHU TO TENG-YUEH

Shang-Po Tsu—Divide between Salwen and Irrawadi—Fung-Sui Ling—Monkeys—Tai-Ping Pu—The Loong Kiang—Yan-Tan Chai—Khan-Oo Tsu—Chin-Chai Pu—Yeh-Peh—Teng-Yueh plain and city—The jade industry—Items of news—Kindness of the Deputy-Prefect—Wrath of the Chun-T'ai—Through the Chinese lines—A safe conduct arranged - - - - - - 214—219

CHAPTER XLII
TENG-YUEH TO JU CH'ENN

A vast necropolis—A Phlegræan Field—The 'Rumbling Bridge'—Roads turned into reservoirs—Lang-Sung Kwan—Large stone bridge—The deadly banana—Corporal Lion-in-the-Path again—Cheap fuel—Nan T'ien—A Shan village—Chi-Tai Kai—Diversion of the road—N'Yow Kan—High-level gravels—Landslip—Shan village of Tang Fang—Man Pu—Lever reservoir rice-hammers—Shan village of Pah-Yi Tang—Ju Ch'enn—A threatened boycott—The Toussa's Shintai yamen - - - - - 219—225

CHAPTER XLIII
JU CH'ENN TO MANWYN

Shan customs—Kachin merchants—Man-Chang Kai—Peepul-trees—The Toussa's elephants and their function—Betel-chewing—The Tai Ping ferry—Shan villages—Manwyn—We discover Sin Kai - - - - 226—231

CHAPTER XLIV
MANWYN TO BHAMO

Margary's monument—The last mountain range—Kachin villages and tribal dwellings—A military cantonment—Pongsi—Hill fortalices—Across the frontier into Burma—Nampoung telegraph-office—In touch with the world—Myothet—By boat to Bhamo - - - 232—237

CONTENTS

CHAPTER XLV
THE LAST CHINESE CAPTURE OF BHAMO

A sort of a hero - - - - - 237—239

CHAPTER XLVI
THE RETURN JOURNEY

Precautions which miscarried—Inaction of British Consul—Good faith of Chinese officials—Return of our Chinese party—Our return to Shanghai - - - 239—243

CHAPTER XLVII
INDIA TO CHINA

Railway projects - - - - - - 244—245

CHAPTER XLVIII
THE DECLINE OF CHINA

Its causes—Virtues run to seed—The written language—Ancestor worship—Ignorance—Traffic in public offices—Opium—Coinage—Hair-dressing—Foot-binding—Status of women—Breeding of animals—Degenerate Buddhism—Bad roads - - - - - - 245—255

CHAPTER XLIX
A REJUVENATED CHINA

Speculations on the future of the Empire - - 256—260

INDEX - - - - - - - 261—269

ILLUSTRATIONS

PLATE		PAGE
I.	PORTRAIT GROUP OF OFFICIALS AND PARTY	*frontispiece*
II.	LIFEBOAT ('RED BOAT') WHICH ACCOMPANIED THE PARTY FROM I-CHANG TO CHUNG KING	
	GEOLOGICAL PARTY'S HOUSEBOAT IN MIDDLE RAPID, CHIN-TAN (HUPEH), YANGTSE RIVER	*to face* 11
III.	BOW PILOT OF HOUSE-BOAT	
	HOANG LING GORGE, YANGTSE RIVER	,, 18
IV.	SALT AWAITING TAXATION AT LIKIN STATION, KWEI-FU	
	BRINE WELL IN BED OF YANGTSE RIVER, KWEI-FU, SZECHUAN	,, 22
V.	BRIDGE AT WAN HSIEN, SZECHUAN	
	BRIDGE EAST OF NING SHIH, YANGTSE RIVER	,, 30
VI.	PAGODA ENCLOSING STAIRWAY TO TEMPLE OF SHI-PAO SHIH, YANGTSE RIVER	
	PAGODA AT N'GAN-KIN, YANGTSE RIVER	,, 34
VII.	CROWD ON BANK OF YANGTSE WATCHING THE LANDING OF FOREIGNERS	,, 38
VIII.	GORGE ON YANGTSE RIVER	,, 42
IX.	UNDERSHOT WATER-WHEEL (BAMBOO) USED FOR THE IRRIGATION OF RICE-FIELDS, SZECHUAN	
	A COURTYARD IN THE YAMEN OF THE MINING BUREAU, CHENGTU	,, 58
X.	CHINESE WOMEN AT FRIENDS' MISSION, CHUNG KING	

PLATE		PAGE
	MILITARY OFFICIALS AT AN EXAMINATION, CHENGTU - - - - -	,, 62
XI.	CAMP OF THE PARTY AT TUNG-LING TSE, WITH THE ESCORT FROM CHENGTU THE WAI-YUAN MOUNTAINEERING - -	*to face* 70
XII.	PAI-FUNG, OR MEMORIAL ARCH TO A VIRTUOUS WIDOW, HAN-JU CHOW BACK OF HIGH ALTAR, TEMPLE OF KWANG-TI	,, 74
XIII.	ORNAMENTAL GROUNDS OF THE CANTONESE CLUB-HOUSE, AN-HSIEN MANTZÜ VILLAGE OF CHAERGH-N'GAI - -	,, 86
XIV.	WOMEN AT LI-KIANG LOLO WOMEN, YÜNNAN - - -	,, 152
XV.	TERRACED RICE CULTIVATION, SHUN-NING FU VALLEY, YUNG-CHANG - - -	,, 218
XVI.	SHAN GIRL, YÜNNAN SUSPENSION BRIDGE OVER LOONG KIANG -	,, 226

MAPS

I.	PART OF THE PROVINCE OF SZECHUAN (CHUNG KING TO YUEH SUI), SHOWING AUTHOR'S ROUTE - - - - -	,, 98
II.	TRAVERSE ACROSS THE YA-LUNG, YANGTSE, MEKONG, AND SALWEN RIVERS TO THE IRRAWADI, SHOWING AUTHOR'S ROUTE FROM YUEH-SUI TO BHAMO - - -	,, 242

THE BACK BLOCKS OF CHINA

CHAPTER I

THE START UP THE YANGTSE KIANG

The mouth of the river—Shanghai—Personnel of the expedition—Interpreter—Chinese family names—Signatures and seals—Servants.

MORE than 100 miles south of Shanghai the seafarer is warned by the discoloration of the water that he is approaching the outlet of a mighty river. Shanghai, where the old walled city is jostled by a cosmopolitan settlement, is not situated on the chief mouth of the Yangtse Kiang, but on one of the numerous streams which meander through the delta. This stream falls into the estuary of the river at Wu Sung, about twenty miles below the city. It is crowded with ocean liners, merchantmen, and the warships of all nations, the intervening spaces being filled up with Chinese coasting and river craft. Among the latter we remarked, with admiration, long trains of house-boats, each drawn by a tug, plying with passengers between Shanghai and Su Chow.

Cold and sleety as it was in the first days of January, when we began the voyage, we contented ourselves for some time with the cabin of Butterfield and Swire's fine river steamer, the *Poi Yang*, deliberately preferring the glow of the stove-pipe to the glimpses of the distant mud-banks of the estuary which could occasionally be seen through the haze. The first high land we saw—Long Shan, or the Mountain of Billows—was covered with snow. A pagoda was perched on one of the peaks.

At Chin Kiang the river crosses the Great Canal, which (now in sad disrepair, it is said) connects Hang Chow with Pekin. Here the only passenger besides our own party, an American missionary, left the steamer. We were a party of three, consisting of Mr. John Fossbrook Morris and my son Robert Lockhart Jack (both Bachelors of Engineering of Sydney University) and myself. Having not long before left sunny Australia, we shivered in our furs, in spite of a couple of months of preparation in the almost Arctic cold of a Korean winter. As interpreter we were accompanied by a young gentleman named Chung Chui Lin. In Chinese fashion (which is the same as the Hungarian) his name would be written as above, Chung, the family name—corresponding to our surname—coming first. As a matter of fact, having mixed much with foreigners and having fallen into English ways, he signed himself Chui Lin Chung. He wore a blue button, and stood on the third step of the nine which form the ladder of rank in China. He was a fair shot, a fearless rider, an amateur in photography, and a good accountant, and to these and other accomplishments he added an intimate acquaintance with the intricacies of Chinese etiquette, and the ability to speak a grammatical, if somewhat laboured, variety of 'journalese' English. His rank procured for him a certain standing and the entrée to the yamens of the officials with whom we were to come in contact; and to this circumstance, and to his ability to instruct us in the art of decorous behaviour, we were on many occasions indebted for the ease with which we passed through the ordeals of Eastern ceremonial.

It may be said that there are only 400 family names in China. To each family name are added two or three 'little' names, which serve to distinguish the individual. To a foreigner, however, the frequent substitution of an official name for the family name is very puzzling, while on the other hand many individuals are known as Ah Something—*e.g.*, Ah Sin, a familiar appellation designed for use within the family. Signatures are managed by impressing the paper with a 'chop,' or seal, on which the characters representing the name are carved in jade or other stone. Through the imprint of the seal, which is invariably in red, the signatory scrawls, with a hair pencil dipped in China ink, an ornamental character importing his motto, which is usually some poetic phrase, such as 'The Dragon in Wrath,' 'The Phœnix on the Coals,' 'The Beauty of Literature,' or 'The Opening Bud.'

Next in importance was the cook, Ah Mow, a man of forty years of age, bald except for a few strands of hair, which he carefully tended, as they formed the basis of a false queue. He was a good cook enough, and managed all right on the house-boat, but when it came to travelling and doing his best with the limited culinary appliances of the wretched country inns, his artistic feelings were subjected to such daily outrages as, according to history, King James's cook suffered on the Irish campaign. His dissatisfaction increased when he found in the course of his travels that our system of paying accounts through the interpreter did not present opportunities for the 'squeezes' which the custom of the country recognises as the cook's perquisite. He told me, with engaging frankness, that it was not the paltry wage of 20 dollars per month which induced him to take service with us, but that he had hoped to make a fair thing out of us in the usual way. He spoke a little English.

My own 'boy,' Ah Kow (thirty-six), had been in the service of Mr. Luzzati and Mr. Shockley, and was a good, honest soul. Hoo Tung Sung (twenty-five), a native of Ang Hwy, served my son in a similar capacity, his previous experience having comprised service with Dr. Haberl at Chung King, and an expedition with a Chinese naturalist in quest of feathered game. He spoke a little English. On what ground I am not aware, he had conceived the idea that the post of 'Number One Boy' was due to him, and he sulked because he had been assigned the second place, till we were glad to get rid of him. The only real 'boy' was assigned to Morris. He was a merry, growing lad, but in the course of his travels he grew to be ashamed of the 'familiar' name, Hwa Hwa (Baby), with which he commenced his career. He rather embarrassed his master by the *petits soins* which he had learned in a previous service, and was with difficulty restrained from performing many offices, such as putting on his master's socks, which Europeans often enough demand from servants in the East, but which an Australian prefers to do for himself.

CHAPTER II

NAN KING TO I-CHANG

Treaty port of Wu Hu—N'gan Kai—Orphan Rock—Han Kow
—Gold washings—I-Chang—Yangtse Lifeboat Service—The
Admiral—Chinese ceremonial—A breach of etiquette.

HAVING passed Nan King in the dark, we reached Wu Hu at noon of the second day in the falling snow, and moored alongside of a hulk which had been an Annamese man-of-war. Wu Hu was opened as a treaty port in 1899, and is one of the most important rice-distributing centres in China. In spite of the thick weather, we counted twelve steamers, and there was an apparently interminable forest of the masts of junks. A large and very old octagonal tower and a five-storey pagoda, with trees growing out of its roof, were conspicuous above the town, and Christianity was represented by a fine church and mission-house.

Early on the third day we passed N'gan Kai, a walled city with a large new pagoda. As this is not a treaty port, the steamer shipped no merchandise, although some Chinese passengers came on board. In the afternoon we were abreast of the Orphan, a rocky island in the river, reminding one of Ailsa Craig. A monastery perched gracefully, although it seemed not too securely, on the rocks. Later in the day we passed the outlet of the Poi Yang Lake, and reached Kiu Kiang just as darkness was closing in. We could only make out large buildings and a riverside boulevard, or 'bund,' with rows of well-grown shade trees.

In the afternoon of the fourth day we arrived at

Han Kow, distant from Shanghai about 600 miles. The city is too well known to require much description. The handsome 'bund' which faces the British concession is being extended to front the French concession. There is a large Russian brick-tea factory. The earthwork for the railway which is to connect Han Kow with Pekin in the north, and ultimately with Canton in the south, is under construction.

We had to wait eight days in Han Kow for a steamer to I-Chang. Among others whom we met during our stay was Mr. Archibald Little, the well-known merchant of Chung King, and author of 'The Yangtse Gorges,' to whose perseverance is due the introduction of steam navigation on the reaches of the Yangtse above I-Chang.

Having at length secured a passage by Butterfield and Swire's steamer *Sha Si*, we set out for I-Chang. The river is comparatively shallow in many parts of this reach, which is 400 miles in length, and this circumstance necessitates the employment of steamers of light draught. Ocean-going steamers only come as far as Han Kow. The *Sha Si* had again and again to breast the current, while an oil launch was sent ahead to sound and mark out the ever-shifting channel. The voyage took six days.

The first of the gold washings of the Yangtse was met with at the mouth of the Tai-Ping Canal, about 110 miles below I-Chang. Apparently no attempt is made to reach 'bottom,' the surface of the gravel in the part of the river-bed which is exposed at this season being merely skimmed off year after year.

Fu Ting Shing, Admiral of the Yangtse Lifeboat Service, had intimated that lifeboat No. 36 would be told off to accompany our house-boat on the voyage to

Chung King, and that, in addition, local lifeboats would convoy us from stage to stage, and we set out in state to thank the Admiral for his kindness. Our chairs were carried through many courtyards till we were brought up by a closed gate. It may be remarked that etiquette strictly prescribes the particular courtyard where a visitor to a Chinese official must alight. A visitor of no importance must walk from the outer port. After a few minutes' detention the gate was thrown open and our chairs were carried in at a trot. The Admiral, a well-set-up, personable man of forty-five or fifty, met us in the inner court. Once inside, the ceremonial of reception was relaxed, and our host sat with us at a table. The conversation, after our thanks had been expressed, drifted to subjects of interest to us, in which we found our host was well versed. He exhibited many specimens of ores and minerals—copper pyrites, galena, fluor-spar, etc.—mostly from localities within 100 miles of I-Chang, and samples of a quaint art which appears to be a speciality of the district. The material employed is a black slate containing layers of pyrites crystals. By a process of carving akin to that of the cameo-cutter, the pyrites is made to represent flowers and foliage, interspersed among figures of men and animals, so as to form a pleasing bas-relief. Through the good offices of Mr. Wrench, of the Imperial Maritime Customs, I was able later on to purchase a fine slab of this curious work.

The Admiral entertained us with champagne, tea, and lily roots (a mixture which made me feel very ill a few hours later), and, in spite of the watchful care of Chung, I committed what would, in a less-enlightened Chinese household, have been considered a shocking breach of good manners. Tea, as I learned too late, should not be drunk till a guest is ready to take his leave; in fact, for the guest to raise it to his lips while he 'looks towards' his host is to intimate that he is about to go, and, conversely, when the host invites the guest to drink tea the meaning is politely conveyed that the interview is at an end. Being, as it happened, genuinely thirsty, I was so far misguided as to drink my tea as soon as it was brought in, and to ask for a second cup. The retinue was, no doubt, horrified at the barbarity, but the great man, who was also a good fellow and a man of the world, took it in good part.

The ceremonial of entering a room has reached in China the dignity of a fine art, and its due observance is, I am informed, an infallible test of good breeding. Entering by a door in the middle of one wall, the visitor sees in front of him, at the further extremity of the room, a daïs, with a little tea-table in the middle. Straight-backed chairs line the walls to right and left of the daïs. The seat for the most honoured guest is on the daïs, to the left of the host, with the tea-table intervening. The remaining guests, if any, are seated, in the order of their importance, on the chairs to the left of the chief personage to be received. The chairs against the right and left walls are of graduated value, decreasing from the host's right hand towards the door.

The host meets the principal guest at the door, and greets him by cordially shaking hands—*with himself*, and bending low. The obeisance is frequently carried to the length of knocking the head on the floor. The guest watches the host out of the corner of one eye, and imitates his every motion with the precision of drill. Next he makes believe to 'sit down in the lowest room'—the chair on his own left nearest the door—against which humility the host emphatically protests, motioning with joined hands towards the daïs. The feint is repeated and frustrated at each successive chair until the ultimate destination (well understood from the outset by both parties)—namely, the left of the tea-table—is reached. Each member of the host's train or staff selects, in the order of importance, an individual from the guest's following, and makes him the object of identical courtesies until he is safely piloted to his proper place. When the whole of the party has at length been brought into position, the host motions the guest to be seated, and the real difficulty begins. Host and guest appear to apprehend sudden death if one sits down before the other. After many polite feints, the high contracting parties apologetically subside into their seats at the same moment, and the other members of the party follow their example. I have seen this ceremony take at least ten minutes.

CHAPTER III

THE YANGTSE GORGES AND RAPIDS

The house-boat — Crew and trackers — Chevalier's charts — Tracking — Magnificent scenery — Rapids — Wreck of the *Sui Hsiang*.

FOR the negotiation of the gorges and rapids which lie between I-Chang and Chung King, it was necessary to charter a 'kwadza,' or house-boat, and this matter had been arranged for us by Mr. Wrench. The bow was devoted to the crew of nine sailors and twenty-six trackers, who generally put up an awning when we tied up for the night. A large deck-house was divided into a dining-room and three bedrooms, with a corridor along the starboard side. On the raised stern Captain Chen Chuen Ta slept with his wife and family. The charter-party, drawn up by Chung and duly signed, contained some curious provisions. The hire was to be 250 taels of silver, say £37 10s. Additional trackers, if required (and they often were), were to be paid by the captain. There was to be no undue delay, and even for the New Year celebrations only two days were to be allowed. In case of shipwreck, or in case of being unable to pass the New Rapid, passengers and baggage were to be transferred to another craft. We were not to contribute anything to the inevitable offerings to river deities.

Dipping our flag to His Majesty's cruiser *Esk*, alongside of which the gunboats *Woodlark* and *Woodcock* lay at anchor, we commenced a voyage which was destined to be full of excitement and hairbreadth 'scapes. Our crew fired crackers innumerable on their own account, and red boat No. 36 let off three guns.

The passage of the 392 miles of magnificent scenery and thrilling dangers known as the Yangtse Gorges has been described often and well. Admiral Ho Chiu Shun's famous ' Szechuan Traveller's *Vade-Mecum* ' is full of information. Of the English works on the subject Mr. Little's is not only the first, but the best. Mrs. Bishop has added many graphic touches, perhaps with a trifle of exaggeration here and there. Father Chevalier, S.J., has sounded and charted the river with rare skill, and added a scientifi-

LIFEBOAT ("RED BOAT") WHICH ACCOMPANIED THE PARTY
FROM I-CHANG TO CHUNG-KING.

GEOLOGICAL PARTY'S HOUSEBOAT IN MIDDLE RAPID,
CHIN-TAN (HUPEH), YANGTSE RIVER.

PLATE II.

cally correct narrative. It might be thought that, after so many authorities, there was no more to be said; but it must not be forgotten that the river varies from month to month with the fall of the rain and the melting of the snow near its far-distant heads in the mountains of Tibet. Where there is dry gravel in January there may be a swirling current in March. The dangerous rapid of this month may be passed unnoticed the next. The upstanding rock which fouls the track-ropes to-day, may be the 'wrecking reef for the gallant bark' on its return voyage. The proper channel for the mariner to take will depend from week to week on the height of the flood. It will therefore be understood that the river must be known in every state of the flood before a pilot can be certain of the best course to steer.

The broad sail was hoisted whenever there happened to be a favourable breeze (which was not very often). Generally the captain stood on the top of the deck-house to direct operations, the sailors chanting a monotonous song, sculling with two enormous 'ya-lus' lashed to the bulwarks. The great rudder was not enough for steering, and was always supplemented, when rapid action was necessary, by the long bow sweep, over which the 'lao pan,' or bow-pilot, presided with unerring judgment and a fluency of invective powerful enough to cause his men at any moment to throw down their uplifted chopsticks and spring to their posts. As a rule, which had few exceptions, a gang of trackers on one or other of the banks tugged at a bamboo rope attached to the foot of the mast, and provided with a cotton rope and pulley at the mast-head to lift it clear of rocks or downstream boats, which, by the way, always unship their mast prior to making the voyage. The trackers were directed by the beat of a drum, which was seldom silent, and they were supplemented in different places by drafts from the resident coolies who make their living in this manner. Tracking is not done by brute force, but is an art demanding much skill and judgment. Answering the beat of the drum, the coolies would now and then pull for their lives, and at other times merely hang on till the momentary slackening which occurs so mysteriously even in the wildest swirl of water enabled them to gain a few inches. Tow-path there is none, for in the different stages of the rise of the water the place where the coolies can get a footing varies from week to week. Projecting points of rock are galled with furrows made by centuries of the wear of the rope, and steep cliffs are deeply marked with holes made by boat-hooks. One man has the dangerous duty of being always ready to swim out through the ice-cold water to clear the rope whenever it is fouled by a rock. This happened very frequently, and the man risked his life half a dozen times a day under our very eyes.

The atlas with the sheets of Chevalier's chart lay constantly on the table before me, and I spent the time in converting it into a geological map as the strata on the banks passed us in a panorama. When tracking was slow, and a suitable landing presented itself, the lifeboat took us ashore and we walked along examining the rocks.

The conglomerates and sandstones of I-Chang, which are nearly horizontal, form high cliffs on the right bank of the reach above the town. Just beyond Nan Mien K'eng thin-bedded sandstones come out from beneath the conglomerate, and attain a total thickness of perhaps 1,000 feet in the I-Chang Gorge, which must be very beautiful in spring and summer. Above Ping-K'io Ki the sandstones are seen to rest unconformably on highly-inclined strata which look like limestone. Above Pien-Nao limestone-beds, which attain a thickness of 500 feet, emerge from beneath the thin-bedded sandstones and form the walls of the river up to the tributary To-Hong Ki, where they are succeeded by sandstones from 40 to 100 feet in thickness, which rest upon granite.

The left bank of the river above this junction is formed of low granite hills, while the loftier hills on the right bank carry the limestones to the west till they recede out of sight beyond Hoang Ling. The gorge practically ends at Ta-Hong Ki, and opener country begins to permit of a little cultivation, green trees, and grassy slopes. When we landed at Hoang Ling, we saw some lovely green terraced cultivation, which could not have been seen from the river. The little village of Hoang Ling, with its 'miao,' or temple, is perched on a picturesque site high up on the slopes among fine trees.

Between the I-Chang Gorge and Hoang Ling we passed several of the rapids which are mentioned by Mr. H. M. Hobson (of the Imperial Maritime Customs), who opened the treaty port of Chung King, and Father Chevalier, but in the existing state of the flood they presented no difficulty. There were rather bad ones at Chang-Lou Kio and Ma-Pi Ku, where the red boat and the swimmer had much to do to clear the tracking lines from the rocks. The difficulties increased at Ta-Tong Tan, where we estimated the current at ten knots, and there was a choppy sea, with ugly rocks on both sides of a narrow channel. The trackers in this reach numbered 120. All hands worked well and as cheerfully as could be expected, considering that snow and sleet fell constantly, and icicles hung from every projecting corner of the ship.

At He-Ien Tse the granite is succeeded by a hard blue-gray rock (greywacke?), which occupies both banks of the river as far as Miao-Ho, where thin-bedded gray sandstones, 300 or 400 feet thick, dip at 25° to the south-west, beneath limestones at least 2,000 feet in thickness. The limestone forms the frowning Niu-Kow-Ma-Fei (Liver and Lung Gorge). The bow-pilot pointed out what I took to be the ' lung,' a somewhat lung-shaped rock hanging out above a precipice a few hundred yards below a cavern —not *in* the cavern where Chevalier looked for it.

The island (Kung- or Tung-Ling) at the outlet of the gorge, with the precipitous limestone cliffs for a background, formed the subject of a successful photograph (Plate III.). Ten months later it saw the terrible wreck of the new German steamer, *Sui Hsiang*.

About six miles above Ta-Tong there were boiling rapids at Hsiao-K'ong Ling and K'ong Ling Chow, but the current was not too strong to permit of the sail keeping the ship in position when the track-line slacked.

CHAPTER IV

SIN TAN TO WU-SHAN

The (Lower) Sin Tan, or New Rapid—Wrecks—Mi-T'sang Gorge—I Tan Rapid—Coal and limestone—Unburied dead—Tow-line breaks—Wu-Shan Hsien—Taoist temple—Privileges of a grandfather.

THE limestone continues to near the village of Sin Tan (New Rapid), which is prettily situated on the left bank. Here, just beneath the temple, gray shales and ripple-marked flags, dipping at 45° to north-north-west (and probably belonging to the limestone series which had been continuous from Miao-Ho), are succeeded, with a violent unconformity, by the conglomerate on which the temple is founded. The conglomerate has remarkably large boulders and pebbles of limestone, granite, quartzite, lydianite and jasper. The largest are of limestone; some of them must weigh a ton at least. The joints and bedding-planes on these large limestone blocks were covered with a black coating, which, on being struck with a hammer, gave out a distinct odour of petroleum. The conglomerate (about 200 feet thick) appears to form the base of the thick limestone beds of the Mi-T'sang Gorge, which commences above Sin Tan.

Because of the evil reputation of the Sin Tan, we were landed on the left bank of the river, two wrecks bearing silent but eloquent testimony to the wisdom of the precaution.

There are two rapids. The lower, just above the mouth of the gully, named Long-Ma Ki, was a boiling swirl, but our 'kwadza' surmounted it in safety. A house-boat in front of us was less fortunate than ours, and, knocking a hole in her bottom, had to discharge her cargo and put six men on the pumps.

Having sailed across to the right bank, our 'kwadza' took her place among a score of junks waiting their turn to be tracked up the Upper Rapid. We had to wait a whole day, during which a light snow fell without intermission. The motion of the moored boat was so unpleasant that Chung suffered from sea-sickness. The alert lifeboats hovered about. The crews get a small gratuity for every corpse recovered, and a larger one for every life saved. Many junks shot down the rapid while we waited, and we could not help being wildly excited as one after another they passed us, every man on board straining at the oars and bow sweep. We were told that we were singularly unfortunate in being on the spot so long without seeing a wreck or two, and, indeed, the escape of every one of the ships seemed little less than a miracle. The haulage up the river was done with three or four ropes, which gave a straight pull up close to the right bank. Late in the afternoon the junk in front of us broke her lines and went down the river at racing speed, but was able to pull up among the waiting craft, sustaining no injury beyond the loss of her place in the rank. When our own turn came, we had three ropes out and 200 extra men on them. A steady and very slow pull brought us out into smooth water, where we moored for the night. There is about a foot of difference between the level of the water above and below the rapid, caused by a bar of rock which stretches across the river. On the left bank the difference is perhaps 4 feet in 20 or 30 yards, and our lifeboat, 'just to show us how it could be done,' made the ascent on that side in ten minutes of very hard work and splendid seamanship.

The Mi-Tsang Gorge, which we passed through in the gray of the morning, too early for sight-seeing, is perhaps finer than the I-Chang Gorge, and is certainly deeper. Its walls are composed of a great thickness of white limestone, weathering to yellow. At the upper end of the gorge gray thin-bedded and flaggy sandstones, having a tendency to concentric weathering, are met with. Above Chi Mun is a great thickness of chocolate-coloured and gray shales. At the little walled town of Kwei Chow (province of Hupeh) the gray sandstones reappear. The whole of the strata from the gorge to the town form a continuous series.

The I Tan Rapid was a swift ripple with high waves coming off a cone of dejection on the left bank. It had 2 feet of fall.

The outcrop of a coal-seam was seen high up on the left or northern bank. The coal is made into briquettes with clay. We landed above the outcrop, and saw gray sandstones with thin beds of limestone and some red shales. After we had been taken on board the red boat, a strong breeze sprang up, and we had to chase the 'kwadza' up to the Niu-Kow Rapid. The rapids marked on the chart (Ta-Pa Chow and Hsiao Pa-Chow) did not prove formidable, as both the 'kwadza' and the red boat negotiated them under sail. Niu-Kow Tan was fairly exciting, a strong wavy ripple, coming off the left bank, necessitating the assistance of a good many extra trackers. We passed a very fine gorge in limestone rocks, between Wang-Yei Miao (temple) and Fu-Li Tsi. The town of Pa-Tong Hsien, on the right bank, was guessed to contain about 5,000 inhabitants, and looked prosperous.

At Fu-Li Tsi the banks opened out, and there were some beautiful moss-green patches of old cultivation on the hill slopes, to which narrow limestone gorges succeeded. The latter extend as far as Pu-Tai Kow, where we left Hupeh and entered the province of Szechuan. Anxious to set foot on the sacred soil of Szechuan (which was our goal), we landed on the southern side of the river at Pei Shih. Here some officers, who had taken me for an expected European named Pi (who could he be ?), came on board and presented their big red visiting cards. We found a 'kwadza' belonging to a French missionary, who was said to be at a church ten miles distant. We visited a small temple which was full of coffins. The inmates, we were told, were waiting patiently till soothsayers skilled in 'fung-shui' (atmospheric influences) should discover favourable places for sepulture. A long tracking-road or tow-path was benched out of the perpendicular limestone cliffs above high-water mark. Rejoining the house-boat, we were rowed, sailed, and tracked, through limestone gorges to Wu-Shan Hsien. The limestone beds on the right bank near Lao-Shu Chu were twisted into remarkable contortions.

About 6 p.m., when we were within sight of our mooring-ground near Wu-Shan Hsien, and tracking round a rock on the right bank, the tow-line broke, a spud dropped through a sort of centre-board case in the bows to hold her doubled up under the 'kwadza,' and as we spun round and swept downstream one of the yalus broke with a tremendous crash. In a moment the boat became a floating Babel. The

Bow Pilot of Houseboat.

Hoang Ling Gorge, Yangtse River.

PLATE III.

captain shrieked that we were lost, and everybody shouted orders which nobody heeded. To add to the confusion, the captain's wife seized a bamboo and jabbed for bottom on the downstream side, with the natural result that she lost the pole and nearly got jerked overboard as the ship rode over it. Thereafter she confined herself to shrieking orders. At last, after we had taken the ground twice, a young fellow who had not lost his head stepped into 3 feet of water with a rope, which he tied to a rock ashore, and we pulled up on a shingle bank at the eastern corner of the town.

The following day (January 31) was the Chinese New Year. In the morning we changed our moorings to a safer place above the town. Wu-Shan, a ' hsien' (or county town) surrounded by a wall, was *en fête*, and a deafening noise was produced by crackers, gongs, drums, and flutes. We sent our cards to the magistrate (Pei-Shung Shi), who returned his own with a message that he would send with us a lifeboat and an order enabling us to requisition trackers as required. With an escort of two of the marines of the I-Chang red boat and our boys, we took a walk through the town, followed by an immense crowd of good-humoured sight-seers. We sent a telegram, and visited two Taoist temples, and secured some good photographs. One group of priests included a man who insisted on his right to be taken because he carried his grandson in his arms. Such is the respect for age in China that a grandfather's right to do whatever he pleases is never questioned.

CHAPTER V

WU-SHAN TO KWEI-CHOW

Fossils—Copper ore—Bellows Gorge—Great tracking-road—Kwei-Chow—Salt-works in bed of river—Measure of rise of water—Reception by the Prefect—Finger-nails—British and Chinese gunboats—Mining men—Wrecks—Presents.

WE got away early next morning, and went ashore while our 'kwadza' climbed up the rapid of Hia-Ma, an operation which took nearly two hours, as the rope broke and a good half-mile was lost. After a diligent search for fossils, we found some encrinites, echinus spines, *Rhynchonella* (?), and a bird bone (?), in a limestone on the left bank above the rapid. A small junk was seen going down the river flying the British ensign. Between this point and Kwei-Chow there are many swift rapids, and consequently much hard tracking.

On the left bank, a little below Kin-Ing Ho, we saw traces of copper in red shales. The magnificent Bellows Gorge, about five miles in length, lies between this point and Kwei-Chow Fu. The tracking-road on the limestone cliffs on the north side, above high-water mark, is one of the grandest works in China, although it is open to question if the labour expended on it would not have been better employed on a railway-line. It is built up on high walls, or benched out of perpendicular rocks. Gullies are bridged over with squared slabs of limestone. Where ascents have to be made there are broad flights of stairs. Some of the ugliest bits had parapets, and many more ought to have had them. The rock had been blasted with powder, and the drill-holes and tool-marks were still fresh.

In a rift of the rock, about 100 feet above the road, we saw five boxes, which we took, and still believe, to be coffins. Chung, however, was told that local tradition has it that they are of great, but unknown, age. It is said that about fifty years ago a bold robber removed one of them, from which he abstracted some valuables, whereupon a furious storm arose, and convinced the authorities that some unholy deed had been committed. The Fu (Prefect) of Kwei-Chow, having captured the robber, ordered him, on pain of death, to restore the box, which was done, and the storm was changed into a calm. When we visited the present Fu (Chu Yuen Hse), a man of about seventy-two years of age, he confirmed the story of the robbery, and added that the boxes have been in their present position for 1,000 years. He informed us that the road was made about ten years ago, the cost, 100,000 taels (say £33,000), having been defrayed by public subscription. He said that he had had a letter from the Fu of I-Chang recommending us to his care.

When the 'kwadza' was pulled up at Chow-Yen Tsi, below the city, it was found to be leaking badly, and that some of our goods in the hold were lying in 3 inches of water. A wrecked junk silently testified to the dangers of navigation higher up the river.

The principal industry of Kwei-Chow is salt. The brine well is situated in the bed of the river, beneath the gravelly cone of dejection brought down by the Jang-Ki Kow, just below the city. The river here must rise 200 feet, but half its bed is dry at this season, and the workmen's town, named Chow-Yen

Tsi, is annually built on it beside the well. The well itself and the evaporating furnaces are annually dug out of the gravel with which the floods have covered them. It is sunk a few feet into the solid rock —horizontal beds of gray shale or limestone (?)—and its four sides are built up with steps like a dry-dock. Fifteen naked men stand in two tiers baling out the brine and emptying it into the carriers' buckets. As it comes from the well the brine tastes strongly of sulphuretted hydrogen, and somewhat weakly of salt. The carriers climb up the steps to a level of about 10 feet above the natural surface, where they empty the brine into settling-pits, whence it is run in bamboo troughing into evaporating pans of iron built in over furnaces. Coal for the furnaces comes in long, narrow, flat boats from a place about thirty miles up the Jang-Ki Kow, but, as that river loses itself in its own cone of dejection, has to be carried in baskets for the last half-mile (Plate IV.).

A Chinese gentleman, who represented Butterfield and Swire at Kwei-Chow, called on us and explained that the question of the day was how to get the brine from the well all the year round. We had to admit that the problem was beyond our skill.

The Magistrate (Prefect), it may be mentioned, received our visit with great ceremony, and when we left conducted us personally out of the inner courtyard between two lines of men-at-arms, who carried poles surmounted with griffins, tigers, and other heraldic devices, the gongs and drums making a noble din. Later in the day he returned our call in state, but, as he was unable to walk the plank which formed the communication between the bank of the river and the house-boat, I conversed with him while

SALT AWAITING TAXATION AT LIKIN STATION, KWEI-FU.

BRINE WELL IN BED OF YANGTSE RIVER, KWEI-FU, SZECHUAN.

PLATE IV.

he sat in his sedan-chair. He had reason to be proud of his finger-nails, which were as long as his fingers. In China the nails are cherished as a sign of distinction. When they are 3 inches in length they undoubtedly prove that the owner never performs any manual labour.

On the invitation of a mining engineer named Wong Su, we visited his office and inspected a collection of copper ores from the surrounding district. On the way we met a procession of men on horseback with banners, arms, lanterns, etc., and little children (also on horseback), highly painted and gorgeous as to head-gear, decorated as it was with 5-feet tail feathers of pheasants. The occasion of the display was that the Prefect was going to the temple to make New Year sacrifices.

At Kwei-Chow we overtook a house-boat in which Captains Watson and Hillman, R.N., were making the voyage with a view to judging of the fitness of the river for the passage of their gunboats, the *Woodcock* and *Woodlark*. They had been delayed three days at the Sin Tan. For the remainder of the voyage to Chung King, their and our house-boats made a 'neck and neck' race—if the term can be applied to our tortoise-like progress. An officer called with the visiting-card of H.E. Li Cheng Yung, the Imperial Commissioner for Mines, and said that he had been ordered to accompany us with a gunboat if so desired. We declined the honour with many thanks. The gunboat of the Upper Yangtse is a rowing-boat, carrying a swivel-gun, whose chief use seems to be the firing of salutes, but it is quite possible that its presence may inspire respect and keep off pirates.

Two secretaries of mining companies called on us.

They had hardly made their obeisances and been seated, when, forgetting my previous lesson, I offered them tea, and made a motion with my own cup. To my dismay, they were off in an instant, as the interpreter did not happen to be at hand to explain that it was not my intention to dismiss them. They had time before they left to inform me (through Ho) that a junk belonging to their company had been lost at the Sin Tan the day before we passed it, and that 7,000 taels (£1,000) had gone down with her.

Next day, after we had started, we were overtaken by a boat with a large present of beef and mutton from these gentlemen, so that I am encouraged to hope that they had not taken offence at the premature invitation to drink tea. Presents in China form a point of ceremonial which must not be treated lightly. It is not the custom to take all that is offered, but a portion is selected and an equivalent is returned, or a present of equal value is given to the messenger.

CHAPTER VI

KWEI-CHOW TO THE UPPER SIN TAN

Yeh Tan Rapid—Wrecks—N'gan Pin—Curiosity and hostility—The worst rapid, the (Upper) Sin Tan—Great landslip—Perils of the downward voyage—250 trackers—Our ship afire—Diving—Gold washings.

BETWEEN Kwei-Chow and N'gan Pin, the hills forming the walls of the valley are composed of limestones, sandstones, and gray and red shales, with a few beds of chert-conglomerate. The strata undulate, but on the whole dip to the north-east. We landed on the left bank near Pa-Mu Tse, and walked to the Hao-Kan Rapid. In the limestone at Kwan-Tao Hia we got fossil brachio-pods of the same species as those found at Hia-Ma.

A rather nasty rapid is produced by the cone of dejection formed by the little river just below N'gan Pin. Two junks had met with disaster, one of them just before our arrival. The Yeh Tan, mentioned by Chevalier as having the reputation of being 'dangerous at high-water and still more so at mean-water,' though confined to a narrow passage, we found to be only a ripple at low-water.

As we strolled through the little town of N'gan Pin, visiting the temple and other noteworthy objects, we were followed by a crowd which before we left for the boat, increased to rather troublesome proportions. The chief feeling of the townsmen at first seemed to be curiosity, and they touched my beard, gloves, and clothing, and even wanted to try on my spectacles. When we left, however, and went down the hill, they commenced talking noisily, and a very small stone clattered behind us. Ho said the conversation was about how easy it would have been, as we stood in certain positions, to have pushed us over the cliff or 'bashed' our heads, and so forth.

From N'gan Pin to Miao-Ki Tse, the river follows the strike of the rocks, which dip to the north-north-west at about 30°. They consist of gray sandstones and shales—some of the latter red—and a few beds of limestone. The tow-line broke at one rapid, and we lost a good deal of ground. At another it got fouled on the bottom, and our stern bumped the sandstone cliff on the left bank. As we approached the rapid at Miao-Ki Tse, its character was attested by two wrecks.

Both this and the Tung-Yang Rapid caused a good deal of delay, chiefly in waiting for other junks. Their chief dangers are the rocks on both sides of the passage.

A little beyond Miao-Ki Tse the sandstone strata (with gray and red shales) begin to flatten; thence to Yün-Yang Hsien they are absolutely horizontal. Just below the city they begin to rise to the north; on the opposite bank the rise is about 15°, on the left bank it is 20°, and in the hill behind the city on the north, 40°.

We found that the Magistrate in charge of the city had gone to Wan Hsien, but his secretary, on my application, sent a lifeboat to wait for us at the 'New Sin Tan,' and runners to smooth the way.

The Sin Tan, or New Rapid, is about nine miles west of Yün-Yang Hsien. It is the newest 'New Rapid.' The name is a bad one, but we have our own New Castles, New Towns, New Rivers, and New Cuts, and need not cavil at the poverty of Chinese nomenclature.

An east-and-west reach extends for six miles above Yün-Yang, and the river follows the strike of gray sandstones, with limestones, which dip to the south at a low angle (15°) on the south bank, at a higher (35°) on the north bank, and before reaching the hill-tops on the northern side at an angle which is steeper than the slope of the hills. At the end of this reach (at San-Pa Ki, where there is a rapid) the river turns to the south-west, thus passing to the south of the synclinal axis, and the strata on both banks have nearly the same dip (10° to 15° to the south). Towards Sin Tan the sandstones become more red than gray, and there are numerous partings of red shale, and the dip is somewhat to the east of south.

At the Sin Tan itself the dip of the strata is to the south-east—that is, at right angles to the course of the river, and the angle is equal to the slope of the hills. This geological structure is specially favourable to the production of landslips, as in any period of heavy rain the saturated partings of shale form greasy beds on which the overlying sandstones must ride towards the river. This, according to Chevalier, is exactly what took place in 1896, and his account was confirmed by the residents, and by the pilots and captains of junks with whom we conversed. Part of the topmost bed of sandstone has moved since the slip of 1896, and here the fracture looked new and raw, while the remainder of the cliff was so weathered that I had no doubt that it formed the wall of the valley of a gully. The gully was probably over the line of a 'master' joint in the sandstone, which gave access to the water which converted the shale into mud. The extent of the slip is uncertain, for nobody can swear to the identity of the debacle of sandstone blocks which covers the fallen portion. My impression is that the debacle is the ruin of the lower bed of sandstone, and that the upper bed was denuded away from the spot before 1896. In that case the vertical displacement would be about 60 feet, whereas if the ruin belongs to the upper bed the displacement would be about 100 feet. The outer (western) limit of the slip is not clear. The whole movement has involved an area of about half a mile long, by a quarter of a mile wide. The fallen ground is not crevassed, as might have been expected, and the continuity of the strata in the fallen area has not been much disturbed.

Old trees on it still grow as well as ever they did, and cultivation has taken possession of the whole.

We had to wait twenty-three hours before our ship began to move up, and had opportunities of watching several junks shooting the rapid. One junk broke her bow sweep, and, becoming involved in the whirlpool below the rocks, spun round about a dozen times before getting out of it. Our moorings and those of the naval officers' 'kwadza,' were on the left (northern) bank above the whirlpool. We observed that, as a rule, boats which had come down the river came up to their moorings stern foremost, and there swung round—apparently a ticklish manœuvre.

Coming up the rapid, ships have to be hauled very carefully round a point of rock into quiet water, taking care not to go too far out on account of a bad stone just awash. (Surely this stone could be blown up.) This operation took our 'kwadza' seventeen minutes. Numerous tracking-lines were out, and no less than 250 men were hauling or holding for dear life. To watch the struggle from the bank was enough to thrill us with excitement. I should recommend all travellers in search of adventures to watch the passage of the rapids, as we did, from the shore. It is much safer, and passengers can be of no use on board at such a time, and may confidently leave the affair in the hands of the Chinese, than whom there are no bolder or more skilful boatmen in the world.

The rapid is formed by ripples coming off both banks, and on the north side of the lower end of the northern ripple is the whirlpool. I use the term 'ripples,' but the ripples are high waves, under which if a downward-bound junk once gets her bow she is lost. The waves are nearly, if not quite, as high as those below the falls of the Rhine at Schaffhausen, and to be shot down into them at a rate too rapid for effective steering is to run a great risk. There is an obvious drop of at least 2 feet where the smooth water ends and the ripple begins. Before the lower end of the ripple is reached there may be a further fall of 2 feet.

The passage is entirely forbidden at certain seasons. Three wrecks occurred the day before our arrival, with the loss of as many lives. Chevalier says that in March this rapid is, 'after that of Yün-Yang Hsien, the most difficult to clear, either for junks or steamers.'

We reckoned that all the trouble might be averted (at low-water) by cutting a boomerang-shaped canal in the sandstone to a depth of about 40 feet. Of course, when the water is high the canal would be useless, and the channel would be between the sandstone ledges and the southern bank.

We found plenty of occupation ashore in the busy settlement occupied by the trackers and the coolies whose employment is to shift the cargoes of junks which do not care to take the risk of carrying them up or down the rapid. A handful of orange-peel was thrown at us while our backs were turned.

It was not till the following day that I discovered the cause of our detention. It appears that ships carrying officials or foreigners are entitled to requisition trackers at half-rates. Naturally, the trackers do not like the arrangement (in which there is neither reason nor justice), and take care to be employed on other jobs when they are wanted.

Above the rapid we tracked up smooth water to

Hoang-Pei-Ki Chang. As we ascended, the sandstone strata took a gradually lower dip, which swung round from south to west. On the rocks at Kiu-Tui Tse there were carved three seated and highly-coloured figures, in the costume of the Ming Dynasty (according to Chung), representing the 'Spirits of the River.'

Just as we came to our moorings at nightfall, an alarm of fire was raised. A lamp had burned through the joist from which it hung by a wire, and fell with a crash beside Lockhart, who sat reading. The cabin floor was ablaze in an instant, but the flames were extinguished with wet sand by the crew, and Lockhart threw the lamp out of the window, not without some damage to his hands. The sequel was interesting. I never expected to see the lamp again, as it had gone down in a rapid current over a shelving bottom; but I made what I considered a 'sporting' offer of 1,000 cash (2 shillings) for its recovery, and one of the red-boat men claimed the reward after diving for about an hour—a good piece of work, as the lamp had rolled right under the boat into deeper water.

The sandstones, with partings of red shale, are horizontal, and form hills at some distance from the river between Hoang-Pei-Ki Chang and our next moorings at Pong-Sha Tzi. (It would be incorrect to use the word 'anchorage,' as few anchorages are possible in the rapid current.) Gold-washing was going on all along this reach, on a low beach formed out of the periodical waste of a higher. A 'cradle,' not unlike that which was at one time familiar in Australia, was in common use. Similar rocks prevailed as far as Wan Hsien.

BRIDGE AT WAN HSIEN, SZECHUAN.

BRIDGE EAST OF NING SHIH, YANGTSE RIVER.

PLATE V.

CHAPTER VII

WAN HSIEN CITY, SHI-PAO SHIH MONASTERY AND FU CHOW

Wan Hsien—A pretty bridge—A sleepy telegraph-master—New Year festivities—Shi-Pao Shih—The monastery—Its legend—Its Chamber of Horrors—Wrecks—Fung-Tu Hsien—Fu Chow—Coal and iron.

At most seasons the river has little more to offer in the way of emotions above Sin Tan, and for this reason European travellers generally leave it at Wan Hsien and continue their journeys overland, whether their destination be Chung King or Changtu. Mrs. Bishop's well-known work, 'The Yangtse and Beyond,' describes the overland journey from Wan Hsien to Chengtu.

Wan Hsien,* on the left bank of the Yangtse, really consists of two distinct towns, one within the walls, and the other, connected with it by a bridge across the Tien-Cheng Ki, extramural. On our way to the telegraph-office we were followed by a crowd of at least 2,000 people, who shouted in a derisive tone. We had sent cards to the Magistrate, but had no reply, although a yamen-runner at last appeared and kept order among the multitude. Although it was eleven o'clock when we arrived, the telegraph-master (who spoke English) had to get up and dress before he could receive us; and while we waited in his office the crowd of sight-seers gave us some anxiety for the safety of the walls. The bridge is a peculiarly graceful arch (see Plate V.), and the back-water of the Yangtse, when the river is high, comes up beneath it, as

* Now a treaty port.

is proved by the marks of boat-hooks. We found the Tien-Cheng Ki very low; there was a pretty waterfall just below the bridge, and crowds of women were busy washing clothes in the stream. The walled city is unusually well paved. Coal of a good quality is hawked about the streets in baskets.

From Wan Hsien to Shi-Pao Shih occupied two days. The gray sandstones with chocolate-coloured shales formed both walls of the valley. They were practically horizontal as far as Lao-Kwan Tsi, where the dip is slightly to the north-west. Opposite Shih-Why Chi the strata on the right bank have a dip equal to the slope of the low hills. Mountains dimly seen behind these hills appear to be of a different formation. At Shi-Pao Shih the sandstones dip at a low angle to the west. There was little to note on the journey except a fine stone bridge at Pei-Sui Ki, of the same type as that at Wan Hsien.

The night we arrived at Shi-Pao Shih (February 12) was the last of the New Year celebrations, and we went ashore after dark to see the sights. The main street was gay with paper lanterns and illuminated arches of coloured paper. A paper dragon pranced round and round a block of buildings, supported at intervals by bearers, who carried the wicker-work frame on bamboo poles. The bearers were naked, except for baggy bathing pantaloons, and the fun of the fair consisted in attempts on the part of the crowd to set fire to these rudimentary garments by means of well-directed squibs. In one instance, at least, they succeeded, and, with only one hand to spare for the conflagration, the unhappy bearer danced round in a manner which made his portion of the dragon very lively indeed.

WAN HSIEN CITY AND SHI-PAO SHIH

Shi-Pao Shih (which Gill translates 'Stone Jewel Fort,' and Mrs. Bishop 'Stone Precious Castle') owes its name to a monastery beautifully situated on the top of a tableland of sandstone, the only access to it being by a stairway enclosed in a wooden pagoda leaning against the cliffs (Plate VI.). Local tradition (according to information elicited from natives by our interpreter) assigns a great age to the building, which is said to have been originally the pleasure-house of a King. After it fell into the hands of the bonzes the monks were supported by a miraculous supply of rice, which trickled through a hole in a stone. The hole was pointed out to us in confirmation of the legend. Generations of holy men were content with this provision, and wrecks were unknown on the reach of the river guarded by the monastery. But in an evil day one Abbot thought to increase the supply, so that he might endow the brotherhood with riches derived from the sale of the staff of life. The offended gods stopped the flow of rice, and wrecks have ever since been of frequent occurrence. This story differs in detail from that given by Gill, but my version is probably as true as the other.

We first visited the monastery in the night, after having seen enough of the New Year rejoicings. Visions of 'fair Melrose' as seen by the 'pale moonlight' arose as we climbed the steps on just such a moonlit night as the poet would have loved. Such visions gave place to misgivings as we found the temple untenanted and hesitated to intrude in spite of the encouraging inscription, 'Honest and Benevolent,' which adorned the gateway.

Such ghastly horrors as met our gaze within exceeded anything we had ever read, either in heathen or

Christian annals! The tortures of the hereafter were represented by galleries of life-like painted sculptures. Here a malefactor was tied to a stake and was undergoing evisceration. Another was being pounded in a rice-mill. Others were being boiled. Others were being sawn asunder. Men and women were writhing, impaled on spikes. Perhaps the most horrible of all was a woman being ground in a rotary rice-mill, while a dog lapped the blood. All the gods or demons were anthropoid, with a strong resemblance to Chinese dignitaries. One remarkable and more pleasing group appeared to suggest the transmigration of souls, human beings passing beneath a huge grindstone ('The mills of God grind slowly, but they grind exceeding small'), and coming out beyond in a fan-shaped mass of birds and beasts.

We revisited the monastery early next morning, in company with Captains Watson and Hillman and Dr. Burniston. We were unable to see more of the modern worship than had been possible in the night. There were many hideous life-sized idols, with their mouths smeared with the blood of sacrificed fowls, the feathers stuck in the blood. I purchased for a trifle a wooden Madonna and Child, about a foot in length—a Goddess of Fecundity, I was informed. It had the appearance of great age, and lay neglected among a heap of rubbish, for it had been superseded by a larger and, no doubt, more powerful divinity, almost of life-size, made of clay and painted and gilded, to whom the barren women of to-day pay their devotions.

From Shi-Pao Shih to Fung-Tu Hsien is a long south-western stretch of the river, with many windings, which took us four days (forty-eight miles).

PAGODA ENCLOSING STAIRWAY TO TEMPLE OF SHI-PAO SHIH, YANGTSE RIVER.

PAGODA AT N'GAN-KIN, YANGTSE RIVER.

PLATE VI.

WAN HSIEN CITY AND SHI-PAO SHIH 35

The gray and reddish sandstones with chocolate-coloured shales form the groundwork of the country, the sandstones becoming more reddish to the south-west. They are, on the whole, nearly horizontal, but begin to dip to the north-west near Fung-Tu. Gold-washing was going on on many of the shingle banks or beaches. On the low hills on both sides of the river there was a great deal of terraced cultivation. On this reach, at Kwan-Ki Chang, we noted a well-constructed level stone bridge with five or six arches. There were several pretty stiff rapids, notably those of Fung-Hoang Tse, Tang-Tung Island, and Lan-Chu Island. At the last-named our two tow-lines snapped just as we were rounding a nasty rock. Shipwreck appeared inevitable, but something or other done with the bow sweep brought us off, and we merely spun down the river for half a mile. Others had been less fortunate, as at Tang-Tung three corpses floated by, and a large junk was seen in a sinking condition, her crew and an attendant lifeboat endeavouring to get her on to a beach. We had a view of Chung Chow, a little walled town in a prettily timbered neighbourhood, and having a sort of Swiss-farm style of architecture. Morris and Chung went ashore to post letters, but the postmaster had left for Wan Hsien, and no business could be done.

Fung-Tu Hsien is a poor-looking town. It was inundated by the river about sixty years ago, and a new town, high up the hill, was begun by the building of a formidable wall. The town was, however, rebuilt on the old site, and the wall, too far from the river for trade, encloses only two or three insignificant cottages.

Above Fung-Tu the gray and reddish sandstones

and chocolate-coloured shales dip at moderate angles to the north-east as far as Li-Shi Cheng (a pretty 'Swiss' village), where they are suddenly contorted into a violent anticline. On the eastern side of the axis the dip (to the east) is 40° or more; on the western side the dip (to the north-west) is about 20° for a mile or so, after which it gradually lessens. It, however, reaches 25° (to west-north-west) at Ki-Kong Ling.

Fu Chow (thirty-five miles above Fung-Tu) is situated on the southern bank of the Yangtse, at the mouth of the Kien Kiang, which drains at least two-thirds of the province of Kwei Chow. There are many coal and iron mines within the valley of the river, and coal forms a considerable part of the trade of the city, which is, moreover, the chief opium mart, and contains about 30,000 inhabitants. Li-Chi Yuen, two miles above the city, is an important salt depot and port.

CHAPTER VIII

FU CHOW TO CHUNG KING

Ning Shih—Bridges—'Stoned'—Our passenger intervenes—Chang-Chow Hsien—River-gods—A Chinese hospital—Rise of the river—Coal—Arrival of Mr. Bush—Iron-smelting—Arrival at Chung King—Steam navigation.

FROM Fu Chow to Ning Shih the sandstones and shales have a low dip to the south-west. At Li-Tu Cheng a stream falling into the left bank is spanned by two good stone bridges, one with a level deck (Plate V.), and the other hog-backed like that of Wan Hsien. The beaches of the island named Nui-Shih

Tse had about 100 men on them engaged in gold-washing.

The weather had now greatly improved, and we landed on the right bank, some distance below the island, with the object of seeing the bridge which Parker ('Up the Yangtse,' p. 171) describes as the finest which he had ever seen in China.

Leaving the river, we went inland, under the impression that we were bound to strike a main-road, but found only very crooked paths fringing rice-ponds and fields of poppies and beans. Parker's description of the bridge is inaccurate in three particulars. He says that it is built entirely of granite, whereas it is of the local sandstone; that it is 80 feet wide instead of 27 feet; and that it 'presents no apparent engineering or architectural defect.' The defect may not have been apparent when Parker wrote, but the west end of the structure is founded on the mud of a backwater of the Yangtse, and is now subsiding. The north side is cracking and bulging outward, while one of the ornamental arches spanning the roadway is in a dangerous condition. As to costing '260,000 taels, or nearly £80,000,' I cannot conceive it, although it is possible that that amount may have been subscribed. Three handsome arches span the roadway of the bridge, and are ornamented with carvings of elephants, tigers, and some other animals which belong rather to the domain of heraldry than to that of natural history.

The populace turned out in great numbers, at first curious, afterwards annoying, and at last decidedly threatening. After we had made some notes, measurements, and photographs, we were hooted, and orange-peel, tiny fragments of pottery, and finally small stones, were thrown. As one of the latter struck Lockhart, I turned round and threatened the crowd, but the red-boat man who accompanied us plucked me by the coat, and advised me to 'keep my hair on.' Having done so, we reached the bank of the river, and as we pulled off in a ferry-boat for the opposite bank the crowd stood and gaped.

Just such a crowd is depicted in an admirable photograph by Mr. Davidson, of the Friends' Mission, Chung King, which I am authorized to reproduce (Plate VII.). I learned afterwards that the crowd took us for French missionaries, and that they were encouraging one another to beat us. Some Chinese got into the boat, no doubt attracted by the opportunity for a free passage.

On landing opposite the town, we found a camp of vendors of small wares, and Wong Lien Sing, a merchant to whom we had, on Chung's introduction, given a passage from I-Chang. He proved on this occasion a valuable ally. He had, it appears, walked on, and, seeing from the hubbub in the town that we were in difficulties, 'stuffed' the people opposite with tales of our good qualities. He met us, as we disembarked, with a ceremonious courtesy, which, as it was unusual, puzzled us at first, although we soon guessed its object. He had, of course, no English, but he and the red-boat man explained matters in Chinese. We had tea, and cultivated the goodwill of the camp till our 'kwadza' came along and took us on board.

As this was the third occasion (and the last but one) when we were 'stoned,' a few words on the subject of the hostility of the Chinese towards foreigners may not be out of place.

Crowd on bank of Yangtse watching the landing of Foreigners.

PLATE VII.

This sort of manifestation generally commences in a petty and insignificant way, and the treatment of foreigners is not worse than Chinese meet with from time to time at the hands of mischievous boys and larrikins in America and Australia. As a rule, somebody incites somebody else—by preference a small boy—to throw a tiny pebble at the stranger from behind, and, if no notice is taken, larger and larger stones will follow till it is seen how much the stranger will stand. Should the assailed turn round and storm, he will see nothing but a look of intense innocence on the faces of the crowd. Should he prove violently resentful, there are, of course, the elements of a promising riot, and there is no saying where such a riot may end, but the instigator of the mischief will take good care to be out of it. It is, I think, probably only in the event of absolute fear, or obvious helplessness, being displayed by the victim that the stoning will become serious. When I read (as I have read) of a traveller being stoned for two hours, I cannot help forming my own conclusions regarding the nature of the transaction. The stoning to death of St. Stephen and of the missionaries lately murdered in Hunan—in which cases murder was contemplated—did not take hours.

Mo-Pan Tan, three miles above Ning Shih, is a pretty bad rapid, with very broken water and a strong current. Above it our crew executed what seemed to us a very delicate and dangerous manœuvre between two rocky islets outside of a point of rock projecting from the right bank. Gold washings were again seen on the shingly beaches.

The sandstones gradually rise to the north-west (upstream), till at Fan-Sui Ki, where a bed of limestone occurs, the angle is 45°. About three miles further, between Hoang-Tsao Hia and Chang Ye, they are bent in a sharp anticlinal fold, on both sides of which are seen the outcrop of a seam of coal overlying a bed of limestone, both worked.

Chang-Chow Hsien is a very little city without a wall. A wall, however, crowns a table-topped hill behind it. Probably this is a case parallel to that of Fung-Tu, or it may be that the wall is one of the fortified places where the population of a district take refuge in times of trouble, as is common enough in China. There were gold washings on a low island above the town.

Some 'river-gods' were carved on the rocks, and gaily coloured, about a mile below San-Pei Tu. At Mu-Tung Tse a fine hospital (Chinese) was perched on the right bank. The river at its summer level reaches the hospital steps, a rise of at least 100 feet.

Above this hospital the south-west course of the river ends, and a series of violent bends begin which extend on a generally western course to Chung King. The change in the course of the river corresponds with an alteration in the disposition of the gray sandstones and shales. These, which for a long distance had been nearly horizontal, now gradually assume a dip to the south-east, which is reversed on a violent anticline about two miles above the hospital. Exactly as at Chang Ye, a coal-seam, with a bed of limestone below, crops out on both sides of the anticlinal axis. The occurrences are so much alike that I am inclined to think the seams are the same. The coal here is somewhat extensively worked.

Mr. J. Holton Bush, the representative of our company at Chung King, came on board at Ye-Luo

Tse, and was welcomed, not only for his own sake, but also as a herald of the approaching termination of our voyage. The north-west gorge of Ta Mo, nine miles below Chung King, has been cut clean across an anticlinal fold in the sandstones. We had quiet water in the gorge, which is said to be very dangerous when the river is high, the downward passage of junks being then entirely prohibited. Above the gorge there are iron smelting works on both sides of the river.

Passing the gigantic gilded Buddha carved on the rocks at Ta-Fu Tse, we moored alongside the hulk of the Imperial Maritime Customs, on the right bank of the river, opposite Chung King, late in the afternoon of February 22, and the following day came to our final resting-place at Mr. Little's 'hong.' The voyage of 392 miles had taken us thirty-two days.

Chung King lies between the Yangtse and the mouth of the Kia-Ling Kiang (known to Europeans as the Little River), is enclosed by a high wall, and is said to contain 600,000 inhabitants. The streets are narrow, and, where they rise from one ledge of sandstone to the next, frequently steep. There is no wheel traffic, and, indeed, our sedan-chairs more than once stuck in the narrow lanes. The port has a considerable traffic in coal, salt, oil, rice, opium, and all the products of the rich province of Szechuan, besides foreign goods. The most conspicuous street industries were wood-carving and the stamping out of paper money and other offerings to the gods. Liquid manure seemed to be the chief commodity carried about the streets, but this article of commerce is naturally apt to attract an amount of attention out of proportion to its actual bulk.

For many years Mr. Archibald Little had proclaimed the importance of the steam navigation of the Yangtse between I-Chang and Chung King, before he succeeded, in 1898, in bringing up a launch. Having managed to interest an English syndicate, a larger steamer, the *Pioneer*, was built and brought up in the summer of 1900, but it had been preceded a few weeks by the flat-bottomed gunboats *Woodcock* and *Woodlark*. The *Pioneer* arrived in Chung King just in time to be 'commandeered' by the British Government, in view of the Boxer troubles, to take down a load of refugees to I-Chang. On her return she was retained as a gunboat, and under the new name of the *Kin Sha* she now represents British influence on the Upper Yangtse. Her intended rival in trade, the German steamer *Sui Hsiang*, starting up the river after the troubles were over, was wrecked in December, 1900, with considerable loss of life, on the very day she left I-Chang.*

The steam navigation of the Upper Yangtse is still an unsolved problem, and the junks have the river to themselves, now as in the past. Mr. Little, whose opinion is entitled to every respect, has come to the conclusion that the river is safe for steamers only when the water is high, and for junks only when it is low.† My own impression is that a riparian railway, effective at all seasons, would prove less costly in the end than the improvement of the river.

* A French gunboat has since reached Chung King.

† 'The Crux of the Upper Yangtse' (*Journ. Roy. Geogr. Soc.*, vol. xviii., 1901).

Gorge on Yangtse River.

PLATE VIII.

CHAPTER IX

CHUNG KING AND THE JOURNEY TO CHENGTU

Chung King—Foreign residents—Coal—A Mantzü document—Arrangements for overland travel—The 'Red Basin'—Departure for Chengtu—Honours for the cook—Dysentery—Yung-Chang—The Chung Kiang—Transport by river—Nei Kiang—Lung-Chang—Cave-dwellings—Gill's 'best inn in China'—A geological puzzle—Bamboo irrigation wheels—Robbers' heads—Kien Chow Plain—Poppy cultivation—Memorial arches—Brine wells—Valleys without outlets—Arrival at Chengtu.

DURING our stay in Chung King we enjoyed the hospitality of Mr. Little's residence, where his manager, Mr. Nicholson, was in charge. We met the following foreigners: British Consul Fraser, French Consul Bonsdanty, U.S. Consul Smithers, Mr. Morehead (Imperial Maritime Customs), Mr. Hancock (Standard Oil Company), Mr. Bush, Messrs. Hislop, Wilson, Davidson, Roe and Murray, and Dr. Wolfendale (missionaries).

The above may be described as residents, and there are perhaps as many more foreigners connected with the Customs, the Post-Office, and the missions. M. Paul Duclos, late of the Mission Lyonnaise, had also a place of business in the city, but was absent. The following were visitors, like ourselves: Captain Watts-Jones, R.E.; Messrs. Birch, Mathieson, and Grant; Captain Watson, R.N. (*Woodcock*); Captain Hillman, R.N. (*Woodlark*); Dr. Burniston (H.M.S. *Esk*); and Captain Bigham.

The French Consulate is a handsome edifice, and a good building for the United States is nearly finished.

The British Consul is located in a tumbledown Chinese house in a slum. Some of the leading foreigners—among others, the British and United States Consuls, the chief of the Customs, and the Friends' Mission (Mr. and Mrs. Davidson)—have summer houses at 'The Bungalows,' three miles south of the city and about 2,000 feet above it.

We visited, near 'The Bungalows,' a coal-mine, where an 8-inch seam, very dirty and pyritous, was worked in a primitive fashion, and also a walled enclosure designed for a refuge in troublous times.

The following schedule of the costs of transport of coal from a mine forty li (twelve miles) up the Kia-Ling, which was given me by the owner, Lung Wang Toong, may be of interest. Ten li are equal to three English miles.* One ton (2,240 pounds) is equal to 16·80 piculs. One tael of silver was then about 3s., and was exchangeable for 1,130 to 1,190 copper cash.

Coal at pit-mouth	100 cash per picul.
Coolie carriage to river	60 ,,
Freight by boat to Chung King	35 ,,
Coolie carriage into town	40 ,,

A mining engineer named Sung Chi Fung showed me a number of interesting documents, relating to mines, in the Mantzü character. Mantzü is Chinese for 'barbarian,' it may be mentioned. The mines in question were, as a matter of fact, in the Lolo country. Sung's own notebooks were not the least remarkable. Although the writing was Chinese, and therefore of little use to me, the pages were full of spirited drawings, from which it could be seen that

* Theoretically, but in popular language 'ten li' means an hour's walk.

the artist was a natural-born topographer. I was much interested in a long document purporting to be an agreement made with a number of Mantzü landowners, each of whom, at the end of a description (such as 'tall and dark, twenty-three years of age, scar on left cheek'), had signed with a cross, and impressed the paper with a thumb smeared in ink.

Our ceremonial visits to the Chinese officials involved the usual compliments and exchange of small-talk about our age, the number of our children, our honourable country, and our experiences in travelling, besides the more serious discussion of the question of escort. Everything was satisfactorily arranged. We had, besides, some business with a native banker, who had a correspondent at Chengtu, to whom he gave us an introduction. Finally, after long negotiations, we made a contract with the Yünnan Sung Pa Cheong (Yünnan Mail- and Wood-Oil-Carrying Company) for the transport of the party and our luggage and stores. The goods were to be taken to Chengtu by thirty-six coolies and a headman, or 'fu-tow,' in eleven days, for 1,100 cash per man for the journey. The three Europeans and the interpreter had riding ponies as well as chairs, and the cook and our three boys had also chairs of an inferior order. We left Chung King on our way to Chengtu on March 5.

The 'Red Basin' of Szechuan and the 'Szechuan Red Sandstones' have often been referred to by travellers. In coming up the river to Chung King we had noted the prevalence of chocolate-coloured shales between the beds of gray sandstone, and that day by day, as we came westward, the same sandstones more and more often assumed a reddish or, rather, chocolate tint. In the same degree the siliceous particles were replaced by felspathic.

By the time we had reached Lai-Feng Yi, thirty-four miles from Chung King, the sandstones might, for the first time, have been described as 'red and gray,' instead of 'gray and red,' as before. I incline to the belief that the currents which brought the sediments came from the west, and that the coarser and heavier siliceous grains were deposited nearer the western shore than the finer and lighter felspathic sediment, which was probably held in suspension for a considerable distance.

As far as our course was westward—viz., to Lung-Chang Hsien (127 miles)—the strata were, as a rule, nearly horizontal, although in places they were thrown into folds. Between Sang Shan and Er-Lang Kwan they are doubled over a sharp anticline, and a thick series of limestones appears along the axial line. A coal-seam is seen shortly to the west.

West of Yung-Chang Hsien for several miles we could see the horizontal outcrop of a coal-seam on a hillside north of the road. Judging by the samples carried in the baskets of the coolies and in bullock-packs, this seam is thick, and of a better quality than any we had yet seen. The bullocks usually carried three lumps of about half a hundredweight each.

The principal places on this portion of the road may be briefly referred to:

Er-Lang Kwan, a hill fort on a little sandstone tableland, fifteen miles from Chung King.

At Lai-Feng Yi (thirty-four miles) we were accommodated in a yamen, consisting of a handsome court-house and suite of apartments, which is kept for the triennial visit of the Viceroy and for examinations.

CHUNG KING AND THE JOURNEY TO CHENGTU 47

At Ma-Feng Chiao we saw the long wooden bridge, with stalls on each side, mentioned by Parker. A similar bridge was seen at Hoang-Ki Sha, nine miles beyond Yun-Chwan.

Yun-Chwan Hsien (sixty-one miles) is said to be the third city in point of population in Szechuan. We saw little but the Examination Hall, seated for 600 students, where we lodged, as we arrived late and left early. Here the cook had to bear 'the burden of an honour unto which he was not born.' The politeness of the Magistrate had prompted him, as we approached, to send a relay of fresh bearers for my chair, so that I might arrive with, so to speak, 'a gallop for the avenue.' As it happened, the cook, seated in his chair, was leading the procession, and as he was a man of venerable appearance, spoke some English, affected European dress, and generally gave himself airs, and as the load on his chair included the usual coloured paper lantern and the interpreter's official hat, the intelligent coolies, naturally concluding that he was the most important member of the party, relieved his bearers (who had no objection to make), and carried him in triumph into the city. Far be it from me to grudge any attention bestowed on a good cook!

The cold drizzle brought on an attack of dysentery, and I had to stop a day to recruit at Yung-Chang Hsien. This is a walled town with an air of business and prosperity. The river is navigable from the town down to the Yangste, and is crossed by a stone bridge 20 feet in width (as usual, much wider than the road), with pointed arches.

M. Paul Duclos met us at Lung-Chang Hsien, on his way to Chung King. Two miles east of this town

we saw a stone pagoda eight stories high. With
this exception we had seen no pagodas since leaving
Chung King, save such as might be described as toys
or models. Here, also, we noticed a number of
square holes cut in the sandstone cliffs, according to
the Chinese the residences of the Mantzü or aboriginal
cave-dwellers.

From Lung-Chang the road keeps north-west to
Chengtu. In eighteen miles we reached a river which,
between its head and this point (136 miles), is called
by three distinct names—Chung Kiang, Fu-Sung
Kiang, and To Kiang. Here the village of Pei-Ma
Tsin is a port whence the coal of Lung-Chang is
shipped in boats down to the Yangtse. The course
of the river is from north-east to south-east. When,
therefore, our whole equipment was embarked in
boats, I naturally expected that we were about to go
upstream, but, to my astonishment, we were carried
down for four miles, the river having taken a sudden
bend and flowing to the north-west. The river was
very low, and in many places the boats had to be
pushed along narrow channels scooped out of the
gravel. We landed on the right bank, near a ten-
story pagoda, and crossed the narrow neck of the
peninsula enclosed by the bend of the river to the
brine well of Si-An Ji on the river-bank.

Three miles above the salt well we came to the
'hsien' (= county town) of Nei Kiang. The local pronunciation is Loui Kiang. In Chinese the distinction
between the N and L sounds seems hardly to be appreciable. Nei Kiang is enclosed by a substantial wall, and
is the most prosperous-looking town which we have,
so far, met with, having good buildings—the porches
generally decorated with mosaic porcelain dogs—and

well-furnished shops. The drapery shops especially are well supplied, cotton ranking as the chief article of commerce. Ploughing, harrowing, and hoeing were going on briskly in the vicinity of the town. The ploughs were of wood, and were drawn by water-buffaloes. We observed that, when they had to travel for any distance along the paved roads, the buffaloes were accommodated with straw sandals.

According to Gill, the inn at Lung-Chang is ' the best in Szechuan.' We found that it had some good points—for example, a backyard well paved and clean, instead of being, as is the custom, a fetid sink. The hotel in Nei Kiang, however, found greater favour in our eyes, as it possessed a good floor, a wooden ceiling, a veranda 10 feet above the soil, and comfortable chairs, tables, and bed platforms.

The traffic from Chengtu to Chung King is embarked at Nei Kang, and boated down the river to Pei-Ma Tsin.

Yün-Shan Tsin, six miles beyond Nei Kiang, is a large and busy village, with well-built and highly-ornamented temples, and a large gilded Buddha and other gods in rock panels.

After passing a hill-fort, we recrossed the river to the left bank, just below where it divides into two branches, both of which are navigable for boats. The eastern branch, up which our course lay, is navigable at least as far as Chi Chow (or Tsu Chow), a large and prosperous town with two-storey houses, well-stocked shops, and a telegraph-station. Here we found sleeping accommodation in a Buddhist temple.

We were a good deal puzzled, in the neighbourhood of Song-Si Pu, to account for an extraordinary accumulation of large water-worn boulders extending for nearly a mile along the crest of a hill, where the road threaded its way among graves. As there were no conglomerates among the rocks of the district, we came to the conclusion that the boulders must have been carried to the spot, and that they had probably something to do with honouring the dead.

Both below and above the village of Nan-Ching Yi some alluvial gold-diggings were observed in the river. About two miles below the village we saw the first of the Szechuan type of undershot irrigation wheel, a delicate structure of bamboo, with bamboo buckets on its periphery, delivering water into a flume 30 feet above the level of the stream (Plate IX.).

We recrossed the river at Chi-Yang Hsien to the right bank, which we kept as far as Shih Chiao. Chi-Yang has a substantial wall, and is a busy town. The chief industry appears to be the weaving of cotton goods, especially towels. North of the town we were struck by the immense number of land shells (*Planorbis*) strewn over the soil, and were at a loss to account for their abundance in this spot.

Ling-Chang Shih is a large thriving village, many houses being in course of erection. One shop was seen stocked with coal of good quality in large blocks. Outside of the village the heads of five robbers were exposed in cages mounted on poles.

Ten miles further the valley opens out into the beautiful Kien Chow Plain. Poppies were growing luxuriantly, and sugar-cane was being planted. The plain is famous for the quality of its opium. Here, for the first time for months, we met with wheel traffic in the form of the humble barrow. The town evidently does not depend entirely on the agricultural industry, as we saw many hands employed in silver-

CHUNG KING AND THE JOURNEY TO CHENGTU 51

chasing and cotton-spinning, and a good deal of business was done in coal and salt. It is said to be flooded annually.

An affluent of the Chung Kiang is spanned by a wide and lofty wooden arcade bridge, with stalls on either side of the roadway. Here the 'pai fungs,' or memorial arches, thrown across the road begin to be painted and gilded. These arches had been met with hitherto at every town and village, the virtuous widowed mothers and incorruptible magistrates whom they commemorate appearing to have been specially abundant in this district. It is whispered, however, among well-informed Chinese, that an astonishing amount of virtue may be discovered in *any* locality if only the official who memorializes the throne be approached in a proper manner. Three pagodas, two of them of ten stories and square in section, lend dignity to the environs of Kien Chow, and contribute to its immunity from the ' adverse atmospheric influences' known as ' fung shui.'

The town or large village of Shih Chiao, where we left the river, lies about three miles north-west of Kien Chow. It seems to do a good deal of trade in salt (of poor quality), china basins, and gelatine. The river is crowded with boats.

About a mile to the north some ten or twelve brine wells were at work. The brine is flumed into central boileries, of which we saw three. At each well a water-buffalo is driven round a whim, on which a bamboo tape is wound. To this a long, valved bamboo bucket, like the sludge-pump used in boring operations, is attached. By calculations based on the number of revolutions and the circumference of the whim, we estimated the depth of one of the wells at

630 feet. The well at Si-An Ji was 675 feet deep. These are, however, not to be numbered among the deep wells of Szechuan, some of those at Tsü-Liu Ching, eighty miles to the south, being over 2,000 feet deep, and the brine being evaporated by the combustion of gas, which is also obtained from bores.

A very good account of these wells, it may be said, is given in Hosie's 'Three Years in Western China,' and the whole process of boring and manufacture is minutely described by Father Coldré in the *Annales des Mines* for 1891. An official handbook, called the 'Yen Fa Che,' in twenty ponderous volumes, may also be consulted ; but as, according to Father Coldré, it is 'innocent of arrangement and choke-full of the useless and the inaccurate,' readers will probably start with a prejudice against it. Father Coldré estimates the cost of the salt produce of the province, *to the consumers*, at £16,000,000 per annum. When I was informed by the Chinese that the sinking of the deeper wells often occupies more than one generation, and that a well in progress may be bequeathed from father to son, the analogy of the lawyer's bequest of a ' guid gangin' plea ' mentioned by Sir Walter Scott rose to my mind.

From Lung Chang to (and beyond) Shih Chiao the chocolate-coloured or liver-coloured sandstones and shales of the so-called 'Red Basin' are highly felspathic, and the beds are rigidly horizontal. A few miles north-west of Shih Chiao they begin to rise, and the rise continues to increase till it reaches 70°, after which the dip is suddenly reversed on a sharp anticline. It m̀ay be conjectured that the whole of these 'red' strata are more or less saturated with soluble chloride of sodium, although the salt has been leached by rain and rivers from the beds near the surface. In this region we crossed several dry valleys, which were apparently without outlet, and later Mr. Little informed me that this was undoubtedly the case. Such valleys are by no means uncommon in limestone country, but in this instance I am inclined to attribute the subsidences to the abstraction, or subtraction, of salt.

The top of the anticlinal arch, near the valley of Cha-Tien Dza, is practically the summit of the road, and by aneroid we made it 2,700 feet above Chung King, or 3,317 feet above the level of the sea. It is also the parting of the waters between the Chung Kiang and the Min, both of which are tributaries of the Yangtse. From the gap which carries the road over the summit the magnificent panorama of the Chengtu Plain is one to command the admiration of the most callous of wayfarers. We entered the plain at Lung-Chuen Yih, and a short day's journey (fifteen miles) across it brought us to Chengtu on March 17. This portion of the plain appears to consist of a recent alluvial terrace and the ruins of an older one, the levels, by aneroid, averaging 2,000 feet above the sea. The journey from Chung King to Chengtu (299 miles) had taken thirteen days, but would no doubt have been completed in the contract time (eleven days) but for wet weather and the delay at Yung-Chang caused by my illness.

The road is possibly one of the best in China, which is not saying much, as the convenience of the public is, here as elsewhere, constantly sacrificed to meet the demands of the farmers. These lords of the soil do not scruple to carry away the flagstones if required, or to pare or even undermine the path to obtain soil for their fields. The construction of a railway along the route would be easy enough, but it is a question, considering the existence of waterways between Chengtu and Chung King, whether a railway would be much used till it had been continued down the Yangtse to I-Chang, where safe and continuous steam navigation may be said to commence.

CHAPTER X

CHENGTU PLAIN AND THE CAPITAL OF SZECHUAN

Intense cultivation—Irrigation works—Seven crops per annum—Opium cultivation—Bridges—Sin Fan—Pen Hsien—The escort—Sin-Tu Hsien—Shih-Foong Hsien—Mien-Chu Hsien—Chiung Chow—Chengtu city—Bellamy's ideal—Arsenal—Reception by the Viceroy—Chinese officials—Foreign residents—Arrangements for our protection by the Viceroy—A Proclamation.

THE Chengtu Plain, sixty miles long by forty wide, is, without doubt, the most intensely cultivated portion of the earth's surface. During April, May, and June, we had occasion to traverse it in three different directions to the north, and one to the south. and so came to see many of the cities with which it abounds. By far the greater part of it is watered by the Min, a river which heads in the extreme northern corner of the province, and is joined by numerous large tributaries coming from the west and south before it flows past Kia Ting and enters the Yangtse at Sui Fu. On entering the plain at Kwan Hsien, the Min is split up into several main canals, which are again and again subdivided for the purpose of irrigation, to be reunited at the southern end of the plain. It is probable that in the thirteenth century, when Marco Polo was on his travels, the 'great river a good half-mile wide,' flowing past Chengtu, was the principal stream; but in the present day that channel is insignificant in comparison to the one which passes by Ta Hsien, Yung-Chia Chong, and Hsin-Chin Hsien. Of course, these channels are stopped up or opened as occasion requires. As a general rule, they follow such contour lines as will allow gravitation to conduct the water to levels as high as is possible, and when it is desired to raise it higher than it will naturally flow, chain-pumps and enormous undershot waterwheels of bamboo are freely employed (see Plate IX.). Water-power is used for driving mills through the medium of wheels, undershot or overshot, or turbines, as the local circumstances may demand.

The northern and higher portion of the plain is irrigated by the diversion of the numerous rivers which take their rise in the lofty snowy ranges culminating in the Chao-Ting Shan, or Nine Nails —according to Gill, from 18,000 to 20,000 feet high. The channels into which these rivers are broken up feed the Chung Kiang, into which, if the Chinese and existing European maps are to be trusted, even a portion of the water of the Min is diverted. Although I had no opportunity of verifying the latter fact, I do not venture to question it, as the Chinese have learned almost to juggle with water, and on the Chengtu Plain, at least, have trained it to perform apparently impossible feats. North of the city of Mien-Chu Hsien we crossed a dry river-bed, quite a quarter of a mile wide, which was being cleaned and deepened, the water having been temporarily turned into another channel.

This is probably the largest head of the Chung Kiang. It is but seldom that rewards are so worthily bestowed as that which has been given to Li Ping, the engineer who, 2,000 years ago, designed the system of irrigation which enables the Chengtu Plain to support 4,000,000 inhabitants. No mere Companionship of the Bath, Cross of the Legion of Honour, or Red Button, was his meed. His merit was proclaimed with generous enthusiasm; he was invested with the rank of 'First Gentleman' and promoted to the *godhood*. Of the many temples erected, and still maintained, in his honour, that at Kwan Hsien is the most notable.

In the course of our several traverses across the plain, we saw one crop take the place of another with amazing rapidity. I was informed, and can readily believe, that seven successive crops are raised in the course of a year. Many of the crops are beautiful, whether in the intense green stage or in flowering or ripening, but the poppy is the loveliest of all. It is, however, sad to reflect that this flower, produced by the square league, and in every tint from white to dark purple, is not grown for useful, or even for decorative or artistic purposes, but is destined to sap the moral sense, if not to weaken the physical strength, of China's millions.

Confessing, as I must, to a lifelong prejudice (which observation and experience in the British Isles and Australia have only tended to strengthen) against agriculture as a first-class means of losing money and wasting labour, I admit that I may have noted only a tithe of what others might have seen on the great plain, and content myself with giving a mere list of the crops observed from time to time; and I know at least enough of agriculture to be astonished at the occurrence, side by side, of plants for which elsewhere one would have to search many degrees of subtropical and temperate lands. The list comprises oranges, persimmons, apricots, peaches, plums, mulberries, pears, walnuts, poppies, tobacco, saffron, chilis, onions, leeks, garlic, cabbages, kale, lettuces, endives, turnips, radishes, carrots, egg-plant, cucumbers, melons, pumpkins, beans, pease, rape, millet, maize, rice, wheat, barley, oats, buckwheat, sugar-cane, and bamboo.

A district traversed in every direction by watercourses, both natural and artificial, must, as a matter of course, have stimulated the inventive genius of the pontifex ever since the day when the primeval inhabitant first cunningly applied fire to throw down a tree across a stream. We find, therefore, as might have been expected, that the streams of the plain are spanned by structures which appear to have anticipated most of the finest conceptions of modern engineering. The 'arcade bridge' is, perhaps, the most frequent and popular. Roofed with tiles, and built mainly of wood, although often founded on stone piers, it presents not only a passage (invariably wider than the roadway), but also niches and stalls which may be decorated with images and paintings or used by merchants, and pannelled ceilings on which triumphs of Chinese art may be studied at the cost of a crick in the neck. Stone bridges are of every variety. Some are 'hog-' or 'camel-backed,' like the 'Auld Brig' of Doon, only more so. Others have level decks and arches varying from the circular to the pointed or 'Gothic,' resting on piers sunk in the river-bed. One type of the circular arch, which I have never seen elsewhere, is very common. The arch is perfect, but is in no way 'keyed,' and is built of spheroidal water-worn stones taken from the river gravels. Such structures could not be expected to carry a heavy wheel traffic, and, as a matter of fact, there is nothing of the sort heavier than wheel-barrows on the plain. They do, however, very often support the vibration of a mill and the weight of the mill building. In still another type of bridging, the deck and hand-rails (if any) are composed of large stone slabs. The giddy single-rope of bamboo, the cantilever, and the suspension-bridge—of bamboo ropes and iron chains—are reserved for mountain gorges, where it is difficult or impossible to plant mid-stream piers. The Chinese 'accumulate merit,' or, as others phrase it, 'lay up for themselves treasures in heaven,' in many ways, founding libraries, building shrines, endowing hospitals, or providing for the burial of the poor, and, above all, they positively revel in building bridges.

Among the Cities of the Plain visited by us were Pi Hsien, Sin-Fan Hsien, Pen Hsien, Sin-Tu Hsien, Shih-Foong Hsien, Mien-Chu Hsien, Shuang-Liu Hsien, Sin-Chin Hsien, and Chiung Chow.

Sin-Fan is a large town with good shops and fairly wide streets, and is surrounded by a wall. The south gate is protected by a semicircular flanking wall. The north gate is a graceful balustraded structure with a double roof. Just outside of it a busy fair was in progress on April 3.

Pen Hsien is surrounded by a wall and a deep 'practicable' moat. According to the Magistrate, there is a population of 60,000 within the walls, and about as many more outside. Dyeing and grain-milling are among its principal industries. The Foong-Sing Dhen, or Propitious Star Hotel, in which we lodged, was exceptionally good and pretty.

Undershot Water-Wheel (Bamboo), used for the irrigation of Ricefields, Szechuan.

A Courtyard in the Yamen of the Mining Bureau, Chengtu.

PLATE IX.

CHENGTU CITY AND PLAIN

Our entry to this city was marked by a degree of ceremony more imposing than any we had met with before. A crowd of soldiers suddenly appeared as we were travelling after dark, drew up on either side of the road, courtseyed and dipped their paper lanterns, shouting a chorus of 'Chu Djen, Dahren!' (Glad to see you, sir!). On the following morning the local escort which set out with us on our journey carried seven tridents, two swords, and a Lochaber axe. Even this imposing display of force was afterwards outdone by the authorities of Kwan Kow, where we reached the edge of the plain. The local volunteers met us, mustering six black flags, six red flags, two trumpeters, four Lochaber axes, seven tridents, two swords, and twenty-five rifles. They saluted with a low obeisance and the shout of 'Chu Djen, Dahren!' brandished their arms above their heads, and finished off with a *feu de joie*, after which they marched in front, the trumpeters filling the startled air with sounds as of a buzz-fly speaking through a megaphone, while the Pen Hsien guard fell in at the rear.

Sin-Tu Hsien is a town of rather less importance than Pen Hsien.

Shih-Foong Hsien, a centre of the tobacco trade, about the same size as Sin-Tu, is a walled town with a fine wide street and some two-storey wooden houses.

Mien-Chu Hsien, a distributing centre and the seat of important paper and tobacco industries, is estimated to have a population of 100,000 within the wall. Coal and coke are brought down in barrows from the neighbouring hills. The city has more than usually important buildings, including a large examination hall. The wall is strong, and is surrounded by a moat.

The population of Shuang-Liu Hsien is given by Baron von Richthofen as above 50,000. Heavy rain and mud knee-deep made us indisposed to investigate.

Chiung Chow contains, according to Richthofen, over 50,000 inhabitants. It has wide streets well paved with stone flags, and at least one good inn. The turbulence and annoyance experienced by Richthofen in 1872 were not met with by us, although our companions gave the town a bad name. Hosie spent a night in the town in 1883, and was not disturbed. The fine stone bridge of fifteen arches (250 yards in length) mentioned by Hosie has been carried away, and a new bridge of cyclopean masonry is in course of construction. The stone used is red and gray sandstone. The deck is quite level. Thirteen arches have been finished, ten piers are ready for the decking, and it will take ten more spans of the same size to cross the river. The deck is of solid blocks of sandstone.

Chengtu, the capital of Szechuan, where we spent in all forty-five days in March, April, and June, is one of the most important cities of China. Its wall, 30 or 40 feet high and wide enough on top for a company of soldiers to march abreast, surrounded by a dry moat given over to cultivation, encloses an area of about twelve square miles. The population is estimated by Richthofen at 800,000, and by the Chinese at 1,000,000. Which of the figures is to be taken as correct probably depends on how much of the suburbs is included. The main streets are broad, well paved with flags, and almost free from the odours so characteristic of the majority of Chinese towns. Many of them are roofed with matting, so that the traveller may imagine himself in Bellamy's ideal city. Some of the shops have really rich stocks of merchandise, including silks, furs, silver wares, jewellery, and arms, with perhaps still greater wealth in coal, salt, and white wax. A few foreign commodities, such as kerosene, cottons, condensed milk, and glass ware, can also be purchased.

Among public buildings the temples are the most conspicuous. The enormous examination hall probably comes next. Club-houses abound, and in large enclosed spaces within the wall innumerable yamens, tenanted by officials and rich merchants, are embowered in foliage. The arsenal employs 600 hands, contains some fine machinery, and turns out Hotchkiss guns and Martini rifles, as well as matchlocks and culverins. Its steam-whistle was the most home-like sound we heard.

Our arrival having been duly notified to the Viceroy, an intimation was sent that he would receive me on March 20.

Kwei Chun, the Manchu Viceroy of Szechuan, rules over a province as large as France and more than twice as populous.* The authority of the Chinese, however, over the Mantzü and Lolo tribes and the Tibetans of the western borderland is for the most part nominal.

At the appointed hour I proceeded to the palace in all the pomp demanded by the occasion—green chair, interpreter, 'ting chai' or card-bearer, runners and soldiers. After a short pause there was a shout from the interior and the gate was thrown open. An usher, carrying my card, preceded the chair-bearers, and the procession filed through many courtyards—

* He has since been transferred to Canton.

all, especially the outer ones, crowded with chairs and drowsy chair-bearers waiting for their masters—past quaint wall-paintings and still quainter carvings of animals of the dog-tiger-elephant-griffin species, known perhaps to heraldry, but of which the natural history text-books are silent. I am proud of the number of courts which were traversed before my chair was set down, since 'a person of no importance' must walk from the outer court, his immediate superior from the next, and so on, in strict accordance with a well-understood and severely regulated etiquette. As it was, my chair was only set down in the last courtyard but one, and I noticed with some anxiety that the bearers were becoming visibly inflated by the distinction conferred on them as they passed one barrier after another. I was so agitated myself that I lost count of the number of courts, but I had time to notice that the pavements were very old and ill kept.

At the entrance to the inner court I was received by Li Show Tin, Secretary for Foreign Affairs, who conducted me to a chamber in a corner of the court, where, after passing through a lane formed by the Viceroy's suite, I was introduced to the Viceroy himself. He shook hands, and wasting no time in the ceremonies which usually lengthen out Chinese visits, beckoned the company at once to their places at a luncheon-table which had been furnished with dainties for the occasion. Everything was done in 'foreign' style, except that the champagne was of that extra sweet variety which commends itself to the Chinese taste, but is never met with outside of China.

The party having been seated, the Viceroy led the conversation, and did the duties of a host with much

CHINESE WOMEN AT FRIENDS' MISSION, CHUNG-KING.

MILITARY OFFICIALS AT AN EXAMINATION, CHENGTU.

PLATE X.

grace and dignity. His remarks had to be translated either into French by Li Show Tin or by a 'professor' whose name escaped me, or into English by Tong Sing Kow, Liu Chung Yu (Manager of Telegraphs), or Chung Chui Lin (my own interpreter), who were among the guests. Commencing with polite inquiries about my journey, and the treatment received on the way, the conversation led to an exchange of experiences of travel and descriptions of foreign countries. The Viceroy did not see any immediate prospect of a European tour, however much he would like it. A remark on the agricultural wealth of the district and its apparent prosperity led our host to reply that many of his people were wretchedly poor, and that he hoped the introduction of foreign methods, especially in mining, would raise the general standard of prosperity. I said that we had come to Szechuan with the intention of introducing English capital to develop its mineral wealth, if such wealth as had been reported really existed; that we must, of course, first satisfy ourselves on that point; and that we relied on His Excellency's goodwill to let us do our work under the best conditions. He was good enough to say that he was very favourable to English enterprise—that, in fact, the English and the Chinese were 'as one family,' and that arrangements were in hand for putting every necessary official and military assistance at our service wherever we might travel through the province. That these promises were not mere empty compliments was abundantly proved during the five following months of our stay in China.

Viceroy Kwei is rather under the medium height and rather beyond middle age. His features are distinctly refined, and his bearing is marked by courtesy and good breeding.

Subsequent visits to other dignitaries in the city revealed the fact that some of them—for instance, the Tartar General and the Provincial Treasurer—are much better lodged than the Viceroy. The General has his courtyards lined with military officers in gorgeous brocades (*cf.* Plate X.), alongside of whom the Viceroy's retinue would make but a poor display. A few days after my audience I saw the Viceroy at a fair outside the city. His following appeared to have been recruited from the most ragged wastrels of the town. A Chinese bystander to whom I turned for an explanation said that what I saw was 'China custom.' The banners and halbards must be carried whenever a great man rides forth, and it is good form to give the job to the poor men who sit at his gate.

During our three sojourns in Chengtu we were in constant communication with His Excellency Li Cheng Yung (Imperial Commissioner for Mines), and the members of the Szechuan Mining Bureau: Messrs. Li Show Tin (who spoke French, and was also the Viceroy's Foreign Secretary), Chu Ling Kwan, Taotai (a merchant and land-owner who spoke English), Han Shing (a rich land-owner), Chun Kwan Pit (a rich man who had been promoted to high rank for numerous benefactions, among others the gift of 1,000,000 taels for famine relief), and Tong Sing Kow (Managing Director, educated in the United States, who had a perfect command of the American tongue). We were the guests of the Commissioner and Managing Director (see Frontispiece).

Other Chinese dignitaries with whom we came in

contact were the Tartar General, Choh; the Fan Tai, or Provincial Treasurer; General Chü, Director of the Arsenal (who was 'out with Gordon' in his youth); and Liu Chung Yu, Director of Telegraphs (who spoke English).

The resident foreigners were all attached to missions. We met Mr. and Mrs. J. F. Peat and Mr. and Mrs. Holin Cady, of the West China Mission; Mr. T. Torrance, Dr. Smith, Dr. Ewen, Dr. (Miss) Kilham, and Miss Hartwell, of the China Inland Mission; Miss Brooks and Mr. Ferguson, of the Bible Society; and Mr. Ottewell. There were, we were given to understand, in all about fifty foreign missionaries in the city. Of non-residents we met Mr. Archibald Little; Mr. John G. Birch; Captain Watts-Jones, R.E. (Yünnan Syndicate); Mr. Kerr (Yünnan Syndicate); Mr. Herbert Way (Upper Yangtse Syndicate); and M. Domato, of the 'Anglo-French Quicksilver and Mining Concessions (Kwei Chun Province) of China.'

The arrangements made by the Viceroy, in conjunction with the Tartar General, for our protection while travelling through the province seemed at first over-elaborate, and to have a tendency to make us ridiculous; but they proved to have been based on a knowledge of Chinese conditions, and stood the test in the troublous times which followed. It is true that we realized that the show of official authority and sanction was of more value than the fighting strength of our escort, and that in any real emergency the defence of our heads would devolve upon our own arms. First there was a proclamation and a Wai-Yuan. The latter is an official of magisterial rank—*i.e.*, qualified by having passed certain examinations for the post of chief magistrate of a 'hsien.' He sometimes headed the procession in his chair, and sometimes went ahead, like the advance agent of a circus, and posted the proclamation on the gates of the towns through which we were to pass. A permanent guard of soldiers, under a petty officer, armed with rifles, accompanied us all the way, one soldier being specially told off to each member of the party. Each 'hsien,' or county town, furnished a local guard, which was relieved at the boundary by the next, who gave a receipt for us, the magistrate being responsible for our safety. The local guard did their best to stand between us and the curious crowds, but, as they themselves understood that they must never let us out of their sight, privacy was impossible, and any attempt which we made to escape from the ever-present eye was invariably foiled. If one of us took a lonely walk, he was certain, on turning round, to encounter the slow, wise smile that twinkled beneath the enormous straw hat of a wily warrior.

The proclamation read as follows :

PROCLAMATION.

KWEI, of the First Order of Nobility, President of the Board of Revenue, Censor, Viceroy, and Director of Government Affairs for the Province of Szechuan;

CHOH, Tartar General and Commander of the whole Province of Szechuan, and Controller of the Civil and Military Officials of Shung Kien; and

LI, of the First Order of Nobility, President of the Third Rank, Imperial Commissioner of Mines (including Copper Mines) and Mercantile Affairs for the Province of Szechuan :

CHENGTU CITY AND PLAIN 67

WHEREAS the Chinese Empire is in great need of money, the Emperor has conceived a project for making it powerful, for which purpose soldiers and a sufficient food-supply are absolutely necessary. Now the population of Szechuan is large, and many are without employment. Some means must be found to enrich the country and benefit the people. The Tsung-li Yamen has, therefore, notified that the above state of affairs has been represented in a Memorial to the Throne, and that an Edict has been issued to the effect that, although minerals are plentiful in Szechuan, such mines as have been opened have not been successful, as the Chinese either do not know how to find the ore, or, having found it, do not know how to treat it. To amend this condition of affairs the Chinese Mercantile Companies, the Hwa-Yik and the Pao-Fu, have been empowered to acquire mining lands, and to engage foreign engineers to open up the mines. When these engineers go out to inspect mines they are to be accompanied by a Wai-Yuan. When they find a mine or any place which has not already been opened by the Government or Merchants, and when it does no injury to the Fung Shui, then, if the land belongs to private individuals. the latter will be requested to sell or lease the same to the above Chinese Companies, and the price or rent shall be equitably arranged by the Wai-Yuan and the local officials. Should the land belong to a private gentleman, it is to be purchased, and will then become the property of the Government. The mines shall be opened in the most suitable manner, whether by native or foreign methods. In the case of mines worth working, roads will have to be made and maintained for the transport of materials. Such roads, however, must not interfere with any tombs which the owners are unwilling to remove, and in such a case the roads must be diverted.

We enjoin all local Magistrates to protect the foreigners and to post this proclamation conspicuously and copiously for the information of the public, and to see that it is obeyed. It should be made known to that the opening of a mine is a distinct benefit to the place where it is situated, as each mine will only employ a few foreign engineers, and all the labour will be done by natives whom the Chinese have the power to appoint. The land will not be alienated to foreigners. As they are visitors from a far country, the foreigners are to be treated with respect and civility.

> The 1st day of the 3rd Moon of
> the 26th Year of the Reign
> of Kwang-Sui.
>
> [*Seals of the Viceroy, Tartar General,
> and Commissioner for Mines.*]

CHAPTER XI

AN EXCURSION TO THE NORTH OF CHENGTU

Departure for Tung-Ling Tse—Kwan Kow—Irrigation works—Bamboo suspension-bridge—Fine scenery—Alluvial gold—Waterfalls—Monastery of Tung-Ling Tse—Difficult roads—How a magistrate travels—Never taught to walk—Copper-smelting—Turbines—An attempted suicide—Medicinal virtue of mustard.

OUR first excursion from Chengtu was to the copper-mines of Tung-Ling Tse (Eastern Grove Monastery) and back, a journey covering 124 miles, which,

AN EXCURSION TO THE NORTH OF CHENGTU

with the work involved, took us fourteen days. After passing through the walled city of Pen Hsien, we entered, at Kwan Kow, the valley of the Chian Kiang, a river about as large as the Tay at Perth. The notables of the town met us and conducted us to a temple, where we lunched, the streets being lined with thousands of admiring citizens. As the river enters the plain below Kwan Kow it is diverted, by long sausage-like gabions of basket-work filled with stones, into a number of irrigation channels. Above the town it is crossed by a suspension-bridge formed by stretching four bamboo ropes (4 inches in diameter) across five stone piers. Higher up the valley there are bridges of a more temporary nature—gabion piers at intervals, connected by planks or saplings. It is not till the river becomes much smaller, near the monastery, that stone bridges are employed. The valley afforded some lovely scenery, and we sighed as we thought of the Australia which we had left not long before, for there was running water everywhere, and we were hardly ever out of sight of some waterfall, or 'staub-bach,' 700 or 800 feet in height. There is some gold in the alluvial terraces, but from the mode of working I should judge that its value is less than that of the agricultural land which would have to be destroyed to win it.

The monastery is beautifully situated, and supports an establishment of about a dozen monks. A large iron bell in the courtyard is among the most notable of its treasures. We camped in tents, as the accommodation under the roof was insufficient for our large party (Plate XI.).

In visiting the copper-mines we were struck with the daring, though bad, engineering of the paths, which ascended thousands of feet without any attempt at grading, and crossed ravines and climbed precipices by means of bridges or ladders made of a couple of logs or notched saplings. I reached places where the last winter's snow still lay, while Morris and Lockhart made an attempt to visit a group of mines on the Chun-Chan Shan, further north, but were baffled, at an estimated elevation of 12,000 feet, by the depth of the snow. It is needless to say that we did this part of the journey on foot, but our Wai-Yuan rode on a coolie all the way (Plate XI.).

Early in my experience, feeling a little indignant to see a man a third of my own age riding while I walked, I asked how old he was. When he replied, I expressed my surprise, and said, with what was meant for fine irony, 'Ah! I took you to be a hundred.' The shaft fell blunted; the intended victim beamed with gratified pride, and for my part I realized that I had hit upon one of the most graceful forms of Chinese flattery. Subsequently we inveigled the Wai-Yuan into making an ascent of 2,500 feet on the locomotive organs provided by Nature, but we had reason to be ashamed of ourselves, as the effort so exhausted him that he had to be carried down to the camp, and, as it was long after dark before he arrived, a party had to be sent with lanterns in search of him and his mount. He plaintively remarked that 'Chinese gentlemen are *never* taught to walk.' As a matter of fact, they do not walk enough for their health, but the riding in chairs is rather a matter of dignity than the result of physical weakness. Even a coolie, when promoted to be a 'boy,' soon discovers that he cannot, or, rather, may not, walk.

CAMP OF THE PARTY AT TUNG-LING TSE, WITH THE ESCORT FROM CHENGTU.

THE WAI-YUAN MOUNTAINEERING.

PLATE XI.

AN EXCURSION TO THE NORTH OF CHENGTU 71

At Tung-Ling Tse we had an opportunity of watching Chinese methods of copper-smelting. The ore, which was carried in baskets some 2,000 feet down the mountain, consisted of a soft shale carrying oxides and carbonates, and a very little sulphide of copper. A small blast-furnace, built of clay and stone, about $4\frac{1}{2}$ feet high and 2 feet by 3 feet internal dimensions, with a hemispherical well in front, was used. Blast was supplied by a double-acting cylinder of wood, about 9 feet long and 2 feet in diameter, actuated by a sort of open turbine, which drove the piston at the rate of nineteen double strokes per minute. After filling in charcoal till the shaft was half full of glowing fuel, ore and fuel were added alternately till the end of the campaign, which lasted twenty-four hours. The ore was self-fluxing. The slag, which was very clean, was tapped into the cavity at the front of the furnace, to be raked out and thrown away.

The furnace was run down by feeding with charcoal only till the ore was practically all reduced, and then the top hole was cut down and the well was filled with molten copper. This was cooled by pouring water on it, the discoid crusts, ready for market, being drawn off as they formed. After all the copper that would flow out had been obtained, the thin breast of the furnace was removed, and the glowing charcoal was drawn out and quenched. The copper within was then cooled with water and taken out.

The next day the furnace, much damaged by all this water and the cutting action of the slag, is rebuilt, and a new tuyère—a block of sandstone with a hole drilled in it—is cut and fitted. After drying for a few days, the furnace is blown in for another twenty-four hours' campaign. The fuel consumption was given as 1 pound per pound of ore—a most unusual proportion, but perhaps not incorrect when the frequency of starting and stopping is considered, coupled with the quantity burned just as soon as it is fed in.

It is of interest to note that the Chinese use turbines, and smelt their copper in blast-furnaces. At a later period we saw the roasting of sulphide ores in a nest of stalls, preparatory to smelting. The Chinese have, in this remote region, evolved a metallurgical process similar in its essentials to the modern copper practice of the West, although no doubt infinitely crude.

Ores of copper are assayed by smelting with charcoal in a miniature blast-furnace of clay, a few inches in height. The copper, after cooling in the hearth, is taken out and weighed.

An incident of the return journey showed the belief of the Chinese in 'foreign medicine,' in spite of their conviction of the questionable methods employed in its preparation. I found the village of Hsiao-Yui Toong in an uproar because of the attempted suicide of a woman who had taken an overdose of opium, and the relatives implored me for an antidote. Opening a tin of mustard, I gave directions for the preparation of an emetic—which was 'exhibited,' as I was informed, with the happiest effect.

CHAPTER XII

JOURNEY TO LUNG-AN

Departure from Chengtu—An Appian Way—The White Cloud Range—Killing devils—Bamboo water-wheels—Alluvial gold—An Hsien—The Cantonese club-house—Execution of robbers—The new broom—Missionaries—Fishing with cormorants—Chu Shan—Shih-Chuen—Bamboo suspension-bridge—Single-rope bridges—We empty a theatre—Wool from Tibet—Coal—Tung Kow—Kiang-Yu Hsien—Confusion of place-names—Rafting timber—Chiu Chow—Pontoon-bridge—Iron bridge—Lung-An—Temple—Praying by machinery.

OUR second excursion from Chengtu—a 'round trip' of 607 miles to Lung-An and Sung Pan and back viâ Kwan Hsien—took us from April 25 to May 31.

Commencing at the north gate of Chengtu, the road through the suburbs, lined with monuments, is for some miles a veritable Appian Way. As it proceeds further out into the plain, however, it speedily becomes a bog, and the bare-legged coolies are clothed in 'skin-tights' of mud. We met a long caravan of Tibetans on mules, returning from Pekin, and a prisoner, clothed in red, carried in a chair with an official seal across its front.

Leaving the Pekin road at Sze-Te Chow, we struck northward through Mien-Chu Hsien, crossing numerous heads of the Chung Kiang. Ploughing operations were going on busily. In one place we saw four men raising water by means of a treadmill pump from a lower field to flood a higher, in which a buffalo was dragging a wooden plough through the mud. Between Shoh-Sui Ho and Song-Chao Yuen, the road skirts the outliers of the red foot-hills, the mountains in the background (the White Cloud Range) being covered with snow. The strata consist mainly of soft gray sandstones, weathering to red, and some beds of the limestone-conglomerate with which the roads of the neighbourhood are flagged, the whole dipping to the south-south-east at 20°.

A busy market or fair was going on at Song-Chao Yuen, where a much-carved and highly-gilded temple is dedicated to Kwan Ti, the warrior who conquered this district in the days of the Three Kingdoms. The river which ought to be crossed north of this town, and which is correctly laid down on Széchenyi's map as flowing (in its natural state) past the east side of Lo-Kiang Hsien, has been diverted to the north-east (after taking toll of it to water the Song-Chao Yuen Plain), and directed through a cutting in a low gap in a range of limestone-conglomerate hills. In this gap, for some reason or other, every traveller makes a point of digging his staff or spear-shaft into the rock to kill the devils, as the soldiers explained, with the result that it is pitted with holes, reminding one of the marks made by the boat-hooks on the Yangtse. Our followers duly performed the rite, which seems to be demanded by custom. Beyond the gap the bamboo wheels for raising water are unusually large and numerous.

We camped for a few days to visit the terrace and stream gold-workings in the neighbourhood of An Hsien, which, although it had defensive ramparts and an elaborate training wall of concrete for the prevention of floods, is, like Zoar, a *very* little city. By the courtesy of the officials we were lodged in the comfortable club-house of the Cantonese Guild, in an

PAI-FUNG, OR MEMORIAL ARCH TO A VIRTUOUS WIDOW, HAN-JU CHOW.

BACK OF HIGH ALTAR, TEMPLE OF KWANG-TI.

PLATE XII.

enclosure tastefully laid out with rockeries, shrubberies, temples, and ornamental water (Plate XIII.).

The Hsien, a brisk and energetic official, called on us. He was in high spirits, and evidently considered that he was making his mark. Having just been appointed to a district with an evil reputation for highway robberies, he had set to work after the customary manner of new brooms, having hanged two robbers, and arranged, before making his call, for the execution, on the day following, of a third.

The gold-workings are said to extend from An Hsien down the Fu Kiang to Lo Chow, near Chung King.

We enjoyed in An Hsien the company and hospitality of the Church Mission, meeting Mr. and Mrs. Knipe, Miss Mitchell, and Messrs. Hamilton, Seaward, and Beach. Mr. Knipe was Mrs. Bishop's guide to 'The Yangtse and Beyond,' and told us some interesting tales of their adventures.

Fishing with cormorants, as practised in the neighbourhood of An Hsien, is the most exciting sport which I have ever had the opportunity of witnessing. On a tiny open canoe stood a man armed with a paddle, and accompanied by a score of cormorants. Merely to balance himself as the boat rushed down the shallow rapids was a feat of which any acrobat might be proud, but the sportsman did much more than this. As he struck the bottom from time to time with his paddle, the cormorants, on seeing a fish rise, would jump overboard and seize it, whereupon the boatman would stretch out the paddle for the bird to step upon, and with a dexterous sweep bring bird and fish on board. This was repeated again and again, to our amazement and admiration. When the cormorants warmed to the work, the whole flock would spring into the water and, while swimming with the canoe, scramble for the prey. The moment one of them had secured a prize he made for the canoe and was taken on board. The birds must be as highly trained as the man.

We met a few high-born sportsmen walking out with hawks on their wrists, but never had the good fortune to see a flight, feathered game being rare. Hawking is even more common in Korea than in China.

After travelling for fifteen miles to the north, through limestone country, we camped in a pretty temple in the village of Chu Shan, where the Chi-Chuen River, after coming from the north-north-west, takes a wonderfully sharp bend to the north.

From Chu Shan to Shih-Chuen (where we spent two days on some alluvial gold-workings), the road leads up the right bank of the Chi-Chuen Ho, commencing with a steep ascent. The river is a foaming rapid all the way. The country is composed of clay slates and blue crystalline limestones, which have a steep dip to the north-west. The local escort was armed with matchlocks. The city wall and a suspension-bridge, 240 feet in length, built of bamboo cables strained on vertical capstans, were among the most notable of the public works of Shih-Chuen. The bridge swayed considerably, but the ponies had no difficulty in crossing it. It is said to require renewal every three years, which must be a severe tax on a community numbering at most 10,000 souls. Two missionaries, the Misses Thompson and Knight, were resident in the town, and theirs were the last white faces we saw on this journey.

JOURNEY TO LUNG-AN

A few miles up the river above the town, we saw the first of the so-called 'Himalayan' or 'Tibetan' bridges, composed of a single rope. As we were passing, a woman attached a load of wood to the rope by means of a thimble, seated herself on the load, glided like lightning to the bottom of the sag, and pulled herself and the load, hand over hand, to the opposite bank.

Walking through Shih-Chuen, on our way to call at the mission, we had to pass the crowd assisting at a theatrical performance in front of a temple. We were sorry for the poor players, who were in a moment left to 'strut and fret' without an audience, the fickle crowd having deserted them for the superior attraction offered by the uncouth foreigners.

Returning to Chu Shan, we took the road to the east. Although this road goes down the valley of the Chi-Chuen, it commences by making an ascent of 2,150 feet (*i.e.*, to 5,350 feet above the sea) in a mile and a half. Up this steep some hundreds of coolies were toiling, laden with bales of wool from Tibet for shipment at Tung Kow, which is reached by a steep descent after passing some coal-mines. Tung Kow, on the Chi-Chuen River, has a very fine bamboo suspension-bridge, and the boat harbour is decidedly picturesque. The river falls into the Fu Kiang a few miles lower. Travelling east and north-east, with limestone hills on our left, we reached the Fu, at Kiang-Yu Hsien, in twenty miles.

In this pretty little town (which, according to the Hsien, who called on us, contains 2,000 families) the Fu, or Prefect, of the Lung-An District now resides. The place is consequently often called Lung-An Fu, whereas the town of Lung-An is seventy-nine miles to the north. The Chinese custom of naming a city after the chief magistrate leads to confusion and a difficulty in identifying places.

In a hill west of the town we noted that gray sandstones and red shales were unconformably overlaid by a limestone formation. About a mile north of the town no less than eleven large bamboo water-wheels were turned by the river. Some four miles further up the valley, the limestone which formed the pavement of the road was full of fossil shells.

At the village of Ping-I Pu, Ho, one of the boys, contracted chicken-pox, and asked for and obtained his discharge. On a shrine in the outskirts we were interested to see an inscription which we could read, although it was only a proper name such as the British tourist pencils on walls everywhere. The inscription was 'T. Wong, 1897.' From one of Litton's Consular Reports I learn that Wong was a Chinese naturalist who had his training from the Abbé David.

A weir crosses the river at Hsiang-N'gai Pa, which is probably, as Gill says, the head of navigation—in a sense. It seems hardly possible for anything to come up the river, but rafts of timber logs shoot down, loaded with merchandise. Chiu Chow is notable as possessing a pontoon-bridge, the only one which I have seen in China. At Pay-Chow Hy we saw the remarkable wrought-iron suspension-bridge mentioned by Gill (vol. i., p. 398).

All the way from Ping-I Pu to Lung-An gold has been worked in the high-level alluvial terraces. On approaching the city, schists replace the limestone and shales, and occasional lenticular masses of shale are met with.

Lung-An is a small but busy town. According to Litton, the inhabitants number 9,000, but I think this must be an overestimate. We were at first conducted to an inn so small and dirty that we protested against the indignity. After some delay we were assigned a suite of rooms attached to the temple. This is said to be one of the ' seven great temples of China,' and it certainly is a fine piece of wooden architecture. I was informed by a Chinaman that it is dedicated to the 'President of Purgatory.' It is doubtful whether there is a Buddhist purgatory, and perhaps the term may be taken as an evidence of the infiltration of Western ideas. There is a Catholic, and at one time there was a Protestant, mission. We called on Father Berrodin, but found him absent.

A remarkable construction was observed within the temple. A wooded pagoda, 40 feet in height, and plastered over with prayers on red paper, was built around a vertical beam, which at the lower end (and presumably at the upper end also) was hollowed into the shape of a cup. The lower cup was balanced on a wooden knob, so that the pagoda could be revolved by the touch of a hand. I am inclined to regard this ingenious contrivance as a concession to, and an improvement on, the llama form of worship, as the prayers can be rotated wholesale, and by machinery, instead of by the tiny hand-wheel used in Tibet.

CHAPTER XIII

HSUEH SHAN RANGE, SUNG PAN, AND RETURN TO CHENGTU

Valley of the Fu—Fortifications against the Mantzü—Suspension-bridges—Alluvial gold—Mining by fire-setting—Primitive milling—'Bits' for artists—The Hsueh Shan Pass—Mountain sickness—Death of a soldier—In the Mantzü country—Sung Pan city—Chinese road kept open through Mantzü territory—Death of Captain Watts-Jones and Mr. J. G. Birch—We bully the Ting—Privileges of travelling officials—Valley of the Min—Mantzü villages—Mantzü fortifications and Chinese garrison towns—Mantzü people—Alluvial gold—Goitre—Mao Chow—'Drive out the foreign devils'—Yen-Hung Ping—Lapidaries—Imitation jade—Coal—Sui Chang—Dragon festival—Return to Chengtu.

From Lung-An to the snow-clad pass of the Hsueh Shan, the valley of the Fu is a gem of beauty, to which, it is to be hoped, artists will direct their attention when they have exhausted Switzerland, Italy, and Norway. Seven miles up the valley from Lung-An the river divides into two branches of equal volume. The branch coming from the north is crossed by an iron suspension-bridge, decked with very rickety planking. The road beyond the bridge crosses a high and steep ridge, on the summit of which a fortified, but dilapidated, gate commands the pass. This is the first of the aforetime defences of the Chinese against the inroads of the 'savages' from the west.

Near Ko-Ta Pa, two villages on the opposite banks of the river are connected not only by a single-rope bridge, but also by a ferry, a boat swinging on a thimble which travels on a rope stretched across the river.

At Sui-Ching Kwan an iron suspension-bridge carries the road over a tributary of the Fu. There are high-level gold-workings in the neighbourhood. The Wong-Shan Kan mines, near Sui-Ching Pu, are worked in a primitive manner. Fallen blocks of quartzite (very poor in gold) are split up by 'fire-setting' and fed into mills of the type in common use for rice-husking. An undershot waterwheel, with two wooden cams, lifts an iron-shod pestle, with the daily result of a few pounds of sand, which are washed in a dish.

There is a bamboo suspension-bridge at the village of Yeh Tang, and an iron one, with fortified gates, at Hso-Pa Kwan. Beyond this village we saw the first cantilever bridge.

Hsiao-Ho Ying is a fort supposed to have a garrison of a thousand soldiers, but actually housing thirty. Its defensive wall (which, by the way, is commanded by the hills on the east and west) is almost perfect, though overgrown with weeds. One corner of it, as well as most of the houses, was carried away a few years ago, but has been repaired. A snow-clad mountain is visible to the south. About ten miles further up the valley the river makes a gorge at least 1,000 feet deep. The foaming water, the covered bridge, the luxuriant vegetation, and the peeps of snow-clad mountains in the distance, form one of the loveliest 'bits' which any artist could desire to see.

Having reached the single inhabited hut now representing the ruinous hill-fort of Hsia-Kwan Tse, we assigned it to the coolies and set up our tents.

Torrents of rain commenced to fall soon after we had camped, and the defects of the roof of the hut became painfully apparent. There was not a dry corner except under our calico. A mile beyond this village a ruinous square stone tower was seen—the first of the ancient strongholds of the Mantzü people. A little further on was the Mantzü village of Kwo-Feng Yeh, with a few sheep. The Mantzü are essentially a pastoral people, while the Chinese prefer agriculture. In the adjacent Chinese hamlet of Win-Tsen Lu we remarked hedgerows of gooseberry-bush.

After another wet camp at Hoang-N'gai Kwan, we commenced the ascent of the Hsueh Shan Pass. There was already a foot of snow on the ground, and we had barely started, when a blinding snowstorm assailed us. Most of the party (Morris excepted) had some experience of the 'mountain sickness' before the summit (13,360) feet was passed. My feet seemed to weigh a hundred pounds each, and my heart beat like a sledge-hammer whenever I made the slightest extra exertion. The Chinese, however, suffered more than we did, which may be attributed, I think, partly to the weakening effects of opium, and partly to 'funk,' for they ascribe the malady to the mountain devils. The Interpreter became black in the face, although he and the Wai-Yuan rode in their chairs while the others walked. Two of the coolies lay down in the snow in a state of collapse, and had to be carried down. One of the soldiers (Corporal Chi) died a few days afterwards while being carried in a chair to the nearest hospital. Morris's pony, although it had been ridden very little, died on the mountain. The white faces of our company peeled for some days after we had crossed the snow. A ruinous hut, or watch-tower, on the summit afforded no shelter, as it was buried deep in snowdrifts.

We lost no time on the inhospitable mountain-top, but slid down, as rapidly as was consistent with safety, through 1,000 feet of snowy slush into better weather and on to grassy slopes, where the sheep and yaks of the Mantzü aborigines pastured at their ease. In the first inhabited hut west of the pass we were hospitably entertained by an aged Mantzü couple, and the milk and scones which they sold enabled us to forget the pangs of hunger, for the coolie with the bread and hard-boiled eggs which were to have been our luncheon was still somewhere in the straggling tail of the procession.

A steep descent brought us, in seventeen miles, to Sung Pan, after passing three Mantzü villages. The houses had mud walls and slate roofs, the slates protected from the wind by heavy stones. High poles, fluttering with paper prayers, denoted that we were among a people who professed the religion of the llamas.

Sung Pan is the furthest outpost of Chinese civilization—the last stronghold or edge of the wedge driven into the heart of Sifan 'barbarism.' Except in this strong military post and on the road up the valley of the Min, which is kept open by the maintenance of a chain of military 'kwans,' or fortified garrison towns, the Chinese have little hold on the Mantzü population. They cultivate the valley and keep the road open, while the Mantzü, who are essentially hunters and pastoralists, have retreated to the mountains. The arrangement recalls the relations subsisting, not so long ago, between the Celts and the Anglo-Saxons.

The principal trade of the town seems to be in woollen stuffs, including blankets. The wall of the city encloses a portion of the river, and runs high up the hill on the right bank. The population is a mixture of Chinese and wild-looking Tibetan and Mantzü people clad in sheepskins. The features and manners of the Mantzü pleased us more than those of the Chinese. They have a distinctly Southern European cast of countenance, and frequently have cheeks as ruddy as any to be met with in England. The people were, however, very shy, and our intercourse with them was limited, as we could only converse with them through the Chinese, who profess to look upon them as beneath their notice.

We learned that Captain Watts-Jones and Mr. Birch had stayed in the town for ten days, and had only left the day before our arrival. The latter was drowned in the Hoang Ho, near Lan Chow, on June 24, and the former was barbarously murdered at Kwei-Hua Cheng a few weeks later.

On our arrival we were taken to a filthy disused temple. The Wai-Yuan and the Interpreter, having been consulted, agreed that a stand must be made. Their methods, which were decidedly un-English, they assured me were strictly in accord with Chinese official ways, and I could do nothing but chime in with them. A strongly worded protest was dispatched to the Ting, or Subprefect, who sent a runner with the reply that he was at the theatre and could not be disturbed, and wished to know what was the matter with the temple. A second remonstrance, accompanied by details of the inconvenience, elicited the rejoinder that the great man was dining out, and that the temple was good enough for us.

This was not to be borne, so the party of five called for chair-bearers and were carried up the hill to the official residence. Invading the yamen and taking possession of the seats of honour on the daïs and the chairs on the left, we intimated to the servants that 'there our fixéd feet should grow,' and that their master had better be sent for. The poor man speedily arrived, and, to my amazement, was treated *de haut en bas* in his own house, the Wai-Yuan and Interpreter pointing out that he was 'bound' to do everything in his power for us, and that our credentials had everywhere else procured for us very different treatment. The lecture had its effect, and in a short time the official was protesting with tears in his voice that it was all a mistake, that his poor house and everything in it were at our disposal, and that at least we should allow him to pay for chair-bearers and coolies to take ourselves and our belongings to suitable quarters. We accepted the new quarters gratefully, but declined the other offers with thanks, and, after profuse compliments, went supperless to bed, as the coolies with the provisions had not arrived. Next day the Ting called on us in state, and all was peace and politeness. The General in charge of the marches and other military dignitaries also paid us ceremonial visits and sent presents of choice viands.

It may be remarked here that it is the custom for resident officials not only to lodge travelling officials, but also to pay their way to the headquarters of the next district. We had been placed on an official footing, and the Wai-Yuan was undoubtedly within his rights in taking the stand which he did on our behalf, and a firm stand was doubtless the best policy; but although I had to put the best face on it and brazen it out, I felt myself blushing at the high-handed proceeding. On our first trip from Chengtu the Hsien of an important city sent me a parcel of silver to pay my expenses to the next 'hsien,' but I declined the gift, and explained that it was the custom of the English to pay their own way. I believe that the fame of this act of self-denial must have gone forth—although, apparently, it had not reached Sung Pan—and must have been the reason that we were, as a rule, so well received by the officials. I heard tales of Europeans similarly placed whose servants, unknown to them, made a practice of exacting 'travelling money' from the officials, and it can be readily understood that such a course would be provocative of ill-will.

The 235 miles down the Min Valley, from Sung Pan to Chengtu, took us ten days. Chinese villages and 'kwans' (fortified garrison towns) alternated with Mantzü villages and high square towers. The Mantzü villages in the valley are now for the most part occupied by Chinese, but we passed within sight of many on the hillsides or in lateral valleys which were still in the possession of the old race. The loop-holed buildings with overhanging balconies and flat roofs were generally two storeys in height, and strongly built of stone, the entrance being invariably high, so high in some instances that a ladder must have been necessary. They were always a-flutter with the llama prayer-flags. Cha-Ergh-N'gai (Plate XIII.) is typical of such villages, although it is tenanted by Chinese.

Captain Gill's description of the Min Valley is so complete that it is unnecessary to repeat it. In a few points, however, changes may be noted. Gill

ORNAMENTAL GROUNDS OF THE CANTONESE CLUB-HOUSE, AN-HSIEN.

MANTZÜ VILLAGE OF CHA-ERGH-N'GAI.

PLATE XIII.

gave the impression of a general decay, which has happily given place to prosperity, if the number of new buildings may be taken as a sign. The forests below Sung Pan mentioned by Gill have almost disappeared. Single-rope bridges are very numerous. Near Seh-Da Kwan we saw a bridge which was an ingenious combination of the suspension and the cantilever. In one place near Cha Ning the road, after struggling for some time along a bench on a cliff, is boldly taken through a tunnel. Cultivation does not begin on the western bank of the river, which is purely Mantzü, till about forty miles below Sung Pan. Potatoes are met with at intervals, grown for non-Chinese consumption. The Mantzü are largely employed by the Chinese as carriers, the road being crowded with pack-yaks driven by men, and women carrying loads in baskets. Even the poorest of these women wear a profusion of silver ornaments, including large brooches and earrings from which discs of jade are suspended. There are frequent workings in the alluvial terraces, from all accounts very poor in gold. Some cases of goitre were observed near Mao Chow.

While we slept in Mao Chow the doors of the inn were placarded with inscriptions inviting the people to 'combine against' us and 'drive out the foreign devils.' There were many other remarks which excited Chung's indignation, but nothing would induce him to translate them or give us their purport beyond admitting that they were 'very bad words.' By order of the Wai-Yuan we were not told of this anti-foreign (Boxer?) demonstration till we were clear of the city. Mao Chow is a city of some importance, situated where the valley opens out into a wide plain.

The walls are unusually strong. The north gate is protected by round towers resembling—or at least suggesting—Fort S. Angelo at Rome. The south gate is remarkable for a Gothic arch.

The village of Yen-Hung Ping employs a considerable number of quarriers and lapidaries in the manufacture, out of a white, green, and red marble, of armlets and pipe-mouths. These articles are chiefly purchased by the coolie classes as a substitute for the jade ornaments worn by their betters. Three miles lower down the valley, at Sui-Wen Ping, the existence of shops where rice could be purchased delighted the hearts of our coolies. The Chinese regard the want of rice as an intolerable hardship, and a dependence on such substitutes as maize, millet, wheat, barley, and oats, as little better than starvation.

At Ta Kwan a coal-mine is worked for the supply of a limekiln. Gray shales and fireclay dip at a high angle on the hillside. In 2 feet of these materials there are scattered films and streaks of coal, aggregating in all perhaps 2 inches. The whole is handpicked, and subsequently washed in troughs for the concentration of the coal, which is partly briquetted and partly made into a wonderfully good coke. In another locality, lower down the valley, an 8-inch seam is made into a high-class coke, for sale in Chengtu (forty miles), whither it is carried in baskets or transported on rafts. Nothing but the badness of the roads and consequent costliness of transport between Chengtu and fields of good coal can account for the admission of the product of these insignificant seams to the market.

Entering the Chengtu Plain at Kwan Hsien, we

reached Chengtu on May 31. In the village of Sui Chang preparations for an approaching 'dragon festival' were in progress. The single street—at least a mile in length—was covered from end to end with an awning of red bunting, bordered with blue, about 10 feet wide. Here and there elaborately embroidered valances of silk depended from the awning.

CHAPTER XIV

FAREWELL TO CHENGTU

Boxer rumours—Joined by Mr. Way—The start—Extra precautions for our safety—Arms of the escort—The Wai-Yuan and his court—'Not guilty, but don't do it again'—Pei-Chung Cheng—Count Bèla Széchenyi's maps—Ya-Chow—Missionaries—Broken telegraph-line—Captain Ryder—Yung-King Hsien—Leprosy—Bridges—Cyclopean masonry—Kwang-Ni Pu—Iron smelting and founding—Artistic castings—Ching-Chai Hsien—Peculiar tombs—Fu-Lin—A French missionary—Ping-Yi Pu—Small-pox in the camp.

DURING our stay in Chengtu, while preparations for the next journey were being carried on, we learned first of the murder of three Germans in Shantung, and of the supposed murder of twenty officials of the Tientsin Railway, and next that Chengtu itself had been placarded with notices intimating that 'the foreigners must quit.' On the night before our projected departure for Maha, Mr. Bush telegraphed from Chung King the news of the destruction of the railway from Tientsin to Pekin, the murder of the Belgian engineers, troubles in the neighbourhood of Chung King, and the interruption of the telegraph-line to Yünnan, and asked me to consider if travelling was safe under the circumstances. I resolved to wait for further details, and requested that the British Consul at Chung King should be asked for his advice. No further news reached us, however, and we left for the South on the morning of June 19, our business being, in my judgment, urgent. We had added to our company Mr. Herbert W. L. Way, representing the Upper Yangtse Syndicate.

In consideration of the disturbed state of the country, the Viceroy directed that we should be accompanied by a party of soldiers from Chengtu as well as by local guards, each of which was to be charged with the duty of taking us across its own military district, and bringing back a receipt for us from the guard of the next district. These escorts varied greatly in numbers as well as in armament and ornament. Some carried Winchester rifles, others merely fans, pipes, and umbrellas, while others had gas-pipe matchlocks. The 'cut-and-thrust' equipment varied from bayonets to swords, spears, pikes, halbards, Lochaber axes, and tridents. Most of the companies carried also brilliantly coloured flags as well as long brass trumpets of the pattern which, according to medieval artists, is in use among the angels in bliss.

We were also accompanied as far as Shaa Ba by a Wai-Yuan named Chü Hung Chi, who held the rank of Hsien, or District Magistrate, and whose red umbrella and green chair had a most imposing effect at the head of our straggling procession, and no doubt procured for us an amount of consideration which we should have missed had we travelled in a private capacity. Chü was a very capable man, who had held magisterial office as a Hsien. He carried with him, as part of his equipment and as a souvenir, the sword with which two malefactors had been decapitated under his orders. On the journey he acted, when necessity arose, in a magisterial capacity, giving judgment in all small disputes which might arise. In one instance one of our chair coolies was jostled or kicked off the road by a mule and injured. The owner of the mule was brought before the Wai-Yuan, and evidence was led, the Writer acting as assessor or *amicus curiæ*. It seemed that nobody was to blame, as the badness of the road and the 'cussedness' of mules were sufficient to account for the disaster. At the suggestion of the assessor, the accused having done no wrong, was dismissed with a caution, and warned not to do it again. He seemed inordinately grateful for this leniency, and made the tour of the room on his knees, knocking his head on the floor in front of the judge and the other members of the party one after another. One of the 'boys,' it may be mentioned, was forced to walk, and the wounded man was carried in his chair, his fellows grumbling loudly at the indignity of having to carry a mere coolie, a man of no more importance than themselves.

At Pei-Chung Cheng (eighty-three miles) there is a handsome stone bridge with five pointed or Gothic arches, a level, well-flagged deck, and steps at both ends. Here we found, on the walls of the inn, a relic of Széchenyi's expedition in the form of a pencilled signature of the late Lieutenant Kreitner, his accomplished topographer, with the date October 16, 1879. It may be said here that we found Széchenyi's maps, so far as we travelled by them, wonderfully accurate and a never-failing comfort. Fortunately, we had had them enlarged, before leaving Shanghai, to the scale of eight miles to an inch, so far as they referred to the province of Szechuan. We had not then foreseen that his maps of Yünnan would have been of at least equal value, and later on it was a matter for constant regret that we had left them behind.

On our arrival at the prefectural city of Ya-Chow, on June 24, we met Dr. Corliss and Mrs. Upcraft, Mr. Upcraft being on a journey. They belong to an American mission, the southmost outpost of Protestantism in Szechuan. We have since learned that this party joined in the retreat from Chung King to Shanghai.

A telegraph-line had been erected by Viceroy Liu Chuan Liu* from Chengtu, viâ Ya-Chow, to Ta-Chien Lu, and we had anticipated that the telegraph-station at Ya-Chow, which could be reached by a messenger from Maha in six days, would form a convenient base of communication. Our disappointment was great when we found that the line was in disrepair, and that dispatches, when received, were forwarded by runners in the time-honoured Chinese fashion. Our communication between Maha and the world was, therefore, always through Chengtu, a journey of ten or twelve days for an express runner.

Ya-Chow is situated on the right bank of the Ya Ho, a considerable river which falls into the Min at Kia Ting. We learned afterwards that Captain Ryder's party arrived at Ya-Chow from Ta-Chien Lu on the day we left (June 27), and that, on hearing of the condition of the country, he dropped down the river by boat to Kia Ting and Chung King.

While we were travelling on the following day, we

* Liu was Grand Councillor at Hsian Fu during the exile of the Court from Pekin.

FAREWELL TO CHENGTU

were overtaken by a telegram informing me of the capture of the Taku Forts and the march of the allies on Pekin. We resumed our journey, puzzling over the question of who was at war with whom.

The long town of Yung-King Hsien (which has a poor low wall) is chiefly dependent on iron-working, hoes and knives being manufactured in great quantities. A leper was seen at the river before we entered the town. At the five-arched stone bridge of Ching-Kow Chow we had the curiosity to measure the stones forming the deck. They were $25 \times 4 \times 2$ feet, and therefore must have weighed about 12 tons each.

At Kwang-Ni Pu, while waiting for the arrival of our belongings, we learned that the town was famous for its iron cooking-pots, and we sallied forth to investigate. Crossing the river to the foundry was rather a ticklish task, the state of the wooden bridge making it a matter of considerable doubt whether we should go over or through it.

The works turned out to be not only a foundry, but also a smelter, operating on hæmatite, limonite, and a clay-band ironstone, the latter of which had been calcined at the mine. We were informed that the grade was 40 or 45 per cent.—of course on the basis of extraction. A quantity of limestone was stored for flux. At the time of our visit the furnace was not in blast, all hands being busied on the conversion of the pig-iron into pots in the foundry. The blast, as at Tung-Ling Tse copper-works, was furnished by a turbine and wooden, double-acting cylinder of considerable size. The furnace was about 30 feet in height, 5 feet at the tuyères, and 10 feet at the boshes, and was fed through a very small opening at the top.

It was built in part of hewn stone, and was not unlike the old English charcoal furnaces. The iron was cast into plates about $4 \times 2 \times 1\frac{1}{4}$ inches, and was fine-grained, and appeared to be of good quality. After breaking up the plates, the iron was melted in small cupolas with hand-bellows, and carried in iron hand-barrows to the casting department. The moulds were made of clay on wicker-work, and were in two parts, which, fitting together at the edges, left a space from $\frac{1}{16}$ to $\frac{5}{16}$ of an inch for the iron. The pots were, from a caster's point of view, beautiful constructions, ranging up to 30 inches in diameter, by 1 foot in depth, and of a mean thickness of probably less than $\frac{1}{4}$ of an inch. At any rate, they were so thin that a travelling pedlar could carry no less than ten of them, weighing in all, perhaps, 500 or 580 pounds.

Very fine art castings in iron are also made by the Chinese, chiefly, so far as we saw, in the shape of bells and urns for temples. Perhaps the most beautiful example of all those that came under our observation was an urn in a temple just outside the walls of Chengtu,* used as a crematorium or fireplace to burn the remnants of joss-sticks and written prayers that had been offered to the gods, and were consequently more or less sanctified. From the intricacy and originality of the design, and its large size, the urn in question may well be regarded as a triumphant evidence of the Chinese founder's skill.

The pass between Kwang-Ni Pu and Ching-Chai Hsien is 9,650 feet above sea-level. Nothing worse than a slight shortness of breath, reminiscent of the 'mountain sickness,' happened to us as we climbed

* A photograph of this urn is reproduced in the *Journal of the Royal Geographical Society* for March, 1902.

up, and at tea-houses on the summit the party was regaled with delicious potatoes, 'all hot.' A small mob of strange little, humped, yellow cattle was met with on the top.

Ching-Chai Hsien does not nearly fill the walls which enclose it. It consists chiefly of one long street, which is a succession of stone stairs. The manufacture of straw hats appears to be one of its principal industries. The tombs of this district are peculiar. They have oval whitewashed walls about 6 feet in height, leaning slightly inward, with a door and memorial tablets at one end. Here the telegraph-line to Ta-Chien Lu and the principal tea route to Tibet leave the main-road. This tea traffic must assume considerable proportions, as an almost unbroken string of coolies had been passed for some days, each man carrying on his back a load which we estimated at not less than 2 hundredweights, and in some cases at as much as 350 pounds.

At Fu-Lin, on the Ta-Tu River, a French priest, the Père Gallay, was located, but, as he was away on duty, we missed him. We left the coolie who had been jostled by the mule, as already mentioned, with a Chinese convert in temporary charge of the mission, with a sum of money sufficient to pay for his keep.

We had all been vaccinated on the eve of our departure from Shanghai, and so successfully that the one great effort of self-denial demanded of us on our voyage to Chung King was to refrain from scratching. In spite of this precaution, however, Lockhart developed small-pox on the way, and we had to halt for a day at Ping-Yi Pu after he had suffered for five days. The attack, however, was a mild one, and the disease was not communicated to any other member of the party. The Chinese suffer a good deal from smallpox, although they practise inoculation with the scab taken from patients.

CHAPTER XV

PING-YI PU TO SHAA BA

Boxer news—Arrival and detention of s.s. *Pioneer* at Chung King—Yueh-Sui—Alleged famine—Prayers against rain—Lolos capture and enslave Chinese—Lolo customs—Richthofen's tracks—A blood-red river—Lu Ku—Iron foundry—French missionaries—A *feu de joie*—Shaa Ba.

WHILE we waited in Ping-Yi Pu, a telegram arrived from Chung King, asking if I thought it advisable to continue the journey, and informing me that the s.s. *Pioneer*, which had just reached Chung King, had been detained, with a view to possible contingencies, by the British Consul, Mr. M. A. F. Fraser, with the consent of the other foreign representatives. The telegram gave some details of the bombardment of Tientsin. After mature conversation, I replied that we were going on, as we could not bear to return with our work unaccomplished, and that I believed that, in the event of trouble, we should be safer at Maha than at Chengtu or Chung King.

We had looked forward to our arrival at Yueh-Sui with some anxiety, on account of the famine which was said to be devastating the district and causing riots. We had been informed that food-stuffs had risen greatly in price, and might, indeed, not be obtainable at any cost. We had, therefore, loaded up a number of mules with rice for the purpose of letting

Near Lu Ku there is an iron foundry, where great cooking-pots and salt-evaporating dishes are turned out. Inside the little walled town we visited the last Europeans we were destined to see for some time— two French priests. They told us that they had heard of the 'rabbling' of the mission houses in Tali Fu, and that the French had advanced from Tonquin and occupied Mengtze, on the road to Yünnan Fu. It may be said here that we afterwards learned that our two friends had been sent for by the Prefect of Ning-Yuan Fu, and lodged in his yamen for their protection. The valley of the An-Ning or Kien Chang Valley is believed to be identical with Cain Du referred to by Marco Polo.

A few miles southward, down the An-Ning from its confluence with the Hoong-Sui, we crossed the river in boats, and arrived at the town of Shaa Ba (Grass Place), where there is a branch office of the Szechuan Mining Bureau. We were met at the An-Ning ferry by a company of the Maha Volunteers, who saluted us with the waving of flags, the blare of trumpets, and a *feu de joie* from their smooth-bore, muzzle-loading, percussion-capped muskets. This was almost the last of the pomps and vanities with which we had been surrounded for some months.

CHAPTER XVI

SHAA BA TO MAHA

Bad news from Pekin, Ning-Yuan and Chung King—Lolos—A mountain pass—Chinese gold-reduction works—Maha gold-mine—Tong Sing Kow—Transport of machinery—Orders to leave China—Preparations—The currency—A new interpreter—Pidgin English—A bid for fortune.

AT Shaa Ba (July 11) I received a telegram, dated July 2, from Chung King, informing me that the German Minister had been murdered in Pekin, and that the situation was very serious. There were also letters from a friend in Chengtu, dated July 3, which informed me that the Viceroy had been very anxious about our safety, and had consulted Li Cheng Yung, the Commissioner for Mines, who gave it as his opinion that the Maha district was for the present safe, and that our best course would be to finish our work as quickly as possible, and then return to Chengtu. We decided to go on with the business.

Shaa Ba (5,355 feet) is a large village, and, as it happened to be market-day when we arrived, we had the opportunity of seeing many of the Lolo people in their gala attire. The women wear a black head-dress, which takes something of the form of a Tam-o'-Shanter bonnet, the rim profusely decorated with silver ornaments. Over a loose vest, clasped with a belt, which is fastened with large silver buckles, they carry broad square silver brooches. A pleated and flounced petticoat completes their attire, and they carry themselves gracefully on their natural feet. The contrast between this costume and the shapeless lower garments of the Chinese women has for ever volved, I am surprised that it takes less than a century.

We observed that the Lolos went barefoot, and they are said to hold the Chinese in contempt for being 'soft' enough to require sandals. They do not encourage this effeminate habit among their captives, but considerably burn the soles of their feet by way of hardening them. I do not know how much of this is true, and I may say that on further acquaintance I found the Lolos a hardy and manly people.

Be this as it may, the road from Ya Chow to Yünnan Fu is hardly considered safe by the Chinese even now, and certainly was not a few years ago. The Lolos occupy the whole of the mountainous country known as the Ta-Liang Shan, east of the road, as well as large districts to the west, having been ousted from the rich lowlands by the Chinese.

Beyond Yueh-Sui we met great numbers of Lolo women carrying baskets of coal from the south. Evidently the Lolos form the bulk of the rural population of this district, and are engaged in agriculture or carrying, while the towns and villages along the road are inhabited almost entirely by Chinese.

About twenty miles from Yueh-Sui we crossed the pass known as Hsiao-Shao Ling (9,315 feet), where Richthofen was turned back in 1872. We were more fortunate than the pioneer, our only trouble being the rain, which fell in torrents.

On the southern slope of this range we struck the Hoong-Sui Ho, or Red River, and ran it down westward to its junction with the An-Ning River at Lu Ku, south of Meinning. The Hoong-Sui River is a striking object—a blood-red streak across the green landscape.

our carrying coolies and other followers (who usually 'found themselves') have it at Chengtu prices.

We found, to our relief, that the sufferings of the district had been exaggerated, for although 4,000 people were reported to be in receipt of charity from the officials and the Famine Committee, we saw little sign of scarcity beyond a slight increase in the usual number of beggars. Rice and potatoes were certainly almost three times their normal cost, but few seemed to be without the means to buy food. We saw no such living skeletons as the illustrated papers have made us familiar with in connection with Indian famines.

Yueh-Sui, a town of perhaps 20,000 inhabitants, is enclosed in a very good wall of dressed sandstone. In accordance with custom, the north gate of the city was closed at the time of our visit, and the magistrates were offering sacrifices and petitions for a cessation of the wet weather, which was threatening, if continued, to ruin the season's crop. In the market we saw many fine leopard-skins and quantities of black salt.

The Hsien, or District Magistrate, told us that only a couple of days ago two Chinese had been killed by Lolos within two miles of the city, and their cattle driven into the mountains. Such occurrences, as well as the carrying off of the Chinese themselves into captivity, are said to be quite frequent. Raids and acts of violence are said to be specially common when, as was then the case, the retiring and the new magistrate are both on the spot, and no one is in recognised authority. It takes, it is said, a year or more for the retiring official to hand over his office to his successor. If questions of money and accounts are in-decided in our minds the vexed question of 'rational dress' in favour of the skirt. The market presented a great show of fruit—chiefly apples and pears—and of mutton. We were received by the Wai-Yuan and other officials in charge of the branch of the Mining Bureau, in their office, which is a converted temple.

On July 12 we left Shaa Ba, and crossed the pass which divides the An-Ning and Ya-Lung Rivers. A few miles out our guard was relieved by a party of twenty spearmen, who before falling in fired three shots from a culverin attached to a staff, like a rocket. About eleven miles from Shaa Ba we had tea in the residence of a Lolo chieftain, who must be a man of means, judging from the number and condition of his cattle and the profusion of silver ornaments worn by his womankind. The serious business of the ascent commenced a few miles further on, and the straggling of our followers became very pronounced, for which it was impossible seriously to blame them. At the summit the index finger of our aneroid, which was only graduated up to 10,000 feet, was 'jammed hard-a-port.' The altitude cannot be under 12,000 feet. We camped for the night at the Native Reduction Works on Ko-Lo Lo Creek, a tributary of the Ya-Lung, where eighty head of stamps, driven by forty overshot water-wheels, were at work crushing stone from the Maha gold-mine. It was not till ten o'clock on the following day that the last of the carrying coolies reached the camp, and, as the night had been marked by a terrific thunderstorm and torrents of rain, they must have spent some wretched hours on the mountain.

An ascent of 400 feet and descent of 1,000 brought

us (July 13) to the modern mill attached to the Maha mine; and here we made our headquarters till August 10, examining the mine and exploring the neighbourhood. The erection of a Huntingdon mill, or, rather, the transport of its heavy parts to such a position as this, is an enterprise which must have severely taxed the patience and ingenuity of the manager, Mr. Tong Sing Kow. This gentleman left China at an early age, and only returned, to take the management of the Szechuan Government mines, after he had received a scientific education in California. With the permission of the Commissioner for Mines, Mr. Tong had accompanied us on our travels since April, and had given us the benefit of his knowledge of the country, the people, and the mines. We were from the first, till we parted on August 10, greatly indebted to him for the vigour and discrimination with which he overcame one difficulty after another. When we finally left, our company's interests were entirely in his hands, and he pushed them zealously.

Although alluvial gold had been worked in the neighbourhood of Maha and the Ya-Lung for many years, the quartz-mine itself had only been at work for twenty. It is said to have employed at one time as many as 15,000 men. Probably the pay-sheet would form the best basis for a census of the employés at any time, for besides the actual miners there are the hands employed at the Huntingdon mill, the Native Reduction Works, and other works at the Lolo village of Ko-Lo Lo. where tailings are treated, and a crowd of Lolo carriers and timber-getters.

The transport of the machinery from Ya Chow

to the mine must have been a work of stupendous difficulty. One casting of 500 pounds in weight is said to have been carried by a single coolie across the range between Shaa Ba and Maha.

All was peaceful in our happy valley. Day after day we awoke to look down upon the upper surface of a fairy cloudland, which on the advent of the sun melted away and revealed the silver streak of the Ya-Lung three miles to the west, and the more than Alpine beauty of the mountainous region beyond. In the outside world, however, events were thickening. The Prefect at Ning-Yuan wrote to our Wai-Yuan, who had remained behind at Shaa Ba, that the Prefect of Ya Chow had informed him that affairs in and near Yünnan Fu were critical, and he warned us that it would be unsafe to go far from Maha, especially southward, without first informing him, and giving him the opportunity of sending more soldiers for our protection. The Prefect continued that on the twelfth day of the fifth moon (June 8) there had been a rising of Boxers in Yünnan Fu, and the houses of the missionaries had been burned down. He added, further, that popular rumour had magnified our four selves, then encamped at Maha, into 300 foreign soldiers.

On July 29 a bombshell fell into our camp in the form of a telegram from our correspondent at Chung King, dated June 30, which, when translated from the cipher, read as follows :

' Revolution increasing. All women and children to be withdrawn from river ports. British Consul most strongly advises you to go to Burma. Europeans and Consuls ready to leave Chung King at a moment's notice. It is probable that all foreigners at Pekin have been killed. Women and children in the river ports are to be sent abroad immediately.'

Later telegrams and letters gave details of the occupation of the native city of Tientsin, of disturbances at Yueh-Sui, and of incendiary fires in the suburbs of Chengtu itself.

The time had evidently arrived for flight, and as the British Consul and other European residents had probably left Chung King before we heard of their intention to do so, no other course was open to us but to take the Consul's 'strong advice' and make for Burma. Letters from other friends advised us merely to 'keep west,' and, as it appeared that the south, east, and north were unsafe, it was evidently the right thing to do.

My knowledge even now of the true state of affairs in the Yangtse Valley is very imperfect, but no doubt Mr. Fraser, the British Consul at Chung King, was in possession of information which appeared to him to render the evacuation of Chung King a necessity. The fates proved kinder to us than to many of our compatriots. The hardships and sufferings of the missionaries who left for Chung King, and the death of many of their number, are now known. The death of Captain Watts-Jones and Mr. Birch, who left Chengtu in the end of April with the intention of travelling, viâ Sung Pan and the Ko Ko Nor, to Pekin, has already been referred to.

Fortunately, thinking that our stay at Maha was likely to be prolonged, I had sent from Ping-Yi Pu, on July 4, to a Chinese banker at Chengtu for a further supply of money, and it arrived at Maha on

August 8. We borrowed some more (which had to be sent for to Li Chow, near Ning-Yuan), for which we gave drafts on Chengtu, after which we reckoned that we had enough to take us beyond the limits of China. Chinese money is received from the bank in the form of 'sycee,' or oval ingots of silver, weighing about 10 taels. In every 100-tael packet are included some smaller, thimble-like ingots of 1 or 2 ounces each, and a number of chips or shavings of silver, to make up the exact weight. It is found to be a convenience, which is adopted by most travellers, to send a number of ingots to the blacksmith, who hammers them out and cold-chisels them into rectangular pieces. It is unnecessary to enlarge on the subject of the Chinese currency. Each city has silver differing in fineness; each has its own scale. The exchange is somehow always against one when converting silver into copper 'cash,' which in their turn vary in value in every district, while in some there are only 82 cash to the reputed 100, and in others there are as many as 98. Lastly, a certain number of bad coins to a string (varying in each district) is allowed. All previous travellers have made merry over the Chinese currency, but I confess it was only when we were in our happiest moods that we saw the humorous side of the question. Our silver money amounted, all told, when we started, to two mule-loads, and as a string of cash—1,000, or reputed 1,000, of the value of about 2s.—weighs 9 pounds, we never carried more of it than we were absolutely compelled to.

As it was necessary to reduce the number of our party as far as possible, we sent back all our boys except two of Mr. Way's, one of whom was to be cook. My interpreter, Chung Chui Lin, also returned to Shanghai, and we took only Mr. Way's interpreter, Nee Sui Ching, who volunteered for the service, but who, because he was only entitled to wear a white button on his hat, had a much lower official standing. It may be said here that Nee, who was generally known by his 'familiar' name of Ah Foo, fully made up for this deficiency by his push and tact, and above all by his good-humour and ready wit, which, we noticed, always sufficed to convert a sulky or timid official in a few minutes into an interested and ready helper. On more than one occasion the gates of a yamen, otherwise closed to him, opened wide on his plausible representation that he was familiar with the official's native town, and had gossip to retail, his extensive travels in China having made him well acquainted with the life and dialect of most of the provinces. By the camp-fire or in the guest-room of the village inn he frequently entertained us with his reminiscences. A single specimen of his pidgin English will suffice. It was a tale of a bid for wealth on the Shanghai Races.

'I go sometimes longa laces, look-see lacing, side show, evellything. You savee "side show," gentlemen? Yes? You have got shooting gallely, evellybody come pay five cent, supposee ling bell catchee one dollar. 'Nother place sell plenty tickets, makee wheel go lound, somebody takee one piecee gun—bang! Hit number on wheel: man with same number on ticket he catchee first-class plize. 'Nother place have got tent and men makee fight and plenty people look see. Evellywhere all about have got plenty stand; evellybody go catchee tiffin. I walk about, look-see side show. Evellybody makee plenty money chop-chop. I say to myself, " Welly good pidgin!" Next year I buy license, put up stand, tent, evellything. Welly big expense; I think welly big plofit too. Then I get twenty, maybe thirty, foreign gentlemen—not number one foreign gentlemen allee same you—some black foreign gentleman. He stop outside tent, topside table alonga side show, makee plenty noise, call out and makee people come spend plenty money. You savee that kind foreign gentleman? I makee cook too, plenty chicken, maybe twenty dozen for tiffin. Supposee man have got good tiffin, he feel velly good, go shoot, go side show, spend plenty dollar. Welly good pidgin! I have got evellything welly nicee.' Here the jubilant note is exchanged for a wail more in sorrow than in anger. 'Then laces come, three days' laces, and it lain allee time: nobody come, no can sell anything, side show can catchee no pidgin. Welly hard luck! When I makee pay, no have got nothing. I luined. I think my Joss welly bad, maybee he angly. I lose my business, then go allee same coolie. By'mby I get interpreter to foreign gentleman. By'mby, suppose Joss no more angly, maybe can catchee 'nother good chance, makee plenty dollar.'

CHAPTER XVII

THE FLIGHT TO BURMA BEGINS

Preparations—Descent to Moo-Li Chang—The Ya-Lung River —A mule slips—Lolo village of Lo-Ko Ti—A much-married man—On Bonin's tracks.

IN spite of the fact that our flight ought to have been of the nature which Nee described as 'chop-chop,' many preparations had to be made. Mr. Tong went to Shaa Ba to negotiate for muleteers and guides. We thought he had found perfect treasures in Ta Er Doh, a Tibetan, with his assistant, Li Tae Shing, and Shaa Ba Shan, a Chinese wool-merchant, with an assistant named Dwen Ying Shang, who was to show him the road—rather a curious requirement for a guide, I thought. It was arranged that Ta Er Doh and Shaa Ba Shan were to contract for mules and coolies, and it was supposed that their presence would materially assist us among the Chinese and semi-Tibetan Sifan people. On their arrival at Maha it appeared that they still required some time for their arrangements. Mules and coolies had to be collected from the surrounding district, and horseshoes had to be sent for to Li Chow. Even when these arrived, further delays were inevitable. I never quite realized before how meritorious is the virtue of patience. Now the last requirement was rice, then it was baskets, again it was arms, and once more it was a mule which had not arrived. Finally, on our own account, we waited a few hours for a mail which we had heard was on the way. The mail brought, among other things, a telegram, dated July 27, from our correspondent in Chung King, which relieved us of all responsibility in the matter of leaving China. It read:

'Foreign Office, London, telegraphed yesterday instructions take steps remove all British subjects from China.'

Within ten minutes of the receipt of this dispatch we had said adieu to our good friends in Maha and started for Burma (August 10) in a heavy downpour of rain. The three miles, as the crow flies, to the

THE FLIGHT TO BURMA

Ya-Lung proved something like seven, and involved a descent of nearly 4,000 feet. We camped in the village of Moo-Li Chang, on the left bank of the river. Heavy rain continued throughout the night.

Next morning we started while it still rained heavily, although it had cleared up by the time we reached the ferry, half a mile up the river. The passage in the single boat, which was very small and could only carry four at a time, took the greater part of the day, the swift current always carrying it a long distance downstream. The horses were swum over, two on each trip, alongside the boat. We erected tents at a farmhouse called Hoang-Ta Ping (5,340 feet), which was occupied by our following. The total distance travelled was about two miles. There was heavy rain again throughout the night.

We left Hoang-Ta Ping at 5.45 a.m. The first half of the day was showery and foggy. It was a terrible day's journey, commencing with a steep climb to strike a road which had been visible from our late residence at Maha. Halfway up one of the mules slipped and rolled down a steep slope for at least 100 feet. Our concern for the mule was tempered by anxiety about his load, which consisted of my box of papers and maps and a case of silver. Fortunately, the Chinese pack-saddle is designed to meet such contingencies, and in this instance it came off bodily, and left the mule to pursue the latter half of his downward course unencumbered. The case was smashed, but the silver was all recovered. The mule, which must have had more than nine lives, was got on his feet apparently little the worse, but proved unfit for further work. We struck the road at last, but had only followed it for about a mile to the south, when we were pulled up by a landslip. We then made for a higher road, in which we succeeded after nearly losing some of the mules and riding-ponies. We were hospitably received and temporarily sheltered from the rain in a farmhouse called Chang-Ko Lo. The highest point of this road, according to the aneroid, was 7,620 feet, and was just above the cliff where the road, as seen from Maha, disappears. The road then sidles down into the creek up which one looks from Maha. It had been washed away in many places, and we had to cross a raging torrent seven times within half a mile. Our impatience was such that we got ahead of the horses, and I never expected to see them again, but I did.

About two miles up the creek we left it and zigzagged up its right bank till we reached a house with a clearing and some cultivation, at an altitude of 8,470 feet. In about three miles we reached the Lolo village of Lo-Ko Ti (9,120 feet). In ten hours of travelling we probably walked ten miles; but I estimate, from bearings, the distance between Moo-Li Chang and Lo-Ko Ti to be five miles. We put up our tents at the end of the village, our followers occupying the inn. The inhabitants were somewhat darker than the Chinese, and were said to be half Sifan, half Lolo. Our Chinese followers were obliged to converse with them through the medium of Ta Er Doh. The male villagers wore sheepskin cloaks. The women had a dress gathered in at the waist with a silver-buckled belt, earrings of silver from which depended jade discs, and a Tam-o'-Shanter cap decorated round the brim with large silver marbles. The married women wore broad silver rings on the usual ring finger. We were told of a silver-mine a few miles across the mountains to the west, which may have been the place of origin of so much feminine finery. The innkeeper, who is also the headman of the village, owns the mine as well as a good deal of land, and is said to have no fewer than five wives. The inn had a raised wooden floor, and was furnished along the side with benches for beds, and a great fireplace in the centre with two large boilers. There was, of course, no chimney.

I was at some pains to inquire into the knowledge of foreigners possessed by the villagers, as I had been informed that Captain Watts-Jones had made the village one of the trigonometrical stations on his survey of the proposed railway from Shamo; but they had never heard his name and knew nothing of his visit. They distinctly remembered, however, the advent of a foreigner, whom they named Po Ta Ning, about five years ago. The syllables sounded like Potanin, but are more likely to have meant Bonin.

CHAPTER XVIII

LO-KO TI TO SHU-PA PU-DZA

A road in the bed of a torrent—Practical engineering—Wet skins and dry throats—Goitre—Irate coolies—Sifan hamlet of Shu-Pa Pu-dza—Flight of the natives—Friendly relations established.

AFTER leaving Lo-Ko Ti, we ascended, for about a mile to the north-east, to a grassy clearing 9,770 feet above the sea, then went along a ridge for about a mile to the east and down again into the creek which we had left the day before. Our road, for five miles west-south-west, lay up and in the creek, and presented many serious difficulties. In one place we were confronted by a waterfall, about 10 feet in height, which plainly said '*non possumus*' to the muleteers. It took us a couple of hours to pile logs and stones in front of the fall till we had made a grade up which the animals could be led—through a 'douche' which, however, could not make us wetter than we were already.

Above the fall the creek opened out to some extent, and we were able to travel for the most part on the alluvial flats which bordered it. Here we saw a bear in a tree, and one of the party, a keen sportsman, was so fortunate as nearly to shoot it. This was the only wild beast of a presumably dangerous character (insects excepted) seen on our travels. In about five miles west-south-west, during which we passed a herd of yaks, we headed the creek and attained the summit of a ridge which we estimated at 13,600 feet, and in another mile found, just at nightfall, a place sufficiently level and free from boulders for a camp. Unfortunately, although water had been superabundant during the greater part of the day, the camp was dry. We had to send back, after the moon rose, more than a mile for water enough to make tea. The coolies kept dribbling in with their loads up to midnight. Some idea of the toil of the day's march may be conveyed by the fact that we only gained eight miles in ten hours. Towards the morning the skies gave us the moisture which the earth had refused, and even more of it than we desired.

Next day's journey commenced with a rapid descent of about 2,000 feet into the head of a creek which we could see falling into the Ya-Lung about ten miles east-south-east. A rise of 3,000 feet followed before the track emerged on the summit of the ridge which divides the north-running, or Kwa Pit, upper reach from the south-running, or Moo-Li Chang, lower reach of the Ya-Lung.

A nearly level road, over bleak moorland country, on the north-west side of this ridge, was a welcome change after the land of mountain and flood of the previous days, as we were able to ride for nearly five miles to the south-west. In a region like this we might have expected to meet tigers or leopards, or at least pheasants or grouse, but the moorland was destitute of life save for the presence of two parties of Sifans whom we met driving goats and cattle. Game, indeed, was remarkably scarce all the way, till we approached the borders of Burma. There were a few patches of pine-forest, many of the trees dead, and all liberally festooned with drooping lichens.

In three miles to the south-west we had rounded the head of our valley and dropped down its right bank to Shu-Pa Pu-dza (10,070 feet), a Sifan hamlet of half a dozen or so of houses enclosed by a low wall and gates. Our noble guide, Shaa Ba Shan, led us still further down the valley to a house (8,970 feet) inhabited by a Sifan woman, with a frightful goitre on the front of her neck, and a pretty little daughter of about fourteen. The house was mainly furnished with vessels containing buckwheat. It appeared that we had left the proper track at Shu-Pa Pu-dza, and the unnecessary steep climb of 1,100 feet back to the village made us all very cross, especially the carrying coolies, who remonstrated with Shaa Ba Shan till he dissolved in floods of tears.

If the gentle reader has ever finished up a hard day's work by carrying a heavy load down 1,100 feet only to carry it up again, he will be in a position to understand the feelings of the coolies. Shaa Ba Shan made his peace in the evening by the purchase and present of a goat, but for some weeks afterwards it was easy to see that his pretensions to guidance were a fertile source of wit in others, and that a constant policy of pin-pricks and pelting with chaff made his life a burden to him.

Our arrival in the village created some consternation among the few inhabitants who were at hand, mostly children and old men. We learned afterwards that the able-bodied men had fled (though they left the old men and children) through fear of being killed and eaten by the invading foreigners. We found a comfortable camping-ground on a green slope above the village, and then proceeded to establish friendly relations with the villagers. We bought, among other things, a goat, from which, on its being dragged out for slaughter, the mistress of the house plucked a handful of hair which she placed on the lintel—an act which had, probably, some religious significance. We found that the majority of the houses in the village were designed for the accommodation of the sheep, goats, cattle, and horses, which are gathered in nightly and housed for their protection from thieves and beasts of prey.

Shu-Pa Pu-dza, it appeared, was the first village on our route within the jurisdiction of the powerful Toussa of Kwa Pit. The headman informed us that a large number of hands were employed in silver-mining across the mountains to the east of the village. The creek which we had headed earlier in the day has, by the time it reaches Shu-Pa Pu-dza, cut a deep ravine. On the left bank of the creek rises a sheer cliff of dazzling white marble, which must be at least 3,000 feet high, and from which the constant fall of fragments of rock keeps up a tinkling clatter which can be heard from the village.

CHAPTER XIX

SHU-PA PU-DZA TO KAI-JA PU-DZA

Marble mountains—A dry valley—Lolo cave-dwellings—A natural tower—Village of Ta Pu-dza—Valley of Mai-Tzu Ping—Lolo villages—Intervillage warfare—An old grudge —Kai-Ja Pu-dza—Capons—Feminine curiosity—Prisoners.

AFTER crossing the creek at an altitude of 8,670 feet, we climbed up to a gap (9,770 feet) on its left bank, about a mile below Shu-Pa. Bearing to the south-south-east, we then sidled down into a tributary valley, which we ran up on the right bank, crossing the creek (at 9,570 feet) just above where the water commences to flow. This creek has its head among the marble mountains, which rise to a height of at least 5,000 feet above the point where we crossed.

Half a mile to the south, up the left wall of this valley, brought us through a gap (10,270 feet), and into the valley of another tributary which falls to the west. This we ran up eastward for two miles to its head (14,000 feet), where the limestone rocks carried a stunted vegetation of pines and evergreen oaks. From this pass we could look down into the heads of an unusually rugged valley, falling to the south-east, and taking its rise from a series of sheer precipices which must have been 4,000 or 5,000 feet in height. A zigzag descent, of about 4,000 feet by the aneroid, brought us to the bottom of the valley in a horizontal distance of not more than a mile, after which we followed the valley down to the south-west by an easy track. This well-defined valley, enclosed between walls varying from 1,000 to 5,000 feet in height, has not a drop of water, or even a definite watercourse, for the first five miles.

Shortly after entering it we came on two Lolo boys tending a small mixed mob of horses, cattle, pigs, and goats, and, a little lower down, two Lolo men engaged in a similar pastoral occupation. At three miles we met with the first patch of cultivation (maize) and some Lolo dwellings. The latter are very peculiar, and I am not sure if they have been described before. They are situated, as a rule, on a ledge of horizontal sandstone rock, where the lower portion of the stratum above has weathered out in such a manner as to leave caverns or rock shelters. These natural shelters are, when necessary, made into complete dwelling-places by the addition of a minimum of wickerwork wall. A sort of veranda in front is fenced in, no doubt for the purpose of saving the children from destruction. One of the most primitive of these dwellings, which we ventured to look into because it had no wall, and consequently no privacy to be respected, had for its sole furniture a wooden trough surmounted by a hand-mill consisting of two flat round stones, for grinding buckwheat, and a few handfuls of straw for bedding. The family of few wants, even in the way of clothing, squatted about in leisurely attitudes or busied themselves with rudimentary culinary processes over a heap of ashes on the floor of the cave.

Near the lower end of the long dry reach of the

valley, we passed, but did not enter, a large Chinese house, which was apparently half temple. Its watersupply was a trickle derived from a spring high up on the hillside, and carried for a considerable distance in wooden flumes.

At the end of the dry reach is a most remarkable natural tower, in shape something like the Nelson monument in Edinburgh, but very much higher, resting on a square pedestal, also natural, although quite in accordance with architectural canons. A pretty little monastery leans against the pedestal and looks down the valley. Just below the tower the dry valley falls (if such a thing can be said of a dry valley) into a valley coming from the west, and carrying what may be called a good-sized trouting stream of clear blue water. This can be no other than the same stream which we had crossed below Shu-Pa Pu-dza.

We crossed, by a graceful new wooden arcadebridge, to the right bank immediately below the confluence of the stream with the dry valley, and just above the mouth of another, though smaller, stream coming from the north-east. Here, while rain began to fall in torrents, we ascended by a road on the right bank of the river for about 400 feet, and reached the village of Ta Pu-dza (7,670 feet). Our camp here was in the house of a Chinese farmer of substance named Sin. The house was fairly new and of a superior type for this part of the country, forming a quadrangle enclosing a courtyard, and having wooden floors and a roof of ornamental red tiles. Some of the rooms were full of agricultural implements, such as wooden ploughs with iron shares, like the flukes of an anchor, and harrows with wooden teeth set in square frames. We noticed one woman with a repulsive goitre. The coolies arrived very late, having lingered too long at the mid-day halt, after persuading themselves, as usual, in spite of all that could be said to the contrary, that this was to be a short day's journey.

From Ta Pu-dza the course of the valley can be seen for perhaps eight or ten miles down to the south-east, and the creek no doubt falls into the Ya-Lung River. We left the village next morning, and in one mile to the south had reached the summit of the wall of the valley (9,570 feet). Keeping as close as possible to the foot of a gigantic cliff of marble, the road took us in three miles to a gap (9,700 feet), held by a large party of Lolos armed with spears. The object of the gathering we had to learn later on. In two miles more south-south-east we reached the Lolo village of Shwang-Nang Pu-dza (8,370 feet), in the valley called Mai-Tzu Ping. This village is a strange collection of mud and stone houses, built on half-artificial terraces on a rocky slope, evidently with the object of not using any land fit for cultivation. Here, to our surprise, we met with anything but a welcome. The villagers poured out of their houses in a state of great excitement, and vociferated loudly, of course without our being any the wiser. Tsung Ho Chung,* the most intelligent and resourceful of the Chengtu soldiers, shouted himself hoarse and apoplectic in the Chinese tongue, naturally with no effect. Finally a Chinese inhabitant was found, and through him matters were explained to the satisfaction of all, whereupon we were conducted to apartments on the first-floor of a

* The central figure of the group on Plate XI.

house, our ponies being accommodated on the ground-floor. This system is not without its advantages, as by looking through the chinks in the flooring the traveller can always satisfy himself of the safety of his beasts of burden. It appears that about twenty-one years before some robbers came over from Ta Pu-dza and carried off four goats. Reprisals followed, and ever since there has been a bitter 'ould grudge' between the two villages. A few days before our arrival at Schwang-Nang some silver had been stolen, and two of the thieves had been captured on the day we arrived. A party of 100 men from Ta Pu-dza had come over to rescue the captives, in which, however, they failed. Hence the armed party which we met at the pass and our unfriendly reception at Schwang-Nang, where the inhabitants had come to the conclusion that we were allies of their hated rivals of Ta Pu-dza. After the difficulty had been explained, the Lolos became the kindest of friends. The headman of the village and many others called (not, perhaps, altogether uninspired by curiosity and a desire to inspect our weapons) and left presents, among which were a leg of mutton and a really magnificent capon. The latter was in itself an evidence that we were among a race differing widely in their ideas from the Chinese. A short digression apropos of this subject may not be out of place. The conclusion that no animal must be allowed to die without having first had the opportunity of reproducing itself follows on certain religious convictions of the Chinese; but it works out, notably among horses (in those parts of China where the Chinese follow their religious teachings), in a very unpleasant manner. The creation of a race of 'weeds' or 'wasters' is the natural result of every horse becoming a sire. Then, the fact that all riding animals are stallions makes it imperative that each rider should be attended by a groom to manage, if not to lead, the animal. The deterioration of the race of riders follows as a matter of course, while the grooms are diverted from more useful employments to the service of luxury.

Two yamen-runners arrived in the course of the evening, one from the Toussa of Kwa Pit, and the other from the Hsien at Yen Yuan. After we had retired for the night, we were somewhat surprised by a visit from our host, who opened the door and held a lighted torch for the purpose of affording the ladies of the household, who crowded behind him, an opportunity of inspecting (from the threshold) the remarkable camp-beds used by the foreigners, and the still more remarkable red blankets with which they covered themselves. The curiosity of the ladies was satisfied at last, and they retired with shrieks of good-natured laughter.

Next day we only moved three miles up the valley (south-south-west) to the village of Kai-Ja Pu-dza (8,270 feet), as our escort reported that there was no possible camp between that and Kwa Pit, which was too long a stage. The village was very much a duplicate of Schwang-Nang, although rather smaller, and our quarters were, as there, over the stable. The two prisoners from Schwang-Nang, one of whom was a mere boy, were brought in in the afternoon with chains round their necks. The valley of Mai-Tzu Ping is closely cultivated, the principal crops being buckwheat, maize, barley, and oats.

CHAPTER XX

KAI-JA TO KWA PIT—KWA PIT—A PEEP INTO THE
MIDDLE AGES

A lake—A gold-mine—Divide between Ya-Lung and Upper Yangtse—Kwa Pit—A hearty welcome—Interior of a mediæval castle—The Toussa's family history—A Lolo court of justice.

LEAVING Kai-Ja early in the morning, our road led up the left bank of the creek, with an enormously high wall of limestone on our right. In two miles it entered a gorge, passed a fine waterfall, and skirted a pretty little lake hemmed in by precipitous limestone walls. The lake is certainly not due to the erosion of a glacier, and is probably only a limestone 'sink' on a large scale.

Two miles above the lake is the alluvial gold-mine called Ma-Jong Tzu. All that could be seen was the mouth of a well-timbered adit.

Five miles further, with the lofty limestone wall on our right, and similar, though more distant, walls on our left, we reached the pass (estimated at 12,000 feet) at the head of the Mai-Tzu Ping Valley, and, I believe, on the divide between the Ya-Lung and the Upper Yangtse. A sharp marble peak on the western side of the pass forms a very conspicuous landmark, and is, I think, one of those which are visible from Maha. In and near the pass we noted the presence of pines, evergreen oaks, silver birch, rhododendron, juniper, and other trees, while bluebells grew to a size quite unusual in their better known Caledonian habitat. A village could be seen on a high plateau about two miles east of the pass, and it was notable that this village was approached from the higher lands to the east by an extraordinarily wide track resembling a 'drove-road' in the pastoral districts of Australia.

From the pass we descended rapidly to the south-west and west, crossing (from right to left) a creek which rises in the pass, and is seen falling, about three miles to the west, into a large river running to the north. The road shortly afterwards leaves the valley, and, turning to the south, heads a creek which forms a deep valley, and also falls into the large river. After heading the creek, the road turns westward, keeping well up on the plateau on the left bank, and in about seven miles from the pass reaches Kwa Pit. We had accomplished in nine days of ceaseless toil a total of seventy-three miles.

We were received, about a mile from the yamen, by a red umbrella and a trumpet, the messengers bearing an invitation from the Toussa.

The residence of the Toussa is a veritable mediæval castle, and has in former times been strongly fortified. There is at present a practicable gate, but it is not the only entrance, as there are many breaches in the wall itself. On our arrival five shots from a culverin saluted us, and there might have been more if we had not begged the gunners to desist, out of deference to the susceptibilities of our ponies.

After we had been led through several courtyards, the Toussa, in official dress, met us at the head of the front steps of the residence. We were the first foreigners who had ever passed his gates. One large room and the adjoining courtyard formed an armoury or arsenal, or, rather, museum, for many of the arms must have been centuries old. The cutting instruments comprised, I should think, every variety of sword, spear, and dagger known in the East; while arms of precision ranged from bows and crossbows, through the whole series of matchlocks, flintlocks, and percussion-locks, to Winchester rifles.

In front of the court of justice there were also numerous stands of arms, chiefly spears, halbards, tridents, etc., but the most remarkable were six long culverins of about $1\frac{1}{2}$ inch calibre, mounted on swivels fastened to office stools, and one 4-inch bore 'carronade' on a wheeled carriage. These pieces of ordnance are said to have come from Chengtu about ninety years ago.

The doorposts were hung with raw-hide straps, bamboo laths, and other instruments of flagellation. A peculiar instrument looked like the sole of a boot composed of several thicknesses of raw hide, but only fastened together at the heel. It was designed, as was explained, to procure 'silence in the court' by striking obstreperous witnesses on the mouth. These instruments are probably, for the most part, relics of a bygone age, for the Toussa is, I believe, a just and humane man.

Detached from the court and residence was a Buddhist temple, which might be called the Toussa's private chapel. It was evidently very old, and contained, among other things, valuable bronzes and china vases, suits of leather-plate armour, stuffed bears and leopards, and an ancient book in the Lolo character, which, whatever its subject might be, was held in great reverence by the priests.

The Toussa's family name is Poo Ta, and his official name Chi King Liong. In answer to our polite inquiries, he informed us that his family had reigned for thirteen generations, or 630 years. It may be remarked that the average length of the generations proves the Poo Tas to have been a healthy race. They migrated originally from the Moso country, and conquered the Kwa Pit district bit by bit. The present chief is a comparatively young man. The Emperor has bestowed upon him the right to wear a yellow jacket and two feathers, in recognition of his services against the insurgent, Li Sieh, in Yünnan four years before. He evinced a keen professional interest in our weapons, especially the Winchester repeating rifles and Mauser pistols, and made some excellent shooting with them, killing pigeons and knocking spots off the ornamental tiles of the roof. We were introduced to his father, a paralytic, and also to a brother and uncle, and had a glimpse of the wives (although, of course, we were not introduced to them) when they were called to look at some illustrated papers which we happened to have with us. One of them was decidedly beautiful, with clear-cut Italian features, and was tastefully painted, not overdone like the Chinese ladies.

In spite of our anxiety to be on the move, we stayed two nights with the Toussa, as he insisted that we must allow time for the messenger whom he was about to send along our route to get ahead of us. Besides, his hospitality was so pressing and so evidently genuine that he would clearly have been hurt by a refusal.

On the second night we attended a sitting of the court. The proceedings were orderly and impressive, although, of course, we could only have the gist of the evidence translated to us in whispers. The trial of two men and two boys for murder lasted as long as we stayed. The accused and the witnesses, on being brought in in their turn, fell on their knees, knocked their heads on the floor, and shouted, 'Hail, great chieftain!' The Toussa listened patiently and attentively to the evidence, his body swaying from side to side, and occasionally made a note, or interrupted the witnesses or prisoners (who were heard in their own defence) with a few questions.

All the parties concerned were Lolos, and from the manner in which they gave their evidence they must either have rehearsed it carefully, or have been born orators. First the mother of the murdered man spoke at great length, then a priest who professed to have seen the murder, and finally the accused were examined one by one. The evidence of one boy of about fourteen did not tally with that of the other witnesses, and, after several warnings, he was laid down on the floor and gently—I must say very gently—spanked with a light bamboo lath till he 'confessed.' The upshot of it all was that a true bill was found, and the prisoners were committed for trial at Yen Yuan. I was somewhat surprised that the Toussa did not himself pronounce judgment, but I am inclined to think that such extreme measures are distasteful to him.

CHAPTER XXI

KWA PIT TO YEN CHING

Alterations in the charting of the Ya-Lung River—Hay-Lü Tzu—Lolo escort—Valley without outlet—Were we invaders?—Ka-La Ba—A Lolo tribal dwelling—Wheel traffic—The Kwa Pit Toussa's wars—Pei-Sui Ho—Among Chinese again—Chinese hotels—Yen Ching—Brine wells and evaporation works.

THE morning on which we left Kwa Pit was one to be remembered for the torrents of rain, which made umbrellas, waterproofs, and attempts to keep our feet dry, mere foolishness. We tramped up and down through the slippery mud in a south-west, south, south-south-east, and easterly direction for about thirteen miles, the rain and fog preventing our making minute observations. Once or twice we caught a glimpse of the large river which we had seen before arriving at Kwa Pit, and we were evidently travelling for some time up its valley. The rain ceased about one o'clock, when we reached our camp in the Toussa's 'shintai' (or guest) yamen of Hay-Lü Tzu (translated as Black Ass Place) 7,018 feet. The 'shintai' yamen is situated near the head of a gully which runs westward to join the large river. Our room was over the stable. When the sun shone out shortly after our arrival, we covered the whole roof with our wet bedding and clothing.

The identity and relations of the large river seen to the west of Kwa Pit had been for many days a constant theme of speculation. According to the compiler of the 'China Inland' map, who takes it from Bretschneider, who takes it, I believe, from Hosie, the river might be one of two which flow north-westward into the Ya-Lung—one west of Yen Yuan, and the other through Yung-Ning; but had it been either of these our course must have crossed it, and it did not. I concluded that, leaving Yung-Ning in the position which Széchenyi assigns to it, the Ya-Lung River itself flows southward to the east of Yung-Ning, takes again a northward course to the west of Kwa Pit, makes a long sweep to the north and east, and finally flows south by Moo-Li Chang, where we crossed it. There is no place for the river called the Wu Liang of Bretschneider's and the ' China Inland ' maps—at least, to the south of Yung-Ning, although in the northern part of its course it may be identical with Amundsen's Shu Ye (see map in *Journ. Roy. Geogr. Soc.*, vol. xxvi.).

On my return to Shanghai I took the opportunity of comparing notes with Major H. R. Davies, who travelled in the district early in 1900. It is now certain that the mysterious river west of Kwa Pit is no other than the Ya-Lung. We had crossed its lowest southward reach at Moo-Li Chang, and gone round the southern end of the great bend above that reach, whereas Major Davies, on a more northerly course (from Mien-Ning via Mili to Chung T'ien), had to cross the river, not once, as we did, but three times.

It rained again the following morning when we set out from Hay-Lü Tzu, and showers fell throughout the day. Our course lay due south for five miles to a pass which forms the divide between gullies running towards Hay-Lü Tzu and waters falling to the south. On this piece of road we observed a number of charcoal furnaces of an unusually permanent character, the charcoal being for use in foundries where evaporating pans for brine are constructed. At a block-house in the pass we were joined by a new escort of Lolo warriors, armed with spears and small-bore matchlocks, with handles like that of a horse-pistol, and of such extravagant length that at a little distance the fusiliers might have been taken for a party of anglers carrying fishing-rods. To our astonishment, a wheel-road led down the bed of a gully southward from the pass, and, although we were not yet by any means clear of the mountains, the mere fact that wheel traffic was possible gave promise of more open country. In three miles to the south the creek which we had run down from its head ceased to flow, and the valley (which had by that time been excavated to a considerable depth) closed in, and was absolutely without any outlet. The creek probably has an underground course through a channel in the limestone. At this point we encountered a gaily-dressed and well-mounted Chinese official, who at the head of a party of soldiers came, like the 'fiery Duke,' pricking fast across the plain. I never quite understood what was the trouble, but probably he took our caravan either for a foreign invasion or a Lolo rising. Our interpreter soon satisfied him, however, and the incident ended in his furnishing us with an addition to the escort.

Climbing up out of the 'blind' valley and crossing a ridge to south-south-east, we dropped into the valley of a small stream running southward. Between the block-house and this stream we met first with limestone and then with sandstones and shales of the coal-measures. About a mile further to the south the road ascended to the summit of the left wall of the valley, and here the coal-measures were succeeded by an older formation consisting of vertical slates.

As soon as we had reached the top, the promise held out by the wheel-ruts was fulfilled. We were on the edge of an extensive area of 'downs,' which, although tame by comparison with the mountain scenery behind us, gratified us with the prospect of a few days of good going. In two miles south-south-east, over the downs, we crossed a small river flowing to the south-west. Another mile to the south-east, and we reached Ka-La Ba (9,070 feet), where we camped for the night in a house which is at once the headman's residence and the tribal dwelling. My arrival was undignified. I rode a little black stallion which had only one fault—an uncontrollable enmity towards the little black stallion ridden by my son. We carried open umbrellas and long mackintoshes. As we came to a halt the usual precaution of keeping the ponies far apart had been forgotten, and without a moment's warning the beasts raged furiously together in a hoof-to-hoof contest. The umbrellas went by the board, and my cloak was thrown over my head, completely blinding me. I was more than grateful to the coolies who at last 'saved our faces,' not to speak of our limbs, by dragging the combatants apart. A previous occasion when the two beasts were allowed to come within reach of one another, on a narrow road overhanging a precipice, and fought like demons, to the imminent danger of both riders, ought not to have been so soon forgotten.

The house at Ka-La Ba was typical of the better class of Lolo residences. The front gave on a large paved courtyard enclosed by the buildings. Three sides of the quadrangle consisted of stables and byres in which the cattle of the family or tribe are regularly housed for the night, when the herdsmen also return from their avocations and occupy the men's quarters, in a large hall forming the fourth side of the square. The women's quarters were behind the men's. The interior of the hall had no windows, and was almost pitch dark. There were two fireplaces, but no chimneys. Hams and other provisions depended from the rafters, where they had every chance of being honestly and thoroughly smoke-dried. There was little in the way of furniture, except that trestles and planks were carried all round the walls for beds, and there were a few stools. This hall is the home of perhaps 150 people. With the addition of our party it was, as might be imagined, somewhat tightly packed.

Our hosts were deeply interested in the pictures in our very much out-of-date copies of the *Graphic* and *Sketch*, which had arrived with the mails just before we left Maha, and of which they were quick to seize the points, especially noting that our ladies wore skirts like their own. They found another bond of union between themselves and us in the fact that our printed characters ran across the page, like their own, and not down, like the Chinese. Their special attention, however, was directed to our firearms, which they regarded with admiration and unconcealed envy. The walls were decorated with an imposing array of antique weapons, such as swords, spears, and daggers, together with bows, crossbows, and guns, the latter stopping short at the matchlock stage of development.

The tribe is great at hunting, and must be somewhat formidable on the war-path. Its members—at least, the women—appear to take their religion more seriously than the Chinese. One of our party was quickly pulled up, by an old woman who superintended the cooking arrangements, for the crime of whistling, which, it appears, is offensive to the Lolo gods. He was equally indiscreet in desecrating the hearth by knocking out the ashes of his pipe on the stone rim surrounding the fireplace, which is dedicated to the gods. It was some time before the old lady's wrath was appeased, and the offender was forgiven on the ground of 'invincible ignorance'; but she kept her eye on him, and was evidently nervous about what he might do next.

The buildings were surrounded by a high mud wall, in one corner of which was a three-story watchtower loopholed for guns. By the way, the loopholes in Chinese and Lolo fortifications have always been a puzzle to me, as they are merely straight narrow slits, and a gun pointed through them could only command a very limited range, out of which an invader might easily keep.

In the surrounding district we saw several flocks and herds, which were generally enclosed in a temporary fence of wickerwork, while the shepherds, neatherds, and goatherds reposed beneath a shelter consisting of a mat stretched on four poles. We heard many tales of tigers, but never had the good fortune to see one.

Near the dwelling-house of Ka-La Ba is a small temple which, although Buddhist, gives some evidence of originality, or at least of a departure from the Chinese type. There were several works of art containing human and superhuman figures, outlined and shaded with minute Chinese characters. There was also a book, in Tibetan characters, said to have come from Lhassa, and held in great veneration. Later in the evening, however, the headman sold me a somewhat similar book, which he said had been left with him for sale by a llama from Lhassa.

The next day saw us bounding over the 'downs' by a good road, on which we met some two-wheeled carts drawn by oxen. Five miles south-south-west of Ka-La Ba a large road came in from the northeast, and we were informed that it was the direct road from Shaa Ba. Near the junction of the two roads we were surprised to see a long line of trenches and rifle-pits, which, on inquiry, we found had been used during the fighting of five years ago, when our friend the Toussa of Kwa Pit distinguished himself. Evidently the Toussa was no stranger to modern tactics, and would have been quite at home in South Africa.

At six miles we passed a mud and thatch village on the right, and at seven passed through a village of mud and shingles called Sze-Tang Tse. Three miles to the south-west we passed another village, and in one mile further came on the right bank of the Pei-Sui Ho, a river which had been in sight for some time.* We crossed to the left bank by a bridge, beyond which stood a highly ornate mud and plaster temple. In a mile and half to the south, along the left bank of the river, we reached the village of Pei-Sui Ho, and were in China once more. The

---

* Pei-Sui Ho = White Water River. There are about as many White Water Rivers in China as there are Sandy Creeks in Australia.' The name is given to any foaming portion of a river, and this leads to much confusion. The reach of the Yangtse above Li Kiang is one of the White Water family.

population presented a marked contrast to that of the villages further north, and there was the familiar tea-house. A substantial stone bridge of twelve spans crossed the river opposite the middle of the village street. The road, however, led out of the village to the south, and crossed from right to left, by a bridge of six spans, a small tributary river coming from the south-east. From the crossing to Yen Ching, a distance of four and a half miles, the road led south-south-east up an easy grade between cultivated fields, and was from 1 to 3 chains in width—quite the most business-like road I have seen in China.

Yen Ching (8,470 feet) is a town which I should guess to contain about 20,000 inhabitants. It happened to be market-day, and, no doubt, the best accommodation in the place was occupied. We were taken at first to an inn which, even after an extensive Chinese experience, we unanimously pronounced uninhabitable. So many previous travellers have enlarged upon the nature of Chinese hotel accommodation that it is unnecessary for me to dwell upon its discomforts. Suffice it to say that dirt abounds, and brings with it the usual concomitants. Some of the inns, indeed, could not be described in any civilized language. It may be understood that where travellers have written of 'rooms over the pigsty,' and the like, 'verily the half was not told,' the 'pigsty' being only a delicate euphemism for the indescribable. When there is furniture in the place, it is, as a rule, hopeless to clean it. Nothing short of a jack-plane would remove the ancient impurities from the dining-table.

After a good deal of uproar, we succeeded in finding a somewhat better inn, although it had the drawback of the usual repulsive crowd with its vacant stare.

Salt is the staple industry of Yen Ching. The brine wells are on the left bank of a small creek, about a quarter of a mile west of the town. The brine, which is less salt than sea-water, is raised from four timbered wells close together, and about 15 feet in depth, which may be about 10 feet below the level of the creek. Into these wells a bucket is lowered by a pole, and, when filled with water, lifted by two men. The water is then carried to settling-vats beside the furnaces. Crucible-shaped moulds of cast iron, about 2 feet long and 1 foot across the top, are suspended over the furnaces, and a man with a dipper keeps continually filling them from the settling-vats till the successive layers of salt have formed a solid mass. During our visit a stream of men, women, and donkeys, was constantly arriving with loads of billeted firewood and lignite. On a rough estimate, I should say that there cannot be fewer than 5,000 people directly employed by the works. I cannot be certain whether the Yen Ching brine wells are the same as those described by Hosie* as near Yen Yuan, but I am inclined to doubt it, as his description does not tally with what we saw. He calls the place he visited Pai (or North) Yen Ching. Yen Yuan, so far as I could gather, is about fourteen miles southeast of Yen Ching.

Yen Ching produces an unusually good breed of pigs, and there was a good deal of mutton exposed for sale in the market. I also saw needles and thread, the former done up in packets, which bore an English inscription, but no maker's name or locality.

* 'Three Years in Western China,' 1897.

We were very glad to be able to purchase some gold, and thus reduce our burden by about a half a mule-load of silver. Our inquiries as to the locality whence the gold was obtained only elicited the information that it came from ' all about here.' It varied from fine dust to small nuggets. A good deal of it had been collected with mercury, and the retorted lumps were generally about the size of a large pea.

CHAPTER XXII

YEN CHING TO TAI-YE FANG

Ho-Show Pu—Lignite quarries—Hoang Shaa Ba—The Toussa of Toong-Su—The Pei-Sui Ho—Yen Tang—Brine wells and evaporation works—Into the province of Yünnan—Tai-Ye Fang—The Pei-Sui Ho and the Wu Liang.

In three miles of travelling to the west and one mile to the north-west, to the lignite mines of Ho-Show Pu, which supply the greater part of the fuel for the evaporation of the brine, we met thousands of donkeys, horses, and mules, and hundreds of men and women, all loaded with baskets of lignite. The lignite occurs in a formation which is evidently much newer than the coal-measures. It is exposed in open-cast workings or quarries, with sometimes as much as 30 or even 40 feet of stripping. Where there is more overburden than this, the lignite has to be left alone, as no economical system of underground working whereby the roof of incoherent sandstone could be supported has yet been devised. Consequently, the lignite is unavailable over a large area, as it lies in a nearly horizontal bed, and, in the higher portions of the downs, is covered by a considerable accumulation of strata. The bed was at least 15 feet in thickness, and might have been more, as the lower part of it was concealed by water. While I was examining the quarry, a stone fell at my feet, but I took no notice of it, as I supposed it to be the result of natural causes. The soldier who stood behind me, however, detected a man in the act of throwing a second stone. The culprit, when the soldier turned his eyes upon him, pretended a sudden and intense interest in something else, and there was no more of it.

A mile north-west of the lignite quarries we crossed a fairly large tributary of the Pei-Sui Ho, and in two miles west, over a cultivated flat, reached a large village (7,920 feet) the name of which I failed to ascertain. It had a mud wall and a gate lined with sheet-iron.

In three miles south-south-west we reached the edge of the downs, the greater part of the distance from the large village being under crops of rice and maize.

From the edge of the downs a steep ascent of a mile and a half up a small creek brought us to a col (9,400 feet), from which we descended for five miles in a general south-west direction down the valley of a gradually enlarging gully, till the latter fell into a small river which runs west-north-west. At this point (7,770 feet) we were met by runners sent by the Toussa of Toong-Su, who directed our steps up the river, or we should inevitably have taken the road which led down.

We followed the left bank of this river for about a mile east-south-east, when we crossed the stream by a stone bridge, near which, on the left bank, is the Toussa's residence.

An ascent of a mile and a half to south-south-east brought us to a pass (8,420 feet), and, as night was now at hand, the journey became a scramble. From this pass we travelled south-south-west for a mile and a half to another; but it was too dark to read the aneroid. In a mile and a half further south-south-west we reached the Chinese village of Hoang Shaa Ba (Yellow Grass Place). I may mention, as an instance of how Chinese officials travel, that while we were progressing slowly in the darkness, and the necessity for a light had become pressing, one of our soldiers calmly wrenched a number of pine shingles from the roof of a house, and made torches of them, no one, not even the owner of the house, appearing to consider it a liberty.

Some time after we had settled down in the inn, La Soh Toong, the Toussa of Toong-Su, paid us a visit. He was a cousin of the Toussa of Kwa Pit, from whom he had heard of our projected visit, and was only twenty-one years of age. His mother had been Toussa till about a year before. He was very anxious to assist us, and furnished the usual guard, but evidently did not know the country well.

On the following day, in about five miles north-west, we reached a summit (9,220 feet), after which the descent to the Pei-Sui Ho began. A long steep slope of four miles, to west-north-west and west, brought us to the river at its junction with a large tributary, which is crossed by a bridge of four spans, with stone piers and wooden girders and decked with stone. Here a drenching rain fell, and, while we sheltered and lunched beneath some ledges of rock, we watched the little dry gullies rapidly becoming mountain torrents. When the rain had cleared a little, we continued our journey down the left bank of the Pei-Sui Ho for about two miles west-north-west to Yen Tang (7,508 feet), where we camped. Several coal-seams of good quality, and up to 2 feet in thickness (including bands), are exposed on the left bank of the river for about a mile below the tributary.

Yen Tang is another important seat of the salt industry. The source of the brine is about half a mile south of the town. An underlie shaft is driven into the hill, and from the bottom the brine is pumped in seven lifts of 9 feet each. The shaft was, unfortunately, unusually well timbered, and, beyond the fact that it had been driven through carbonaceous matter, we could see little. About 20 feet below the mouth of the underlie is a vertical shaft, also well timbered, of the unusual dimensions of 17 by 11 feet, up which brine is pumped in five stages of 15 feet each. The remark is often made that the Chinese are ignorant of the use of suction-pumps, and nowhere else have I ever seen them, except on river junks. A fresh-water gully passes the mouth of the shaft, and falls into the river at the town. The brine is carried in wooden flumes from the wells direct into underground tanks at the evaporating works. The first operation is the saturation of hot ashes with brine from the vats, after which the ashes are leached in other vats. The liquor is next concentrated in pans at a white heat, and then ladled into crucible-shaped moulds. The moulds form the roof of what may be called a reverberatory furnace. Sixteen of the largest size cover the greater part of the furnace, the interspaces being filled up with smaller moulds. The iron moulds are cast in a foundry in the town, the fuel used being charcoal. Immense stacks of firewood are piled up in the vicinity of the evaporating works, which must be at a disadvantage when compared with those of Yen Ching, where lignite is available. The Yen Tang works belong to the Toussa of Toong-Su, who gave me an estimate of their annual output at 100,000 piculs (5,952 tons), that of the Yen Ching works being 900,000.

We left the river, after running it down for two and a half miles from Yen Tang, and followed up a creek for seven miles south-south-west to its head (9,370 feet), passing on the way some outcrops of coal. Three miles down the spur of a hill, to the south-west, brought us to a good-sized 'trouting stream,' called Yang-Sui (Winding Water), which runs to the east, and must fall into the large tributary which enters the left bank of the Pei-Sui Ho above Yen Tang. This we ran up for a mile, passing the fortified farm of Lan-Tzü Ko, to Tai-Ye Fang, a little village on the right bank (8,470 feet).

Beyond the information that Yen Tang is in Szechuan and Lan-Tzü Ko in Yünnan, I was unable to locate the boundary-line between the two provinces. It may be taken to pass through the watershed between the Pei-Sui Ho and Yang-Sui. According to all previous maps, the boundary-line is more to the east. I conclude that there is no political boundary, but merely a limit set on either side to the control exercised by the official in charge of the nearest 'hsien,' whether in Yünnan or Szechuan. We camped in a school-house, where (Chinese) writing seemed to be the only branch of learning taught. There were a number of absolutely naked children—a condition of things which, in a comparatively cold climate, must be the result of poverty rather than of choice. The children were said to be of Sifan race, and the village was said to be for the most part inhabited by Lolos; while, as a matter of fact, the majority of the adults whom we saw were Chinese. Our stay was not long enough to enable us to reconcile such contradictory statements and observations. A native gave 'Mo niu pin tze' as the Sifan equivalent of the phrase which we had the most frequent occasion to use, viz., 'What is the name of this place?'

CHAPTER XXIII

TAI-YE FANG TO YA-SHOW PING

Prince Henri's route to Assam—Large limestone sink on mountain—Sifan villages of Peh-Yang Tsung and Ya-Show Ping—Degenerate pear-trees.

It had originally been our intention to make for the nearest British outpost—viz., Kampti in Upper Burma —viâ Yung-Ning, Chung T'ien, Atuntze, and Chamu-tong. This route, according to Bretschneider and the 'China Inland' map, appeared to be not only the shortest, but also to follow, from the Mekong to the Irrawadi, a trade road connecting Batang in Szechuan with Sadiya in Assam. The only information available, when we started from Maha, was the route of Prince Henri of Orleans (1895), as laid down on these maps. Unfortunately, we had not read Prince Henri's book. Never having dreamed of following in his footsteps, we had postponed the reading of it till a future occasion, as we could not find it in Hong Kong or Shanghai. With regard to the portion of the journey from Maha to Chung T'ien, viâ Yung-

Ning, we were assured that our guides, Ta Er Doh and Shaa Ba Shan, knew the road well. It is certain that they did not, neither of them having ever seen either Yung-Ning or Chung T'ien.

We knew that at Lan-Tzü Ko we were far to the south of the position of Yung-Ning, and the conviction was gradually sinking into our minds that in the east one must be content to do what one can, rather than insist upon doing what one will. It had been part of the arrangement that the guides, who were also contractors for porterage, should replace the carrying coolies by mules as soon as possible. With this object, they kept as much as possible to the main-roads, and I suspect that, for trading purposes of their own, they had a natural bias towards the cities of the south, which we, on our part, desired to avoid. I am not aware that the position of Yung-Ning has been fixed by any modern cartographer, and for the present it may be left in the position which Széchenyi has assigned to it.*

The guides now began to talk of getting at last on a 'large road' at Yung-Peh, and as this was fully a degree of latitude further south than we had bargained for, and near the large towns of Li Kiang and Tali, the latter of which, at least, we knew to have been the scene of recent anti-foreign riots, we gnashed our teeth and resigned ourselves to the inevitable.

On August 27 we commenced our journey by climbing south-westward for four and a half miles to a col (9,870 feet) at the head of a creek, the banks of which supply firewood for the Yen Tang brine

* It has probably been located by Captain Ryder. See his paper read before the Royal Geographical Society in December, 1902.

evaporation works. A little beyond the col, on a limestone hill on the right side of the head of a creek which flows to the west, a Lolo village was perched. Our general course still lay south-west, and in about three miles from the col we reached a summit estimated at 11,070 feet, from which there extended southward a large plain suggestive of a dried-up lake, and literally covered with bluebells and a gigantic edelweiss. A mile and a half south-south-west brought us to the opposite rim of the lakelike plain, which has no outlet, and which is evidently an enormous limestone 'sink.' The road next led for a mile and a half up to the south-south-west, through limestone country, and for two miles south-west followed down a gully from its head, to the Sifan village of La-Che Chu. Two miles further down the creek we passed the village of Peh-Yang Tsung. Two and a half miles further to south-south-west we crossed the creek, just above the point where it empties into a much larger watercourse falling to the north-west. Crossing the latter, we reached, in about a mile further, the Sifan village of Ya-Show Ping (9,220 feet), where we lodged in the house of a Chinese farmer. Here, it may be mentioned, there were a great many more dogs than there was any need for, and one of these unnecessary animals bit me, seizing the opportunity and the calf of my leg while I was bending over a box. As a precautionary measure, the wound was washed with a strong solution of permanganate of potash, and no ill effects followed. Heavy rain fell during the night, and as the roof was, to say the least of it, defective, waterproofs and umbrellas were in great demand. One of the party had to take up his bed and walk because the rain had dissolved portions of the mud wall above his cot. Ya-Show Ping is in the district or 'hsien' of Yung-Peh. This neighbourhood was perhaps more noticeable than others for the prevalence of wild pear-trees, the fruit being about the size of a small marble, and gritty and acrid to an almost incredible degree.

CHAPTER XXIV

YA-SHOW PING TO SHOW PING

Sifan village of Po-Lo—A trial for life—Conditional sentence— A dance—Show Ping.

THE morning which followed our sleepless night was wet and foggy, and the first half of the day's travelling was very unpleasant. Three miles to the south-east we reached a col (9,790 feet) at the head of a tributary of the creek. After eight miles to south-south-west, down a gully from its head, we continued on the same course for four miles up another gully to a col (9,470 feet). Three miles further, down a gully to the south-west, we reached the little Sifan village of Po-Lo (8,990 feet), where we camped for the night. Here, it may be mentioned, for the first time in many months, we saw the image and superscription of Queen Victoria—on a rupee. The village street, what with mud and cow-dung, was far from being a pleasant thoroughfare. The dwelling-houses, as a rule, could only be reached through the byres.

Shortly after our arrival in the village we had an opportunity of witnessing the proceedings in a Sifan court of justice. It appears that one of our muleteers recognised a man who was lurking in the jungle by the roadside as one who had stolen a mule from him some time before. The attention of one of the corporals having been called to the thief, he was captured and brought in chains to the village. (All this happened in the rear of our procession, and we knew nothing of it at the time.) The headman of the village sat in judgment, assisted by a few of the elders, and although the seat of justice was only a log in front of a pigsty, it must be admitted that the proceedings were orderly and dignified. The evidence of the muleteer was heard, and there was no lack of witnesses to prove that the prisoner was by habit and repute a horse-thief who had long been 'wanted.' The sentence was decapitation on the following day, unless the prisoner could find two sureties willing to answer with their own heads for his good behaviour.

At night the villagers came in to pay their respects and gratify their innocent curiosity by an inspection of our strange equipments, our weapons, our camp-beds, and the illustrated papers proving the chief attractions. When it grew late, and our efforts at entertainment began to flag, we said (may the white lie be forgiven!) that we had heard, even in far countries, the fame of Sifan music and dancing, and hinted that we would be grateful for an exhibition. After long delay a musician was sent for, and the girls withdrew to another house to make I know not what preparations. A portion of the earthen floor was cleared, and a few pieces of lighted pine-wood were placed in the centre, and around these the performers danced in a circle. Both men and women were uncomfortably shy, and the performance was a good deal more like an incantation than a 'fling,' and may have had some religious significance. The dancers shuffled around slowly, hand in hand or hand on shoulder, following, with something which was nearly a step, the doleful music, which at times resembled an air. The girls, for the most part, kept together, though a few late-coming men joined in among them and broke their ranks. The player's instrument was a set of pandean pipes leading into a gourd. He blew down one of the pipes, and fingered the stops on the other. The scale, I think, was pentatonic; at least, it resembled some discordant sounds which I remember the late Lord Neaves to have made at a *séance* of the Royal Society of Edinburgh many years ago in illustration of the pentatonic scale, which he said was the basis of true Celtic music. Musical adepts will, I hope, pardon my unskilled attempt to convey an idea of my impressions. I freely admit that the good looks and modest bearing of the girls were the chief merits of the performance in my eyes. Had the *danseuses* been scrubbed and well dressed, they would have been a presentable body of *débutantes* in any European ballroom. One of our party, frivolously disposed, asked a girl (through an interpreter) if she would marry him and go to his country. The reply, 'I do not know you, sir,' was all that propriety could have demanded in the best society, and worthy of a pupil 'finished' at Miss Pinkerton's celebrated establishment.

Have the Sifans progressed since Marco Polo and Cooper wrote such damaging accounts of their morals? Marco was scandalized by the practice of the 'caitiff husband' in lending his wives to travellers. Cooper was forced to go through a form of marriage with a woman, who, however, left him after a few days. Judging from our experience, no idea of hospitalities of the kind was in the people's minds.

Po-Lo is about a mile north of the right bank of a small river which flows to the west, doubtless to fall into the Yangtse above the suspension-bridge on the road from Yung-Peh to Li Kiang. The 'China Inland' map makes this the mouth of the Wu-Liang Ho. The latter name is given to a large river which rises in Tibet, and is called the Li-Chu below Litang, and which cannot flow south of Yung-Ning, for the simple reason that the Yangtse meanders across its supposed course. The Li-Chu, if it does not feed the Ya-Lung north of lat. 29°, may be the Shu Ye of Amundsen. Three miles south-south-west of Po-Lo we reached a gap (8,940) at the head of a gully, and in a mile and a half further a summit at an elevation of 9,170 feet. In eight and a half miles west-south-west we reached Show Ping (8,600 feet), a village of half a dozen houses, built of mud, logs, and shingles. Show Ping has—at least nominally—a garrison of twelve soldiers. The country between Po-Lo and Show Ping is fairly well cultivated. The Lolo farmers must sleep somewhere, but they do not appear, in this district, to erect permanent dwellings. We only saw, during the whole day's march, one hut, of logs and shingles, and some 'gunyahs' of matting. The shingled roof of the Chinese house in Show Ping where we camped leaked freely, and a heavy rain in the night-watches again brought our stock of umbrellas and mackintoshes into requisition.

CHAPTER XXV

SHOW PING TO YUNG-PEH TING

A dissertation on Chinese roads—Architectural peculiarities of Northern Yünnan—Yung-Peh.

IN three miles to the south-west (August 30) we reached the head of a creek (9,320 feet) which flows to the north-east, and probably joins the river draining Po-Lo. The descent from this point, for the next two miles to south-south-west, was shocking, as the unpaved track through a slippery clay soil was often cut into deep channels, and as rain continued to fall heavily these had become formidable watercourses. The formation was white sandstones with gray and dark shales, varied by streaks of coal.

This arduous descent brought us to a village on the edge of the Yung-Peh Plain, and we had no sooner got on the paved roads between and around the fields of rice and maize than we heartily wished that they had been left as Nature made them. 'Oh, how can words with equal warmth' (to quote from an Addisonian hymn) paint the amazing badness of a Chinese road, paved with good intentions and solid flagstones, which latter must in many instances be centuries or tens of centuries old ! The wear of ironshod hoofs has rounded the flagstones into smooth boulders and widened the intervening spaces until it becomes a mere chance whether the traveller steps on a boulder or into the mud; or, where it happens that the middle of a flagstone in some far-off time offered the best foothold, the successive impact of hoofs in the same spot has drilled a hole right through the stone into the mud beneath. Men and animals stagger, slip, and flounder over these pavements, which are frequently left, or partially left, by the progress of denudation, standing on ridges of earth. The worst available position is invariably assigned to the public road if the land is of any value whatever for agriculture. A road is never regarded as a means of communication between two given localities, but is only a concession grudgingly made by the farmer to the public convenience. The farmer does not scruple to acquire soil for top-dressing by paring the road away or by undermining it, and even throws a dam across it, whenever he sees fit, to convert it into a reservoir for the irrigation of his rice-field. The road must go round, never through, a rice-field, and nothing is more common than to see a road which ought to be straight going round three sides of a square. An ascent is always negotiated by flights of steps, and although the short zigzag is in common use, the idea of a long zigzag forming an easy grade has never met with favour. The road across the Yung-Peh Plain was a typical example of its kind. Riding over it was a penance which was soon found to be unendurable, and walking on foot was not much better.

In one mile to the south, across the plain, we passed a place where evidently coal had been worked a long time ago. Two miles further we crossed, by a fine stone bridge, a little river coming from the east. The cultivated plain is dotted with farmhouses. The houses in Northern Yünnan are built either of mud, mud-concrete, or sun-dried bricks, with the usual sagging Chinese roof of ornamental tiles, and are decorated as to the gables, lintels, and eaves, with courses of whitewash, scrolls, and paintings.

SHOW PING TO YUNG-PEH TING

We had sent Shaa Ba Shan ahead of us to Yung-Peh, to make arrangements about a change of mules, so that we should not be delayed in the city. In accordance with our general plan, we meant to camp outside, and only pass through this as well as other large towns. The official (Ting) in charge of the city had, however, sent Shaa Ba Shan back with a message that we had better come to the town, where he had an inn ready for us, and where he could protect us efficiently, and he met us at the bridge. The Ting added that, as the country people had heard of the foreign troubles at Yünnan Fu, they would, in all probability, be afraid to give us lodging.

Yung-Peh (7,270 feet), which we entered about a mile south of the bridge, is a Ting, or subprefectural city, with a picturesque but not very high or very strong wall, gay with creepers and flowers. A great deal of the space within the wall is under cultivation, and perhaps my estimate of the population at 10,000 is a liberal one. We observed peaches, plums, walnuts, celery, potatoes, carrots, and mutton, in the market. The Subprefect called unofficially after we had settled down. He was very friendly, and much interested in our movements, having received a letter about us from the Hsien of Yen Yuan, who had written on the bare chance that we might come to Yung-Peh.

He did not think well of our proposed route, via Atuntze (in reality it was beyond his ken), and advised us rather to make for 'Sin Kai,' a place only five stages from Tali Fu, where a steamer from French territory called once a fortnight. This information puzzled us not a little, as we had never heard that any river was navigable from Tonquin or Cochin China to within five days' march of Tali. In any case, we were not going to Tali if we could avoid it.

We tried hard to obtain information regarding the possibility of making for Chung T'ien without crossing the Yangtse, but could elicit nothing; if there was a road, nobody knew anything about it. The universal opinion was that we must go by Li Kiang.

The military officer of the district sent cards, and promised us an escort, but said he was not well enough to call. Colquhoun mentions* the Yung-Peh silver-mine, 'one of the largest in West Yünnan, situated north of the Yung-Peh Ting, and east of Li Kiang, about some seven days' journey north of Tali.' We were not, at the time when we were in the district, in possession of this information, and heard nothing of the mine.

CHAPTER XXVI

YUNG-PEH TO TUI-NA KO

Alluvial plain—Villages of Toong-Choo Kai-ja and Ching Kwan—Egrets—Ta Whan—Camp in a farmhouse—A brawling woman in a crowded house—Crossing the Yangtse—A stiff ascent—Tui-Na Ko—Copious springs.

WE left Yung-Peh on August 31, in a drizzling rain, which, however, ceased before noon. We had a new guard, armed with percussion muskets (converted flintlocks), marked with a crown and the characters 'B 23,' and having a back-sight with a 'protractor.' In one mile west, 30° north, across the plain, we reached a low gap which was followed by a very steep

* 'Across Chrysê,' London, 1883, vol. ii., p. 259.

descent. There was a lovely view to the west over a green valley thickly dotted with villages.

On the descent (two miles west-north-west, by a dreadful paved road), we met great numbers of women carrying baskets of fruits and vegetables to the market. They wore trousers reaching to the knee, and had healthy, natural feet. Foot-binding, which is almost universal in the greater part of Szechuan, becomes rare in the southern part, where the Chinese come in contact with the Lolos, and is seldom seen in the parts of Yünnan visited by us.

Two miles from the gap we crossed the river (5,570 feet), which we had last seen a mile north of Yung-Peh. Here it emerges from a gorge in a limestone range, and debouches on a great alluvial plain, over which it is diverted in all directions for irrigation. It is crossed by an arcade-bridge.

Two miles west-north-west across the alluvial plain we passed through the large village of Toong-Choo Kai-ja. Here a theatrical performance was going on in front of a temple, and in the middle of a street two priests stood on a raised stall, one beating a drum, and another reading from a book in front of some images. Three miles further across the plain (west-north-west), which was covered with a heavy crop of rice, we reached the large village of Ching Kwan (5,470 feet), where we camped.

From the arcade-bridge the river had been on our left, sometimes a considerable distance off, and its volume a good deal diminished by its diversion into irrigation channels. We saw a few egrets on the plain. This beautiful white bird is much valued for its plumage, which, however, was not in season at that time of year.

In two miles to the west we had crossed the Yung-Peh River (here running north, no doubt to join the river from Po-Lo), and also a tributary which comes from the west. Two miles up the valley of the latter, by the left bank (west, 10° south), at an altitude of 6,950 feet, we were opposite a copper-mine on the right bank. After three miles more up the left bank of the creek, westward, we struck north-west up a branch of it, and headed it in two miles. We found oats being cultivated in the gap (8,470 feet). Our road to the Yangtse Bridge now lay in a general west-north-west direction, down the ridge on the left bank of a creek which falls into the Yangtse.

Two miles brought us to the village of Ta Whan, and five miles more brought us, in the rain, just as night closed in, to the farmsteading of Tsü-Li Chang (5,990 feet). The place was only remarkable for the limited proportions of the quarters into which all hands had to pack themselves, and for a scolding wife who objected on principle to everything which was said or done by everybody. After husband, neighbours, soldiers, mafus, and coolies, had each and all retired discomfited from the vain attempt to pacify the virago, she was so far mollified by the gift of a few cash that we were permitted to eat in peace, and she even condescended to make one of the crowd which stood around to witness the novel performance.

In a mile to the west we had descended, next morning, to the alluvial flats of the Yangtse, and a mile to the north crossed the river by a suspension-bridge (4,440 feet). The bridge is 330 feet in length, and is constructed of eighteen iron chains supporting a wooden deck. It is thrown across a point where the river is compelled by the hardness of the rock to

WOMEN AT LI-KIANG.

LOLO WOMEN, YÜNNAN.

PLATE XIV.

cut a very deep and narrow gorge. On the right bank is the little village of Chang P'yen.

We had no sooner left the village than we were confronted by a difficulty of which we had been warned for some time—a small mountain torrent, then in flood, with a ford for the horses (and, of course, their mafus) alleged to be breast-deep, and below it a bridge consisting of a single plank thrown over the swift stream just where it tumbled into a seething caldron, which made one giddy to look at. We were still contemplating the possibility of having to wait till the flood subsided, when Pien Ta San, one of the mafus, who had been there before, came up, and, with the greatest sang-froid, led his horse across. The muddy stream proved to be only knee-deep, although so rapid that it was not easy for horses or men to keep their footing.

Pien Ta San deserves more than a cursory mention. He came from Maha in the humble capacity of a mafu, or groom, but proved such an Admirable Crichton that we gladly put in his way little odd jobs which added to his earnings. As a millwright and blacksmith he had taken a leading part in the construction of the water-wheels at the Native Reduction Works at Ko-Lo Lo, and he was the only one in our retinue who could shoe a horse without laming it. He was keenly alive to the value of money, and used to excite the ridicule of his fellows by the earnestness with which he chaffered over the price of rice or tea. It was ludicrous to see him sprawling in the mud of a paddy-field, in chase of certain large frogs which he regarded as a great delicacy, and cheap withal. Altogether, he was one of the most reliable and manly men in our caravan.

The ascent from the river was very steep, and it was four hours before we attained a summit (8,250 feet) which bore north-west of the suspension-bridge, from which it was estimated to be two and a half miles distant. Half a mile north of the summit, and practically on the same level, we camped in the village of Tui-Na Ko.

During the ascent we looked at times up the valley of the large river which comes from Po-Lo, and which falls into the Yangtse from east-north-east a short distance above the bridge. It had a very deep and narrow valley, which could be traced for a long distance, but we never succeeded in getting a glimpse of the stream itself. For reasons already stated, it cannot be the Wu Liang of the maps.

On the right wall of the Yangtse Valley, below our course, we saw two magnificent springs discharging what were really rivers from synclinal depressions in the limestone strata on the hillside.

CHAPTER XXVII

TUI-NA KO TO LI KIANG FU

Li Kiang Plain and City—Chinese men and Sifan women—Protecting missionaries—Discussion of routes with the officials—Our credentials—The Wai-Yuan's letter—A disturbance.

LEAVING Tui-Na Ko, we crossed a low pass, and, by a crooked but well-graded road (which could never have been engineered by Chinese), reached, in four miles, a col (9,770 feet) at the head of a creek which runs south-east into the Yangtse a few miles above the bridge. There was a temple in the pass. Running down a gully from its head, we reached, in three miles, the edge of an alluvial plain (7,970 feet). In five miles across this plain, in which here and there were 'islands' of limestone downs, each crowned with a village, we reached the 'fu,' or prefectural city, of Li Kiang (8,070 feet).

Li Kiang is a small and scattered town without a wall, and consists mainly of widely separated streets, built along watercourses and straggling up a hill. A peculiarity in its population struck us at once. It appeared to be peopled by Tibetan or Sifan women, who were greatly in the majority, and Chinese men. The former (Plate XIV.) had brown skins, and wore earrings of silver with jade discs. They had peculiar sun-bonnets built up of coils, inside of which the hair was bunched up towards the front of the head. We were informed that there had been disturbances in Yünnan Fu, and that the officials had begged the missionaries to leave the country till the storm had blown over, promising to rebuild their houses on their return; that the missionaries had left (for 'Sin Kai, six days' journey from Tali'), but were stopped by a mob halfway to Tali Fu, whereupon 2,500 soldiers were sent for their protection from Li Kiang and an equal number from Chung T'ien. If this story be true, it explains the scarcity of men in Li Kiang; and it is probable enough that the mates of the Sifan women were sent to the front while the Chinese men prudently stayed behind.

We were at first treated with scant courtesy. After having sent our cards, the interpreter went to see the officials. He was informed that the Hsien, Wu Sin Ku, was not well enough to receive him, and that the Fu and the military official had gone out to dinner.

Later on the last-named sent a servant to say that we ought to go to Tali Fu, and that, as the road to Chung T'ien was dangerous, he declined to countenance our project by sending soldiers with us. We had, however, two documents with us which proved of great service at this juncture and afterwards.

The first was the proclamation issued, as already mentioned, by the Viceroy of Szechuan. The second was a letter from the Wai-Yuan, Chü Hung Chi (whom we left at Shaa Ba), to the Hsien at Yen Yuan, and of which we had a signed copy. It was to the same effect as the proclamation, and added that we were good people, who had been invited to China by the Empress-Dowager to assist the Chinese to open the mines, and that, having finished our work in Szechuan, we were returning to our own country, and requested the Hsien to take all necessary steps to assist us.

Although technically only good for Szechuan, we found these documents, especially the Wai-Yuan's letter, of great assistance in Yünnan.

After a day's delay, seeing that our preparations were not progressing, I waived the point of etiquette which required that the Hsien should first call on us, and went with the interpreter to the yamen. I found the Hsien, an old man in feeble health, suffering from ague, and a present of quinine smoothed the way for negotiations. After reading the proclamation and letter, he offered to give us an escort to Tali Fu or Atuntze, but declined to have anything to say to Chung T'ien, where, he said, the people were of a turbulent disposition, and strangers always got into trouble. On thinking the matter over, and on our refusing to go to Tali Fu, he said we could only go to Atuntze viâ Wei-Si and the Mekong Valley, as not only was Chung T'ien impracticable, but the road up the right bank of the Yangtse had been washed away and was no longer in use. This seemed hard, as Széchenyi had travelled by the one route (1880), and Gill by the other (1877), and Wei-Si, according to the map, was too far west. However, there was no help for it, and the compromise was agreed to, as the Hsien said the Hsien of Wei-Si was his very good friend, and at his request would do his best to assist us. He was also getting as anxious as we were that we should go, and he feared there might be trouble with the people if we prolonged our stay in Li Kiang.

We lodged in the upper storey of an inn, the comparative privacy of the room outweighing the advantages of occupying the place of honour on the ground-floor, which was open to the public. As it was, we had quite enough of publicity: the courtyard was always crowded with sightseers, and upper rooms in adjoining houses commanding a view of our quarters were at a premium. What threatened to become a serious fracas arose at one time out of an attempt on the part of the cook to restrain the ardour of a man who insisted on coming upstairs, after so many others had done so that we had hinted a desire for privacy. The Chinaman clings lovingly to his inalienable right to enter any house when he thinks fit, and 'glower frae him.' A general *mêlée* ensued, with punching of heads, pulling of hair, and much vociferation. The disturbance was put an end to by the intervention of a yamen-runner and an old woman, and gentle peace returned.

Mr. Way, who had a bad sore due to the treatment of a swollen leg with what was supposed to be tincture of iodine, but turned out to be a mixture of that with carbolic acid, now expressed a desire to take the mainroad viâ Tali Fu, and 'throw himself on the protection of the officials.' Our policy was to avoid Tali Fu and all large towns, and such information as we possessed seemed to point to the necessity for keeping together and travelling as fast as we could. Happily for all, he was dissuaded from what I cannot help thinking would have proved a dangerous course of action.

CHAPTER XXVIII

LI KIANG TO SHI KU AND MOO-CHI TI

Return of the guides—A lake—Llamaserai of La-Sü Ba—Foreign trade—Snowy mountains—Shi Ku—Up the Yangtse—Moo-Chi Ti.

As we were now far beyond the region known to Ta Er Doh and Shaa Ba Shan, these gentlemen had obtained leave to return, as well as the 'kumshaw' usual in such cases. When we resumed our journey, they astonished our ponies with a farewell salute of crackers, which always broke out in a new part of the street after we thought it had come to an end. We passed through a portion of the city which we had not seen before. A market-square was followed by steep streets, climbing by flights of slippery stone steps to a hill-top commanding a view of a beautiful cultivated plain extending from north to south. In many ways the 'laying out' of the city differed from the stereotyped Chinese pattern, and proclaimed its

LI KIANG TO SHI KU AND MOO-CHI TI 159

foreign origin. Our road crossed the plain in two and a half miles. The aneroid gave its altitude as 7,920 feet.

Ascending to a gap (8,320 feet) in some low hills composed of melaphyre and limestone, we reached, two and a half miles from the plain, the south-east end of a lake (8,150 feet), bordered by marshy flats. The road wound round the southern end of the lake, and was very boggy, except where it kept on the divisions between rice-fields. Here, for the first time, we saw ploughing with a pair of buffaloes, which for the rest of our journey was the usual custom. The Chinese use only one. Five miles brought us to the llamaserai of La-Sü Ba, on the western margin of the lake. The llamaserai was not old, having been removed not very long ago from a more commanding site on the top of a neighbouring hill. It was in good repair and redolent of fresh paint—very different from anything Chinese. It formed a quadrangle, the temple occupying the side opposite the entrance-gate. It had elaborately carved and painted ceilings which, like the churches of Italy, left a crick in the neck as the most lasting impression. Unfortunately, the temple and all the principal shrines were locked up in the absence of the Chief Priest, who was at Li Kiang. There was a nunnery in connection with the temple, but we only caught a passing and accidental glimpse of one of the nuns. The priests, of whom we saw about a dozen, had shaven heads and bare feet, and wore gray robes reaching to the ankles and confined at the waist with a cord.

Between Li Kiang and the llamaserai, we noticed very few Chinese umbrellas ; nearly everybody carried a steel-ribbed one, covered with alpaca, either of European make or a close imitation thereof.

Just inside of the principal entrance of the llama-serai was a fine incense-urn of brecciated marble, said to be 150 years old.

We set up our beds on the floor of a veranda room, and, although it rained heavily in the night, managed to make ourselves snug by hanging up the 'fly' of a tent to make a fourth wall.

Leaving La-Sü Ba, we reached, in two and a half miles, a gap (8,650 feet) in the range to the west, and a march of about the same distance on the same level, over liver-coloured shales and limestones with numerous 'sinks,' brought us to the beginning of the descent towards the Yangtse. Half a mile farther, to the north-west, we had a view of a snow-clad mountain bearing 33° east of north. This mountain is given in the 'China Inland' map, probably on the authority of Captain Gill,* on very much the same bearing from Li Kiang, but too far south. Unfortunately, it was almost always capped with clouds, and we never got a second bearing to fix its position. Its altitude is given in the map as 16,405 feet, but, for reasons shortly to be given, I believe this to be an underestimate.

In three miles north-west we reached the right bank of the Yangtse River (6,210 feet). From the point where we struck the river we could see the village of Shi Ku, three miles to the south-west, and look straight down the valley for a distance estimated at fourteen miles to north-north-east, and we just caught a glimpse of the snowy Li Kiang Mountain to the right of the last point where the river was visible.

* 'The River of the Golden Sand.' London, 1880.

The river was in flood, and appeared quite as large as it did at Chung King, 600 miles lower.

Following up the right bank, we reached the town or large village of Shi Ku (6,110 feet), and, after a hasty luncheon under a veranda in the courtyard of a little llamaserai, continued our journey up the river. We first crossed, by a crazy wooden bridge, the mouth of a large creek which comes from the south-west. As, according to the map, the way to Wei-Si is up the valley of this creek, we marvelled much that the road still hugged the river; but we were in the hands of an official guide and a muleteer who certainly knew the way, and forbore to make embarrassing remarks.

Two miles up the river we passed an apparently fortified llamaserai perched on a mountain-top, and bearing a striking resemblance to one of the castles of the Rhine valley. Two miles further, we reached Moo-Chi Ti (6,540 feet), a cluster of mud houses, and after having tried the second storey of the inn, and having been fairly driven out by the smoke from the kitchen below, found a resting-place for the night in a hayloft above a farmhouse. True, there was a coffin in the room, but there was nothing in it, and the owner had either got it at a bargain or had it as a present, and was only keeping it safe against the time when it should be wanted.

Up the reach of the Yangtse above Shi Ku, there are many villages on both sides of the river—generally speaking, one on each 'cone of dejection.' I could not ascertain the names of any of those on the left bank, and only noted a few of those, through which we passed, on the right. It is difficult to say exactly which villages should be named on a map and which should be omitted. As a rule, I have only noted the names of those which lay in our path, and not those which we only saw in the distance. Széchenyi,[*] who gives few names, travelled on the left bank, and Gill,[†] some of whose names are identifiable with my own, on the right.

CHAPTER XXIX

MOO-CHI TI TO KU-TU WAH

Villages of San-Shien Ku, Kwo-Tu, Kai-Tsa, Tsu-Kwo Tang, and Ta Tang—Coffins in bedrooms—Foreign trade—Birthday of the moon—Villages of Chow Tang, Chu-Kwo Lia, Pay-Fin Chang, Wu-Lu T'ien, and Wu-Lu Pu—Goldwashing—Chi T'ien destroyed in Mahommedan rebellion—Ku-Tu Wah.

RESUMING our march, we still followed up the right bank of the Yangtse (here called the Kin-Sha, or Golden Sand) for sixteen miles north-north-west, and, after passing the villages of San-Shien Ku,[‡] Kwo-Tu, Kai-Tsa, and Tsu-Kwo Tang, reached the village of Ta Tang (6,670 feet), where we camped again in a hayloft, and this time in company with two coffins. At Mai-Tsa a considerable stream falls into the river from the west, and is spanned by an arcade-bridge.

[*] 'Die wissenschaftlichen Ergebnisse der Reise des Grafen Béla Széchenyi in Ost-Asien, 1877-1880.' Wien, 1893-1899.
[†] 'The River of the Golden Sand.'
[‡] Ku is a 'clipped' form of Kwan (fortified garrison). The inhabitants of the highlands of Szechuan and Yünnan 'clip' their words. Another instance noted was the gradual transition of 'Ti-fang' (place) into 'Tifa.' The well-known treatment of the German language by the Swiss, who, for example, shorten 'bube' into 'bu,' is analogous.

Between the village and the river is what may be called a 'toy' pagoda, the first of any kind which we had seen for some time.

Believing that any indication of the course of trade in such comparatively unknown regions is worth noting, I make no apology for the observation that on this day's march we saw nothing but foreign umbrellas, and that one of them bore the brand 'Dunlop and Co., Rangoon.'

This date, September 8, being the fifteenth day of the eighth moon of the twenty-sixth year of Kwang Hsü, turned out to be the birthday of the moon, and, in accordance with Chinese custom, we had to present the muleteers with a goat, to enable them to celebrate the occasion in a fit and proper manner.

On leaving Ta Tang, we kept a general north-north-west course for eighteen miles up the river till we were within sight of Chi T'ien, passing the villages of Chow Tang, Chu-Kwo Lia, Pay-Fin Chang (a large one), Wu-Lu T'ien, and Wu-Lu Pu. At Chow Tang, a large creek, almost a river, enters the Yangtse from about 10° to the south of west. Between Wu-Lu T'ien and Wu-Lu Pu some men were observed washing for gold in the river-bed.

The valley of the Yangtse had been gradually becoming more open as we progressed northward, and at Chi T'ien it widened into a large alluvial flat. Here we left it and ran west-north-west for a mile up the right bank of a tributary to the village of Ku-Tu Wah (6,485 feet), where we camped for the night, again in a hayloft, in which the only piece of furniture was a well-preserved coffin.

We only saw Chi T'ien in the distance, but it appeared to have grown into a town of some size;

it was totally destroyed during the Mahommedan rebellion.

From Shi Ku to Chi T'ien the river is navigable, at least for boats, although in one place, about two miles below Chi T'ien, there may be a rapid when the water is low. On the road up this reach we observed that the inhabitants did not carry arms—a fact which spoke well for the orderly character of the district, for the Chinese carry swords on the slightest provocation, although the weapons are oftener used for splitting wood or cutting grass than for any other purpose. We met, indeed, a few parties of Tibetan carriers who carried lethal weapons, but this was no reflection on the Yangtse Valley, as they must have passed through a less settled country.

CHAPTER XXX

KU-TU WAH TO WEI-SI

Villages of La-P'si Ku and Ta-P'ien Ta—Sifans—Goitre—Crossbows—Llamaserai of Lu T'ien—The Llama—A consecration and its cost—Om Mani Pami Hum—The divide between the Yangtse and the Mekong—Wei-Si.

IT was raining heavily when we left Ku-Tu Wah, but the sky cleared in a few hours, and we were dry when we reached (in fifteen miles) the llamaserai of Lu T'ien. Within the first four miles we passed La-P'si Ku and another village of which I could not ascertain the name. Both had the long masts and dependent banners inscribed with prayers which are part of the apparatus of llama piety. A steep ascent brought us to the village of Ta-P'ien Ta (8,320 feet), after which we again descended to the valley of the creek, which we ran up till the confined valley was seen issuing from the cultivated plain of Lu T'ien, on the northern side of which the llamaserai (8,440 feet) is situated. There is no village of Lu T'ien, but the whole plain is dotted over with farmhouses or groups of farmhouses, which in some cases attain the importance of hamlets. There is a white pagoda on the southern edge of the plain opposite the llamaserai. The people are for the most part Sifans, and the men wear the usual 'horn' of coiled hair on the front of the head. We observed one woman with fine features who would have passed for an Italian. Goitre was alarmingly prevalent here and all the way from Shi Ku. The tendency to goitre may or may not be hereditary, but we only saw a single exception to the rule that it is developed in adults alone. The disease is ascribed in some districts to the lime in the water, and in others to the quality of the salt.

We met in the course of the day a good many men armed with crossbows. These weapons are of the simplest possible character. The bow is let into the end of a barrel and stock, which are in one piece and rudely cut out of a $\frac{1}{2}$-inch plank. The sportsman lifts the string from a notch in the barrel, either with his forefinger or by a trigger. The arrow, which is feathered with a small twist of bamboo leaf, is about 14 inches in length, and not much thicker than a knitting-needle.

There seemed at first no chance of getting accommodation in the llamaserai, as the llama was absent when we arrived, and had taken the keys with him. After we had waited for about an hour, and just as we were preparing to make the best of a cold and draughty, unenclosed shed with a stone floor, the llama and his assistant arrived with a large following of neophytes and coolies, laden with guns (matchlocks converted to percussion), besides a big drum, two trumpets, gongs, censers, baskets of books, and other paraphernalia of worship. It was interesting to learn that a rich man, who had erected a new house, had bestowed 10 taels (say 30s.) on the monastery in order that the house might be properly consecrated, and that the cost of the journey and ceremony, which occupied three days, were covered by this donation. The llama must have been over eighty, and had the manners of a gentleman (the expression is used in no ironical sense). He had the best room (a granary) prepared for us, offered us snuff, sunflower seeds, and the spirit of the country, entertained us with intelligent conversation, and encouraged us to talk of our home—and withal was simple as a child. He and his assistant wore red serge robes and red plush jackets. He invited us to look at the temple itself, in which were a gilded Buddha, a brass censer, and some carvings, the whole rather tawdry. The buildings, which formed a quadrangle, were nearly new. The woodwork of the walls beneath the verandas which opened on the central square was ornamented with spirited carvings, the favourite subjects being flowers, birds, fishes, monkeys, and an undescribed species of elephant with a horse's tail. Later in the evening the old priest settled to his orisons, and intoned his 'Om mani pa-mi hum' (The jewel is in the lotus) in a rich bass voice, which would be certain, in spite of his age, to make him the darling of a fashionable congregation if he could only be translated to some such sphere of usefulness in the West.

We set out next day with the addition of a local escort of six crossbowmen to protect us from the robbers who are said to infest the pass between the Yangtse and the Mekong. Leaving the monastery, we crossed the Lu T'ien Plain in two and a half miles, and began the ascent, which proved very laborious, occupying nearly two hours, although the horizontal distance could not have been more than two miles. We estimated the altitude of the pass at 12,000 feet. Unfortunately, the day was cloudy, and we had no such view as we had counted upon. The summit is surrounded by a double trench, said to have been made during the Mahommedan rebellion (1856-1874), when the insurgents held Li Kiang and the Imperialists Wei-Si.

West of the pass the road crosses a boggy plateau for two miles and a half before the land begins to slope rapidly towards the Mekong. On the plateau were a few shelter-sheds for the use of the nomadic Sifan herdsmen, of the same type as those which we had met with further east, but roofed with shingles instead of matting.

The descent of seven miles to the west was accomplished without incident, unless there be reckoned the frequent tumbles of the party on the slippery slopes, and the meeting with a perspiring crowd of Chinese, who had still the greater part of their uphill work before them. The guide indicated that there was a copper-mine some miles to the south-west.

Wei-Si (7,480 feet) lies well up on the left bank of what may be called a fair-sized 'trouting stream,' and may either be regarded as a large village or a small town. It is said to have been of much greater importance prior to the Mahommedan rebellion than now. The town population and merchants are mainly Chinese, while the suburban people and labourers are chiefly Sifans. Numerous shops line both sides of a steep paved and stepped main-street.

CHAPTER XXXI

WEI-SI

Cooper's troubles—Discontent in our camp—A missionary besieged—Flint and steel.

THE position of Wei-Si, as will be seen from the map, differs greatly from that assigned to it in previous maps.* I conjecture that the compilers must have located the town from Cooper's account of his journey,† to which no map is attached, and that Cooper had overestimated his daily progress to the south. Cooper had troublesome experiences at Wei-Si, and probably little time to devote to mapping. Foiled near Atuntze in the attempt to cross Tibet to Assam, by the opposition of the llama, he passed Wei-Si (held at the time by the Imperialists, although it had changed hands often, and suffered much in the process), only to be turned back at Lan Chow by the Mahommedan rebels. Returning to Wei-Si, he was thrown into prison by the civil officials. He escaped once, but was recaptured at Ka Ga and brought back to prison, to be afterwards rescued by a friendly chief from the north.

* Considering its true position, the advice of the Hsien of Li Kiang to go to Atuntze viâ Wei-Si was not so unreasonable as it seemed at the time.

† 'Travels of a Pioneer of Commerce,' by T. T. Cooper. London, 1871.

No such trials were in store for us. Our worst difficulties arose from the quality of the accommodation provided for us in the first-floor of a wretched hovel of an inn, and the growth of discontent among our followers. We had previously, at their own request, promised our Szechuanese soldiers to take them back with us by water from Assam to Shanghai, and send them to their homes up the Yangtse; but now the coolies and mafus, who had been listening to blood-curdling tales of robbery and violence, declared their determination to go no further unless the soldiers were to return with them. We had to promise them also a return passage by sea.

A tale was current in Wei-Si of a missionary attacked by 'wild men' at Chiung, the crossing of the Mekong between Atuntze and Chamutong, about eleven days before. The missionary was said to have escaped, but the 'wild men' captured two sons of the Toussa who were protecting him. This tallied with information which we subsequently received.

We had to delay a day in Wei-Si while negotiations went on touching the supply of mules and other arrangements. The muleteer agreed to take us to Chamutong, or at least to the left bank of the Salwen, beyond which, he said, beasts of burden could not go. If we thought fit to go further, he said, we would have to get Tibetan coolies at Chamutong; and as to whether it was worth while to go so far, he advised us to consult the foreign missionary at Hsiao (Little) Wei-Si, on whose advice he also was prepared to act.

It may be said here that we first heard of this priest at Yung-Peh, where he was said to inhabit Li Kiang. At Li Kiang, however, we found that he had moved westward to Wei-Si, and that he had been magnified into *eleven* priests. It was only at Wei-Si that we learned that the eleven priests were still one and indivisible, and that the one was, and always had been, located at Hsiao Wei-Si.

Between Li Kiang and Wei-Si matches are scarce, and every man carries flint and an elaborate steel case. Looking through the market for indications of foreign trade, we found few except some buttons marked 'S. P. & Co.,' and umbrellas, one of which bore the name of a Calcutta maker.

CHAPTER XXXII

WEI-SI TO HSIAO WEI-SI

Villages of Pu Ah and Ka Ga—Camping in a hen-roost—Village of Toong-Show Ah—A gorge—The Mekong River—Villages of Pay-Chi Sui, Chin Shan, Lo Kwo, Zing King, Lo-Chi Pu, and Hsiao Wei-Si—Bamboo rope bridges—The Abbé Tintet—Exchanging news—Prince Henri's journey—Manifold and Davies at Hsiao Wei-Si.

From Wei-Si to the Mekong, a distance of twenty-five miles, the road keeps the right bank of the creek, on a pretty straight north-west course. Seven miles from Wei-Si we passed the village of Pu Ah, and six miles further camped in the larger village of Ka Ga. The latter is the place where Cooper was captured after his escape from durance at Wei-Si, and where he was married against his will. Cooper refers to the inhabitants as belonging to the Lei Su tribe. I cannot say that we saw anything to distinguish them from other Sifans, but his knowledge of the people was much more intimate than ours, our principal aim being to travel as far as we could in the day, and secure the best possible accommodation for man and beast at night. Our quarters at Ka Ga were in a hen-roost which formed the first floor over a hay-shed, and required a good deal of sweeping before it was fit for human habitation, and a good deal of vigilance afterwards to keep out the *de jure* owners. The mistress of the house carried herself with a commanding air, as was natural in a country where polyandry is said to prevail. We could not help speculating as to which of the old women we saw at Ka Ga was the one who married Cooper by force and then left him.

Between Ka Ga and the Mekong there was little to note. At six miles we passed the village of Toong-Show Ah, and in three miles further the creek entered a fine gorge, down which it tumbled, till in three miles more it fell into the left bank of the Mekong. Following up the river to the north, we passed, in one mile, the village of Pay-Chi Sui. On the opposite or right bank was the village of Chin Shan, where it is reported that gold is obtained both in the river-bed and in reefs. I fancy it is, as elsewhere within my experience, a question of licenses or miners' rights; but local gossip says that the officials can collect no revenue from these mines, and that when their approach is announced the miners and diggers transfer their energies to other mines further to the west. A mile and a half to the north-west is the village of Lo Kwo, connected with a village on the opposite or right bank by a single-rope bamboo bridge. Half a mile further north there is another village on the right bank, named Zing King, with a single-rope bridge. Four and a half miles more to the north-west the large village of Lo-Chi Pu, on the left bank, is connected by a single-rope bridge with a village on the right. Two and a half miles further north-west we reached the village of Hsiao Wei-Si (5,813 feet), where important issues awaited us.

My diary of September 14 now bore the unsatisfactory entry: 'Total from Maha (in thirty-six days) 394 miles.' Had it been possible to carry out our original plans, we ought to have been in Upper Burma by this time and within this distance.

We lodged in the house of the headman of the village, in a capacious apartment on the upper storey —of course without a front wall, as is the case with all the second storeys in this part of the country.

Here we met the Abbé Tintet, the French missionary to Tibet, of whom we had first heard at Yung-Peh. For some months he had had no communication with the Bishop at Ta-Ch'ien Lu or the French Consul, and knew nothing of the rising of the Boxers (whom, by the way, he classed, like a good Catholic, with all secret societies, as 'freemasons'). When he heard such news as we could give him, including the orders of the French Consul that all French subjects were to leave Yünnan, and we invited him to accompany us, he replied with a *non possumus* on the double ground that he could not leave 'his people' unprotected, and that he could not move in any case without orders from the Bishop. The Abbé had been in Hsiao Wei-Si for twelve years, and had been at his post when the late Prince Henri of Orleans arrived in 1895, and had since read the Prince's book, 'From Tonkin to India.' The book had been lent by the Abbé, with the usual result. He was able to give us information about the journey from Hsiao Wei-Si to Kampti (Burma) and Sadiya (Assam) which would have been worth a great deal to us when we were making our plans at Maha. The Prince, it appears, after having abandoned his ponies and mules, and left everything behind which he and his party could not carry on their backs, had plunged into ' *des difficultés énormes* ' in the shape of snow-clad wastes, hunger, fatigue, fever, tigers, etc., and had had to abandon some members of the party till relief could be sent to them, and some of them had died.

It was now getting late in the season, the Abbé continued, and the snows would soon begin to fall, in which case, if we did not perish in the mountains, we might consider ourselves lucky if we got back to put in the winter at Chamutong. One of the Abbé's confrères (probably the missionary we had heard of at Wei-Si), according to his latest information, was then defending himself behind an entrenchment from the attacks of the Tibetans; but a Chinese official had gone to straighten things out.

I have since had an opportunity of seeing Prince Henri's book, ' From Tonkin to India,' in the library of the Rangoon Literary Society (an admirable institution, it may be remarked in passing), and the reader may be referred to it for the details of an interesting and remarkable journey. The Prince found no road, and had simply to make his own way; but I was informed in Burma, on reliable authority, that there is a road from Wei-Si to the head of the Burmese railway system at Myitkyina. This road is, however, chiefly used by salt-smugglers, and it is likely enough that Chinese officials know, or care to know, nothing of it. Had we heard of it in time, the chances are we should have attempted it.

I afterwards learned from Major Davies in Shanghai

that Colonel Manifold, with a party of sepoys, had passed through Hsiao Wei-Si on his way to meet Major Davies and Captain Ryder at Atuntze. The intention of the conjoined party was to follow Prince Henri's route as far as the Salwen, and to run the valley of the Salwen up into Tibet. They were, however, stopped (in April) by snows in the pass between the Mekong and Salwen. Returning to Atuntze, they went to Batang viâ Yerkolo. Returning to Yerkolo towards the end of May, they tried to cross the Mekong there, but were prevented by the Tibetans cutting the bridge. They then bent their steps to the east, keeping south of Batang, and striking the main Ta-Chien Lu road near Li Tang. They had no trouble either at Atuntze or Chung Tien.

Their routes to Atuntze were as follows: Colonel Manifold from Yang-Pi by the same route as that which we took from Hsiao Wei-Si to Yang-Pi; Captain Ryder from Hui-Li Chow through Yen Yuan, Ying-Ning, and Chung T'ien; Major Davies from Mien-Ning through Mili and Chung T'ien.

CHAPTER XXXIII

HSIAO WEI-SI TO SHI KU

Shall we abandon everything?—No; try the Bhamo road—Return to Wei-Si—Pediculi—Loss of a mule—Crossing the Mekong-Yangtse divide—Military exercises—Robbers with poisoned arrows—Snowy mountains—Ku-Tu Wah, Ta Tang—Single-rope bridges—Cantilever bridges—The Yangtse near Li Kiang—Shi Ku.

As we were not travelling solely for amusement, and were not prepared to sacrifice our papers, maps, or money (having started with what we considered an 'irreducible minimum'), not to speak of a possible sacrifice of human life, and as Mr. Way was unfit for a journey on foot across rough country, we reluctantly gave up the attempt on Kampti, and resolved to make for Bhamo. After lightening our load by making over to the Abbé, for the benefit of his 'people,' a few blankets with which we had prepared to face the mountains of Tibet, and sharing with him the contents of a little medicine-chest (the latter of which he declared would be of the greatest service), we turned our faces to the south and bade adieu to Hsiao Wei-Si and a valued friend. It may be mentioned that Cooper refers to the inhabitants of Hsiao Wei-Si as belonging to the Mooquooi tribe.

The Abbé Tintet had informed us that the robbers who infest the Lu T'ien Pass must be taken seriously, and that their custom is to collect in bands, sometimes numbering as many as forty men, and to 'snipe' travellers with poisoned arrows discharged from crossbows. The poison is said to be almost immediately fatal, although death may be prevented by the prompt amputation of a limb. The robber guild is said to preserve jealously the secret of the poison, as well as the secret of an antidote. Camping once more at Ka Ga, we returned to Wei-Si on September 17. We heard of five gold-mines (reefs) and also of alluvial gold in the vicinity of Lu-Tzu Chiang, between the Mekong and the Salwen.

The authorities at Wei-Si had made up their minds that we were to be protected with vigour, and filled the inn with soldiers, who slept in the room adjoining our apartment. Whether we got it from these soldiers, or direct from the walls of the hostelry, it is idle to speculate, but we carried with us, in the shape of a swarm of pediculi, a souvenir of Wei-Si which it took us some weeks to get rid of. It became the custom, night and morning, to examine clothing and bedding with scrupulous care, while one of the party, who was musical, hummed the in-the-circumstances-rather-irritating refrain, 'We'll all go a-hunting to-day.' The precaution of guarding the inn did not prevent the theft of a riding mule belonging to Mr. Way. When the loss was discovered early in the morning, and before the town gates were opened, the official confidently expected to recover the mule in a short time, as he sent runners to watch every gate. A city, however, may have the most irreproachable gates, and yet, if the walls only connect houses, and every house has a front and a back door, the escape of a thief with his booty need occasion no surprise. We never heard of the mule afterwards.

The Hsien had announced his intention of sending an escort of thirty soldiers across the pass with us, but the actual number turned out to be eight. A Chinese army never has, in the field, quite the strength it has on paper. Falling back on some ancient experiences of volunteer drill, and bearing in mind such lessons of recent South African warfare as had reached me, I resolved that, whether we were attacked or not, the day's march should be of some educational value to the soldiery, both provincial and local. It was decreed that straggling was for the day absolutely forbidden; that the van, however fresh, was not to run away from the main body; that every one was to keep the place assigned to him; and that the rearguard was to keep in touch with the party in front, and that nobody was to be allowed to fall behind. One of the Europeans took charge of each of the van, the rear, and the treasure in the centre, and each had with him a small party of soldiers. There was a good deal of trouble at first, especially with the petty officers, who could not see why they should not go where they pleased or stray or stop as they felt inclined, and I had to make a stern show of violence on more than one occasion. All Chinamen have an innocent but irritating habit of regarding unpalatable orders as meant for somebody else. We were not attacked by the banditti; but the day will be long remembered in the valley of the Mekong as the one when soldiers actually obeyed their orders.

The retiring Hsien of Wei-Si was travelling in the same direction with us, and one of the reasons given for the extra military precautions promised was that *he* had his enemies, who might molest us. We overtook his equipage on the plateau on the range, and kept it company as far as Ta Tang.

Fortunately, this time it was clear weather, and from the entrenchments or fortifications on the summit of the pass we had a magnificent view, and were able to take a series of compass bearings. Beyond the Mekong a snow-clad mountain lay $5°$ to the south of west, and there were others both to north and south. To the east of the Yangtse, the highest peak, which rose some thousands of feet above the snow-line, lay $5°$ south of east, at a distance which we guessed at fifty miles. There appeared to be a continuous chain of mountains, all high above the snow-line. One of the most conspicuous peaks bore $40°$ north of east, and another $8°$ north of east. This is what we should have had to encounter if we had been lucky (?) enough to carry out our intention of going across country from Yung-Ning to Chung T'ien.

I am led to assign to the highest of these peaks an altitude of about 20,000 feet by the following considerations:

We had no instruments with us for accurate determinations of altitude, having left everything of the kind behind except an aneroid barometer. But the winter had not set in; no snow had fallen, and the heat of the sun must have still every day been melting the lower snows. As long before as May 20 we had found the snow-line at 13,000 feet in the pass of Hsueh Shan, 5° of latitude north of where we were now. After leaving Maha we had passed close to heights of at least 15,000 feet on which there was not a particle of snow, and, of course, we were prepared to find the snow-line rising as we approached the equator. Now, if a long experience in judging of mountain heights has been of any service to me, I am prepared to assert that the highest peak observed from the pass on which we now stood rose at least 5,000 feet above the snow-line.

Once we had cleared the pass, discipline was relaxed, and it was 'go as you please' till we reached the Lu T'ien llamaserai a little before nightfall. Our friend the old llama was absent on duty, and his lieutenant did the honours in his stead, with much less of grace and dignity.

One of the local soldiers informed us that there was a quicksilver (cinnabar) mine beyond the right wall of the valley below Ta-P'ien Ta. He so minutely described the process of distillation that I think there can be no mistake about it, although we saw no specimens. There was a heavy thunderstorm in the night.

We left Ku-Tu Wah on September 20, and reached our old quarters at Ta Tang. The river had fallen about 6 feet since we passed up, and we could see that there was, and had been, a good deal of gold-washing in its bed between Ku-Tu Wah and Wu-Lu Pu. Besides a raft taking men across to some washings on a gravel bank, which had emerged since our previous visit, we saw a cargo-raft floating down the river.

On September 21 we arrived at Shi Ku, and camped in the little llamaserai. We counted ten men working gold on the left bank, between Kwo Tu and San-Shien Ku. There was a thunderstorm in the night and heavy rain.

The bridges, each composed of a single bamboo rope, which span the Mekong every two or three miles, are of the type which has already been described. The passage in mid-air over the foaming river must be trying to the strongest nerves, and the pull-up from the bottom of the sag must be very laborious. The latter is avoided on the Min and other rivers in Northern Szechuan by having two ropes wherever the banks are high enough. Each rope is so arranged, high on one bank and low on the other, that the impetus given by the initial glissade is just sufficiently checked by the sag on the opposite side to enable the passenger to step off on the landing-stage without fatigue. The great width of the river and consequent expense of ropes are, no doubt, the reasons why this plan is not adopted on the Mekong.

All the way between the Mekong and the Yangtse

the bridges over the smaller streams are of the cantilever type.

The course of the Yangtse below Shi Ku differs considerably from that which will be found on the best published maps. The bend of the river is very abrupt, and its course below Shi Ku is to north-north-east, after which it turns to the north. It must curve round again very abruptly and flow to the south. From the slopes above the suspension-bridge between Yung-Peh and Li Kiang the valley could be followed up by the eye for many miles to the north-west.*

CHAPTER XXXIV

SHI KU TO KIEN-CH'UAN CHOW

Divide between Yangtse and Mekong—Snowy peaks north of Li Kiang—Loong-Sui Valley—Pay-Han Chang Lake—Kwan Shan—Loong-Yu Tsun—Tu Ho—Kwo Tung—Kwo Tsi—May-Tze Sha—May-Tzu Show—Kien Ch'uan—Opportune orders from Viceroy of Yünnan—Magistrate issues a proclamation—Telegrams sent from Tali Fu.

FROM Shi Ku we followed Gill's route to Kien-Ch'uan, and it is unnecessary to linger over what has already been so well described by him.

* Since the above was written I have seen Bianconi's 'Carte Speciale de la Chine,' Paris (no date, but evidently very new). It gives to the Yangtse above Li Kiang the same bend as in the map attached to this volume, but continues it north-eastward almost to Yung-Ning. This reading of the topography is confirmed by the travels of Mr. E. Amundsen (Royal Geographical Society's Journal for June and November, 1900). It is almost certain that Bianconi's map follows the report of the Lyons Mission, which I failed to procure in the East. I

Five miles from Shi Ku we were on the divide between the Yangtse and the Mekong (6,320 feet), after seven miles of crooked uphill travelling. From this point a snowy peak bore 25° to the east of north. This was too far away to be the Li Kiang Peak, which is only lightly, and perhaps not perennially, snow-clad. We must have been looking over the top of this elevation to, I believe, the peak which bore 8° east of north from the pass between Wei-Si and Lu T'ien. Scarcely distinguishable at times from the fleecy clouds around it, at others it flashed in the sun like a silver shield. I am ready to maintain that this peak, at least 5,000 feet above the snow-line, is no whit behind the Matterhorn, Mont Blanc, and Mount Cook, in beauty. Perhaps when artists have exhausted Switzerland, Norway, and New Zealand, the highlands of Yünnan will have their vogue.

Turning to the west, we looked down from our vantage-ground in the pass into the dry, cultivated valley of Loong-Sui, which heads about two miles to the south and falls very gently northward into the Yangtse Valley, and which we had crossed between La Sü Ba Llamaserai and Shi Ku. Descending to the head of this valley (7,980 feet), we passed a ruinous block-house (of mud and timber) between the Yangtse fall and the head of the valley, which is followed by the road as far as Kien-Ch'uan. There is a lakelet

---

remember to have read in a review that the Lyons Mission found the Yangtse above Li Kiang very far wrong in previously existing maps.

I am only able to make Amundsen's mapping fit in with Széchenyi's by shifting the whole of his work half a degree west; and it is probable that Széchenyi is more reliable than Amundsen in his observations for longitudes.

(a limestone 'sink') on the Yangtse side, and a lake about a mile long, on the Kien-Ch'uan side. This lake (7,870 feet), which, as well as the village on its eastern margin, is called Pay-Han Chang, occupies the head of the valley, but has no outlet, and is undoubtedly a limestone 'sink.' Three miles down the valley (south 15° west) we camped on the left bank in a farmhouse (7,700 feet) opposite the village of Kwan Shan, which is on the western side. The Loong-Sui, or Dry Valley, as well as the valley we were now following down, no doubt marks the outcrop of a soft or easily-decomposed vertical stratum among the limestone rocks.

Our further progress to Kien-Ch'uan was on the same course and down the same valley, which from a few hundred yards in width gradually increases to two or three miles of rice rice-lands. We passed many villages, which were mostly on the right bank, while the road was on the left. There was good pigeon-shooting in the morning, and in the afternoon many egrets were seen near Kien-Ch'uan. Five miles from Kwan Shan we saw a lump of limestone impregnated with carbonate of copper, which had evidently come down a lateral valley. At six miles we had the large village of Loong-Yu Tsun on our right, and at seven miles we passed through the village of Tu Ho. After three miles through low limestone hills, we passed a small square five-storey pagoda and the little village of Kwo Tung, the larger village of Kwo Tsi lying on the opposite side of the valley. At eleven miles we passed the village of May-Tze Sha, remarkable in this district for having two-storey dwelling-houses, built of mud and timber. At thirteen miles we passed a five-storey pagoda, and crossed, by a fine stone bridge of five arches, a large creek which comes from the west, and into which the creek which we had followed falls a little lower down. The village of May-Tzu Show is on the right bank of what may now be called the river. Four miles more, down the plain on the right bank, with several villages at the foot of the hills, brought us to Kien-Ch'uan (7,400 feet), where we occupied 'Ma's' inn, which had been highly recommended, and which really was a little better than the majority of Chinese hostelries. Here we found a parcel of good copper ore (azurite and oxide), and, on inquiry, were informed that it came from Lung Chang, one of four copper-mines in the Li Kiang district, four stages from Kien Ch'uan.

The Hsien (Dzo Hai Ching) called after we had settled down, and made arrangements for our journey, having just received a telegram from the Viceroy of Yünnan requesting him carefully to protect all foreigners ('including missionaries'), as China was now on friendly terms with all nations. He advised us to wait a day to give time for his messengers to get well ahead of us with a proclamation for the people and letters to officials and headmen. We afterwards found this proclamation (in which we were described as peaceful strangers who had come to China, on the invitation of the Empress-Dowager, to help the Chinese to open their mines) as far as Tai-Ping Pu, six stages on.

We had hoped to get a change of pack-mules at Kien-Ch'uan, as those now with us had come from Wei-Si, and were nearly spent. This, however, was found to be impossible, and the muleteer agreed to go with us as far as Yung-Ch'ang after purchasing a few fresh animals to replace those which were absolutely unfit for further work.

We still adhered to our determination to avoid Tali Fu, and made up our minds to take the 'small road' which leads direct to Yang-Pi, where it joins the main-road from Tali to Bhamo. We, however, sent a corporal and coolie to Tali Fu, the first telegraph-station which we had been near, with dispatches for London and for the officer commanding the British forces at Bhamo. The corporal was to follow the main-road (Gill's route) to Tali, and rejoin us at Yang-Pi.

CHAPTER XXXV

KIEN-CH'UAN TO CHOW HO

How Chang—Sa-Chi Plain and villages—Smoked out—A lesson in good manners—How to ask for the best hotel—Chow Ho—Brine and rock-salt—News from Tali.

WE left Kien-Ch'uan on September 25. Shortly after we had cleared the city wall we had a last view (north-north-east) of the snow-capped mountain which was seen from the pass between Shi Ku and Kien Ch'uan. The paved road wound in a general southerly direction for five miles among the rice-fields of the alluvial flat, on which were great numbers of egrets. A lake or swamp was just visible to the left, and villages were scattered along the right margin of the valley. Five miles from the city we left the outlet of the lake or swamp on our left, and entered among low hills on a south-westerly course. Here a deer was seen by some members of the party.

In this region, and as far north as our journey had extended, the twin-baskets carried on a pole across the shoulder, so common throughout China, are discarded in favour of a single basket carried on the back by the aid of a wooden yoke, as in Korea. The majority of the carriers are women.

Eight miles from the city we descended to and crossed (from left to right) a small creek fringed with rice-fields, and entered the village of How Chang.

For the next seven miles we crossed low hills till we again came on the right bank of the outlet of the Kien-Ch'uan lake, which had made, since it was last seen, a considerable excursion to the east, and which at this point emerges from a gorge and enters on an alluvial flat devoted to the cultivation of rice. The flat generally is known as Sa-Chi, and has eight or nine groups of dwellings which may rank as villages, and which are all called by the same name. In one of these (6,890 feet), three miles south of the point where we entered on the plain, we made our camp for a night.

We attempted to occupy the second storey of an inn, but were literally smoked out as soon as the kitchen fires below had been lit. We obtained permission to sleep in a temple and spread out our beds at the feet of the grinning gods. The crowd of sightseers was inclined to resent our desire for seclusion, and perhaps our own tempers had been (or, to be strictly just, let me say mine had been) strained dangerously near to breaking-point. At any rate, I let myself go and indulged with zest in a game which I had often seen practised before, but this time it was with all the added refinements suggested by accumulated experiences.

The gaping crowd, which as a rule we suffered without comment, proved unusually trying to the nerves, and I requested all but our own people to withdraw. In every Chinese crowd there are always some men who blandly decline to realize that unpalatable orders can possibly apply to themselves. In this case a ringleader made himself busy in expelling the rest, and after he had finished I enjoyed the keenest satisfaction in ordering him to follow them. He kicked the door from the outside by way of farewell. A few minutes later the usual clearing out of the courtyard of the temple at sunset produced a welcome calm. I am aware that in relating this incident I do not show up in the most amiable light, but I am very human, and the ever-present staring Chinese eye is sure to get upon one's nerves sooner or later.

From this village our course lay for three miles south-south-west to another, also called Sa-Chi, and perhaps the largest village of the name. At five miles the plain ended, and the river entered, at a graceful new single-arched stone bridge (which we did not cross), on a more confined course. The gorge would offer no difficulty to railway construction, as the fall is trifling, and cutting through the soft sandstones and shales would be easy.

At seven miles, where the valley again opens out, we passed a small village, and in another mile crossed to the left bank of the river by a wooden bridge (two villages on the right bank). Here was the first bamboo water-wheel which we had met with in Yünnan, although they are very common in Szechuan. Still following the river, which now turned to the south, we passed, at nine miles, a small village with

KIEN-CH'UAN TO CHOW HO 187

a three-storey temple of adobe and wood. At this point the river commences to flow 10° to the west of south.

At eleven miles the river is spanned by a pretty rustic suspension-bridge. At thirteen miles the course of the river alters to south 30° west, and at sixteen a large tributary falls into it from the west. After three miles of winding through the hills on this course, another mile (south 12° west) brought us to a village where an immense quantity of firewood was stacked for the use of the Chow Ho salt-works, and the river was crossed in a single span by a very fine covered wooden bridge. Chow Ho (6,190 feet) is about a mile south-east of this village, on an alluvial flat.

We were at first taken to a wretched inn, about the worst we had yet seen—which is saying a great deal; but after some demur we were lodged in a slightly better. We occupied a loft, and only escaped suffocation by removing a wall of bamboo matting which converted our apartment into a passage for the smoke from the kitchen. We had got ahead of the English-speaking Chinese and the guides, and our ill-success in the first instance was due to our having looked out, on our own account, with the help of a Chengtu soldier, for hotel accommodation.

Nee Sui Ching took occasion to hint when he arrived that we were apt to lose a good deal through the brusqueness of our manners. We had, no doubt, he said, gone straight to the point, which is never done in good society, and had probably asked the first man we met: 'Where is the best inn in this place?' Nothing throws a Chinese off his balance so certainly as to come straight to the point with him. We ought to have gone about it, he said, like this:

'What is your honourable name?—Mo. Ah! I knew a family of that name in Szechuan, and have very pleasant recollections of their kindness and good breeding' (here draw on your imagination for some facts in illustration).

'My name? My insignificant appellation is Jah. It is not one of the four hundred illustrious names of China, but only a name common among a tribe of foreigners. I shall be eighty-five years old next birthday. I am, as your astuteness has already guessed, a stranger in these parts, but my desire, and that of my companions, is to pass a night in this fine town. Can you, perchance, direct us to a house where we can sleep and eat? We are able and willing to pay for the accommodation. Over there, where the two venerable elders are dry-nursing their grandchildren? Oh, thank you, thank you!'

'Chinese gentleman everytime very polite,' remarked Nee in conclusion. 'F'r example, where English doctor man say, "You puttee this poultice on small of your back," Chinese doctor say, "This concoction of simples will have the felicity of reposing upon the distinguished small of your honourable back."'

We may profit by the lesson after our Chinese vocabulary has been somewhat enlarged. At present it does not run to such graceful flights as Chinese good-breeding demands. As to the eighty-five years and the pleasant Mo family, Nee encouragingly remarked, 'never mind little bit lie pidgin.'

Chow Ho looks like a village of 2,000 inhabitants, and is the seat of important salt-works. We found its products as far west as Manwyn, near the border of Burma. For the first time in China we saw rock-salt, a little dark in colour but fairly pure, and entirely soluble, with the exception of a trifling residue of silica. The rock is sawn into blocks of varying sizes convenient for transport and sale. There are also brine wells, the brine being led down in long conduits from the hillside to evaporation works in the village. The firewood for the furnaces is floated down the river, and caught and stacked at the village above Chow Ho.

We were now near enough Tali to hear some of the gossip of that city. We were informed that the trouble of a month or so before had arisen through the wholesale importation of arms, ostensibly for the use of the French missionaries, and that in consequence of the popular excitement the latter had been requested by the officials to leave the city. How much of truth there was in this story I cannot tell.

CHAPTER XXXVI

CHOW HO TO YANG-PI

Cooper at Lan Chow—La-Tzu Yi—Evidences of depopulation—Lien-Ti—Market-day—Foreign trade—Kwa Chow—San-Cha Tung—Ku-Ah Tse—No purchase in money—Cartridges in request—Ku-Ah Tsin—Ah-Lung—May-To—Ma-Ti Plain—The worst road in China—Yang-Pi.

ABOUT a mile below Chow Ho, a large tributary falls into the right bank of the Kien-Ch'uan river. This may possibly be the creek which Cooper followed down in 1868, after leaving Wei-Si, till he was turned back by the Mahommedans at Lan Chow. Evidently

Lan Chow, like Wei-Si, is placed too far south on the map.

Three miles south-south-east of this tributary, down the left bank of the river, is the village of La-Tzu Yi. Five miles further is another village, with a two-storey mud pagoda. The road then leads in the same direction for a mile and a half over grassy hills, where the extraordinary number of tombs is one of many evidences of a former much closer population than there is in the present day. The depopulation (from which, however, the district is evidently recovering) probably resulted from the Mahommedan rebellion.

A mile and a half further, south-south-west, we arrived at Lien-Ti (6,800 feet), where we camped for the night. This is a very little village, enclosed by a loopholed mud wall. An extraordinarily busy market was being held in its little square. Among the objects exposed for sale were salt from Chow Ho, 'lichees' from the south, needles marked 'Scheele and Co., Hongkong,' shirt buttons marked 'France,' and Japanese safety matches.

Lien-Ti is under the jurisdiction of the Hsien of Lang-T'iung (between Kien-Ch'uan and Tali). We found that the Hsien, who had been written to by the Kien-Ch'uan official, had sent dispatches to Lien-Ti which insured us a good reception. We were lodged in a small temple, the best accommodation which the place afforded, and the leading men made ceremonial calls.

From this village to the Yangtse, between Li Kiang and Shi Ku, a railway could easily be constructed. We could not help remarking that, whether a railway is wanted or not, Nature seemed to have specially made the country from five miles south of Kien-Ch'uan, up the river to the lakes and down the 'Dry Valley' to the Yangtse, with a view to railway construction.

The river is some distance east of the road at Lien-Ti, and is not again met with till the village of San-Cha Tung, six miles south-south-east, is reached. The village of Kwa Chow is about midway between Lien-Ti and San-Cha Tung. Four miles south-east of the latter we pulled up at a temple, where our own people and the escort seemed to have made it up between them that we should spend the night. It is always easier to submit to than to combat such a determination on the part of the Chinese; but the desire to have his own way dies hard in the breast of the Briton, and after infinite trouble and much swaggering we got the unwilling cortège under way. In three miles south-east and one south-south-east we reached Ku-Ah Tse, where an unavailing attempt was made to engage a local guide, as we felt that the 'escort' was playing with us. It was a new experience to find that money had no attraction for the villagers, although some of them professed their willingness to serve us for cartridges. We had none to spare, and if we had they would not have fitted the Chinese guns, and so no business was done.

Our design when we set out from Lien-Ti was to make the regular stage to Ma-Ti, but when night fell and we had still a high range in front of us, we were obliged, in consequence of the delay at the temple, to camp in the village of Ku-Ah Tsin (6,510 feet).

From the temple the road was certainly frightfully rough, what with bad paving and bad engineering, and it is hardly surprising that the coolies, who knew what lay before them, had desired to postpone the evil day of traversing it.

The headman of the village gave us an upper room in his house, where we found a teacher and a few pupils busy over copy-books. Penmanship was evidently all that the teacher professed. We hoped to elicit from the pedagogue some useful knowledge concerning our route, but I have rarely found a man so innocent of general information.

Leaving Ku-Ah Tsin, we reached the summit of a range (6,370 feet) about a mile from the village. After following a gully down from its head, to south-south-east, for three miles, we passed the village of Ah-Lung. A mile and a half further was a village called May-To, and in a mile and a half further we again reached the bank of the Kien-Ch'uan River, into which the tributary we had been following poured out of a narrow gorge. Following down the river for a mile, we reached the Ma-Ti Plain, over which several hamlets were scattered. We had our mid-day meal in one of a group of tabernacles erected on a piece of waste ground conveniently situated as a gathering-place for the dwellers in the plain. Reaping operations were in full swing, and the crop of rice appeared to be a very good one.

From Ma-Ti to Yang-Pi, a distance of thirteen miles to the south, the whole bottom of the valley was under close cultivation. When the track was permitted to descend to the valley, or, rather, could no longer be prevented from doing so, it either followed a grassy ridge, pared by the industrious farmer to a knife-edge, or kept on what had once been a pavement, but was now little better than a series of rounded stepping-stones through the mud. As a rule, however, the track kept on the stony edge of the high land, which is always, according to Chinese ideas, accounted good enough for a road if useless for any other purposes.

Most travellers in China have referred to some pet piece of bad road. That from the temple near San-Cha Tung to Yang-Pi is mine. The head that planned and the hands that laid the pavement have, no doubt, been at rest for a thousand years, and, as their intentions were good, they may sleep in peace; but we felt that we owed a deep debt of ingratitude to the many generations of men who have neglected to repair it. Colquhoun, it may be said, refers to the road from Yung-Chang to Bhamo as the worst in his experience; but, bad as it is, we found it the best which we had seen between the Ya-Lung and the Irrawadi.

Yang-Pi (5,430 feet) is a small and sleepy town on the left bank of the Kien-Ch'uan River. It is said to have been of some importance before the Mahommedan rebellion, when it was taken and retaken many times. Colquhoun mentions* that 2,000 Mahommedans were driven by the Imperialist troops into the mountains, where they perished of cold and hunger.

We were informed that a French missionary had made his headquarters at Yang-Pi till a short time ago, when he left for Sin Kai in consequence of the troubles in the neighbourhood of Tali. There was a French priest at Yang-Pi in 1882 when Colquhoun passed through.

An evidence of the condition of the country was incidentally gathered at Yang-Pi, where we learned that the 'small officials' who, about this season,

* 'Across Chrysê,' third edition, 1883.

usually go to Yünnan Fu and have their annual chance of promotion or a button of higher rank, had this year been forbidden to travel on account of the disturbances.

Beef, the first which we had seen since Maha, was procurable at Yang-Pi.

CHAPTER XXXVII

YANG-PI TO CHÜ TANG

A telegraph survey—Tai-Ping Pu—Ta-Niu P'ien—Shwan-Pi Chow—Hoang-Lien Pu—Trade in cotton—Pei-To Po—Telegraphic communication under difficulties—Tien-Ching Pu—Sa-Sung Sae—May-Hwa Pu—A blood-red river—Chü Tang—Goose-breeding—Yung Ping.

WE were now on the main trade route from Yünnan, viâ Tali and Teng-Yueh, to Upper Burma, called, if my memory serves me (for I cannot lay my hands on the reference), the 'Great Gold and Silver Road.' We set out from Yang-Pi in heavy rain on the morning of September 30, commencing the journey by crossing the river on an iron suspension-bridge 120 feet in length. One of the new guards carried a horse-pistol branded 'Tower, 1848.'

In the telegraph-office at Yung-Chang we found a survey of the telegraph-line from Tali to Teng-Yueh, and the operator was good enough to let us copy it. As it was evidently good surveying work (I believe by Mr. Jansen), and the telegraph-line closely follows the road, I have no hesitation in substituting it for our own, which was necessarily of a sketchy character, and laying down our observations upon it. It is, I have no doubt, more accurate than the mapping of any previous traveller whose work has been published; recent, but as yet unpublished, railway surveys must be better still.

In about six miles from the river the road had climbed, in a general westerly direction, to a shed on a summit 8,070 feet above the sea-level. Sidling down the right wall of a valley from its head to west 10° south, we camped in the little village of Tai-Ping Pu (7,330 feet).

A mile beyond Tai-Ping Pu we first sighted the telegraph-line from Tali to Bhamo, and felt that we were at last in touch with the great world. At two and a half miles we passed a tea-shed, and at five and a half miles a village (Ta-Niu P'ien) with a tea-house.

At eight miles, after we had sidled down to the left bank of a river, which we crossed at Shwan-Pi Chow (5,100 feet) by an iron suspension-bridge, 90 feet in length, the gully (now a river) which we had followed down from its head fell in below the bridge.

Keeping well upon the right bank of the river, the road now went south for three miles and south-south-west for one mile, to Hoang-Lien Pu, a large village with some shops. We were jostled, on the narrow hillside path, by a constant stream of traffic, cotton in bales and officials in chairs. One of the latter, who was travelling with his family, asked us anxiously if we had such a thing as a baby's feeding-bottle. Alas, there was no such thing among our baggage! Leaving Hoang-Lien Pu by a steep ascent, we reached, in two miles west, a temple prettily situated in a pass (6,330 feet). A slight descent, followed by a general rise, brought us, in another mile, to a gap (6,570 feet) in the drainage basin of the Hoang-Lien

Pu River. Two miles further (south-west) by the ridge which forms the left wall of the same river, we camped in a village called Bei-To Pu (6,570 feet), probably the village called Hoang-Sing An in the Telegraph Survey.

Here the corporal who had been sent to Tali Fu from Kien-Ch'uan overtook us, and reported that he had found the gates of the city strongly guarded by soldiers, who inquired strictly into his business. When he arrived at the telegraph-office, the operator refused to transmit our messages till he had consulted the Hsien. The latter sent for the General in command of the troops, and the investigation was repeated, the corporal explaining the nature of our employment and giving the names of our Chinese associates in Szechuan. It turned out that his trump card, so to speak, was a reference to our friendship with General Chü, who, as a young man, had been 'out' with 'Chinese Gordon.' Our *bona fides* was triumphantly established, and the telegrams were sent next morning. The corporal gathered that all the foreigners (three English and two French) had left Tali for Sin Kai, and that a small army was concentrated at Teng-Yueh, watching the Burmese frontier, three Hsiens or Toussas having sent 800 men each.

From Bei-To Pu the road ascends for five miles west-south-west to the village of Tien-Ching Pu on the summit of the range (8,020 feet), passing a tea-house at three miles. Two miles beyond, down a valley (south-west), is the village of Sa-Sung Sae, according to the map, the local pronunciation being Sao-Chung Show (7,420 feet), and four miles further the village of May-Hwa Pu (6,670 feet). Down grassy spurs, forming the right wall of the valley, for three miles, we crossed to the left bank of the creek, where it debouches on the Yung Ping Plain. After skirting the plain, to south-southwest, for three miles, we reached a village on the left bank of the Yung-Ping River, and here again we had to oppose a cut-and-dried conspiracy to stop us. It was raining, and the river to be forded was reported to be breast, if not chin, high. The temptation, in short, to rest was too strong for the resolution of the Chinese, who had started in the morning with the intention of making the full stage to Chü Tang. We persisted, however, and the river, of a blood-red colour, was found to be only a little more than knee-deep at the ford. A mile more over the alluvial flat, by a badly cobbled pavement, brought us to Chü Tang (5,430 feet), a village whose prevailing industry is the breeding of geese. The town of Yung Ping is situated on the right bank of the river, about four miles above Chü Tang, and looks well as seen from the grassy spurs on the opposite side. According to Gill, Yung Ping was entirely destroyed during the Mahommedan rebellion, and he remarked that at the time of his visit (1877) Chü Tang seemed to be taking its place. Nevertheless, Yung Ping was in 1900 the more important of the two. The alluvial plain marked on Széchenyi's geological map ends a little below Chü Tang. For the credit of the village, it may be mentioned that we spent the night in an unusually commodious inn.

CHAPTER XXXVIII

CHÜ TANG TO YUNG-CHANG FU

Tia Tang—Hwa Chai—T'ien-Ching Pu—Sha Yang—Pack-bullocks—Crossing the Mekong River—P'yin Pu—Sui Chai—Ta-Li Chow—Divide between Mekong and Salwen—The Yung-Chang Plain—Po-Lo Ti—Pan Chiao—Cotton-weaving and dyeing—A new fashion in tombs—Yung-Chang—Foreign trade—Foot-binding—Where is Sin Kai?

FROM Chü Tang the road led, up the narrow valley of a tributary stream, south-westward for three miles to a pass (6,330 feet). The hills are composed of a coarse conglomerate, in which the forces of Nature and constant mule traffic have in some cases converted the roads into deep cuttings, in one of which I had to straighten myself up into a corner and wait a quarter of an hour for the passage of a train of mules laden with cotton. In two and a half miles we had descended to a village (6,070 feet) on the right bank of a stream which flows south-eastward and is bordered by a rice flat. The village is locally named Hwa Chai, but is probably the Tia Tang of the map. A toilsome ascent up the valley of a tributary streamlet by a paved road, which climbed from one rice-field to another all the way, brought us, in a mile and a half, to a village (6,570 feet) which the inhabitants called by the same name as the last (Hwa Chai), and which is no doubt the one which the map calls To-Hwai Chai. Here, with some difficulty, we found an upper room which, after much sweeping, was made habitable for the night. The interpreter, always on the alert for signs of the proximity of 'England side,' detected a noise which he was certain was 'belonging to foreign man church.' Sure enough, close attention was rewarded by the beautiful strains of 'Yes, we'll gather at the river,' with variations. The excited interpreter reported, after an investigation, that there were a few native Christians in this place, though for the present, owing to the state of affairs, they were lying low and 'doing a little bit Joss pidgin' to avoid exciting remark. One of the converts, however, had been indulging in musical memories.

Between To-Hwa Chai and the tea-house named T'ien-Ching Pu (8,210 feet), on the top of the range (three miles south-west), we met several teams of mules laden with bales of raw cotton from Burma. A steep descent of four miles (south-west) brought us to Sha Yang (4,970 feet), on the Sha-Ma Ho, a small stream falling to the south-east. Sha Yang is a village consisting of one long street, and has a population which may be guessed at 4,000. It stands out honourably conspicuous among villages of the same calibre by its partiality for whitewash. Its whitewashed adobe cottages and tombs glitter in the sun, and from afar look like a tented field. Like many Chinese things which are beautiful from afar, it does not, however, bear close inspection. Our hotel accommodation was not scrupulously clean.

Half a mile south-west of Sha Yang we had crossed a low ridge, and after a much steeper descent reached a cultivated 'bottom' (4,620 feet) traversed by a small stream, which we crossed by a three-arched stone bridge. We followed down the left bank of the stream for a mile and a half (west-north-west), and left it where it took a northward course and plunged into the mountains. Here we met bullocks used for packing, an innovation indicative of the approach to Burma. In a mile (south 10° west) we reached a pass (5,510 feet) from which the Mekong River was visible. From this pass we almost literally 'dropped' into the Mekong or Lan-T'sang (4,150 feet) in less than a mile of horizontal distance.

The river is crossed by an iron suspension-bridge at a point where it is constricted between limestone cliffs. The cliffs are covered with gigantic inscriptions in the Chinese character, unintelligible to us, but giving rise to much speculation as to the kind of scaffolding which had been employed. The waterway is 260 feet wide, but is reduced by masonry piers to 175 feet, the actual span of the bridge. Colquhoun gives a photograph of the bridge in 'Across Chrysê.' I was informed that the bridge, which is carried on twelve iron chains, dates from 1863.

The ascent of the right bank of the river brought us, in half a mile south-south-east, by a paved road, neglected to a pitch which fits it well for the crippling of beasts of burden, to the village of P'yin Pu (4,770 feet). Here we overtook a party of soldiers in charge of a train of mules laden with silver for the pay of the troops at Teng-Yueh—an interesting event, as it proves that the Chinese do sometimes pay their troops, which has been doubted by many writers.

From P'yin Pu the road led (south-west) up the valley of a small tributary, with some fine waterfalls. The ascent was very steep, but the pavement and short zigzags were better cared for than anywhere else on the journey. In a mile and a half the narrow valley became more open, and a mile and a half more over a cultivated flat brought us to the village of Sui Chai (6,670 feet), where we camped for the night.

Another village of the same name was passed a mile to the south at an altitude of 6,870 feet. A mile further (south-south-west) the road crossed a ridge (7,320 feet). Two miles more, and we reached the village of Tali Chow, and two miles further were on the pass (7,850 feet) between the Mekong and Salwen waters.

A mile beyond the pass (south-west) is a tea-house, from which a magnificent view of the Yung-Chang Plain is obtained. About the same distance from the tea-house is the village of Kwan Pu. Two miles further we descended to the edge of the plain at Po-Lo Ti. Here the farmers had shown that they believed themselves to be in a free country by making free to use the road for their own benefit. They had erected mud dams across it, and one drop was positively dangerous for horses. In countries which I have known, the first teamster who happened along with a spade in his possession would have demonstrated *his* freedom by making short work of the dams.

It was market-day when we passed through the small town of Pan Chiao, one and a half miles beyond Po-Lo Ti. Here we first saw lotus bulbs used as articles of diet. Cotton-weaving and dyeing appeared to be the chief industries of the town. There was an elaborate arcade-bridge over a small tributary of the Salwen. The plain was alive with beautiful white egrets. We noted among tombs of the usual pattern ('Norman'-arched gable, with domed roof sloping to the ground at the opposite end) a few round ones of 'pepper-box' form and built of dressed stone, but so narrow that the coffins must of necessity stand upright. We met a General with his wife, 'small wife,' secretary, and escort of soldiers, returning from Teng-Yueh—' by order of the Empress,' it was said.

Six miles south-west across the plain, we reached Yung-Chang Fu, a small city enclosed by a brick wall on the western edge of the plain (5,720 feet), and here we stayed for two nights.

As Yung-Chang possessed the first telegraph-station which we had seen for more than 1,000 miles (not reckoning Ya Chow, which was on a line not in working order), we put ourselves in communication with London and the authorities in Bhamo. To the latter I said :

'Expect reach Sin Kai eighteenth.—JACK.'

I did not myself know where Sin Kai was, but thought myself justified in assuming that officials in Burma would be better informed. The Acting Deputy-Commissioner's curiosity was aroused, and he set his subordinates the task of finding out, first, ' Where is Sin Kai ?' and next, ' Who is Jack ?' To the latter he never received an answer, as my letter to the Commanding Officer miscarried. Inquiries as to the whereabouts of Sin Kai resulted in the discovery (which I hope has been officially noted) that Sin Kai is the Chinese name for Bhamo itself. No other name is known in China. Colquhoun made the same discovery in 1882, if I had only known it.

In the market of Yung-Chang we noted, among foreign commodities, Anglo-Swiss condensed milk, Price's stearine candles (Liverpool), Bear's bird's-eye tobacco (London), Vienna cigarette-papers, and petroleum.

We observed with regret that foot-binding, of which we had seen little for some time, again began to be the custom in Yung-Chang.

CHAPTER XXXIX

YUNG-CHANG FU

Missionaries, runaways, or bad characters—The Hsien satisfied —A 'crier' sent ahead—The Carriers' Union—Drastic measures—How not to do it—The Li Kiang muleteer to the rescue—The Fever Valley—Corporal Lion-in-the-Path —The foreigner's inside—Opening for an insurance agent— Passages in the history of Yung-Chang.

In due time the officials (the acting Fu and the Hsien) called and assured us of their protection. It transpired that we had no sooner arrived than the leading men of the city went to the Hsien and reported the circumstance, representing that if we were found to be missionaries, runaways, or bad characters, we should be sent to Tali Fu. Happily, the Hsien was satisfied, on the production of the Wai-Yuan's letter, that we did not come under any of the heads of this somewhat peculiar classification.

Besides the usual escort, he took the thoughtful precaution of sending ahead of us, as far as Teng-Yueh, a 'crier' with a gong to proclaim in every town and village that we were travelling with a peaceful, and even laudable, object, and must be well treated.

The acting Fu was an interesting old gentleman, and an expert in palmistry. He read our hands in the most approved fashion, predicting things which may or may not come true, and making some happy hits as to our family affairs and relations.

Notwithstanding the goodwill of the officials, we were destined not to leave Yung-Chang without abundance of worry. A corporal who had been sent ahead of us had contracted with a muleteer for the carriage of our load to Sin Kai. When we arrived, however, and proved to be foreigners, the muleteer declared that he could not carry out the bargain, which would bring him in collision with the Carriers' Union, among whose rules was a clause making it penal to accept employment from foreigners. We had mentioned our difficulty and the threatened boycott to the Hsien, and he had promised to do what he could for us.

As the sequel shows, he certainly acted with vigour. Having sent for the muleteer, and, failing him, for four of the leaders of the Union, he explained that we were an exceptional kind of foreigners—in reality, Chinese officials for the time being. The Chinese are, it may be said in passing, masters of all the arts of trade-unionism, their numerous 'guilds' exercising a despotic authority among the labouring and trading classes. The Hsien's argument failed to convince the four representatives, whereupon he ordered each of them 200 smacks with a bamboo lath. After this infliction the unhappy men professed to be convinced, and promised that mules should be forthcoming, the Hsien, having gained his point, so far relenting that the muleteer was to go no farther than Teng-Yueh, *unless he liked us.*

The mules, as might have been expected, were not forthcoming on the following day, and several moves had been made in the game of delay, which the

Chinaman plays so well, and which we had by this time come to understand a little, when our Li Kiang muleteer came to the rescue, and volunteered to follow our fortunes to Teng-Yueh, in spite of many good reasons which made him anxious to return— among others, the worn-out condition of his team and the approaching wedding of a younger brother, which would have to be postponed on account of his absence. We were much indebted to him for the concession, and very glad to get away, as, however well meant, the Hsien's methods did not seem calculated to increase the popularity of foreign service.

An even more formidable danger was the resolution of our 'permanent' (as distinguished from 'local') soldiers and mafus, of which we were now apprised, to desert us in a body, as they declined to face the malaria of the Lu-Kiang Ba, or Salwen Valley. We had, of course, read in Gill's book of this difficulty, but as we approached the Salwen we had concluded that the scare had been forgotten. We found, to our chagrin, that the dreaded 'Fever Valley' had lost none of its terrors. The valley had a bad name in Marco Polo's day, in the thirteenth century, and its reputation has clung to it ever since, with all the tenacity of Chinese traditions. The Chinaman of the district crosses the valley daily without fear, but the Chinaman from a distance *knows* that he will either die or his wife will prove unfaithful. If he is compelled to go, the usual course is to write to his wife and tell her that she is free to look out for another husband. Having made up his mind that he will die, I have no doubt that he often dies through sheer funk.

The ringleader in this mischief, as in all others, was

Corporal Lung Si Tang, whom Bunyan, had he been with us, would have delighted to nickname Corporal Lion-in-the-Path. Lung had been recommended to us as a warrior almost too bold for anything. Unfortunately, he was well-to-do, and contemplated retiring from active service and taking a farm on his return from this trip, for he reckoned that he could by that time write a cheque for 300 taels (£45), and he saw no reason why a valuable life like his should be risked. Besides, he was confoundedly well informed, and always managed to pick up early information of any difficulty ahead of us which might damp the spirits of his companions.

Many were the arguments with which we sought to combat the fears of our following; but the gallant corporal had an answer to each and all of them. To my inquiry whether an old man like me (in China it pays to make the most of one's advancing years) was not more likely to die than a lot of strong young fellows, he replied that 'foreigners are very strong in their insides.' Mr. Way made a sporting offer of 500 taels to the widow of any man who might die in crossing the valley, but the corporal parried by saying that compensation to a wife would not prevent a man's death, thereby showing that he had never had the pleasure of an hour's interview with an insurance agent. Our best trump, after all, proved to be the promise of a pill which would make every man malaria-proof. At last, after a whole day's discussion, the men agreed to come on, but stipulated that they should *not* return by sea (*for* which they had already stipulated). This seemed rather illogical, as to return overland would imply recrossing the Fever Valley. The corporal's fears, however, as I gathered, had given rise to a suspicion that, if they once set foot in British territory, they would be kidnapped and compelled to serve in the army. I must record that one plucky youth, a mafu named Low Luan, stuck by us from the first, and refused to be swayed by the fears of the others.

Yung-Chang was a place of much greater importance before the Mahommedan rebellion than it is now, and during the Middle Ages was the capital of a large province. A stirring episode in its history is thus related by Marco Polo (whom not everybody reads):

' Now, there was in A.D. 1272 a certain King of Mien [the Chinese name for Burma] and Bengala who was a very puissant prince, with much territory and treasure and people, and he was not yet subject to the Great Khan [the Emperor of China], though it was not long after that the latter conquered him, and took from him both kingdoms which I have named. As it came to pass when the King of Mien and Bengala heard that the host of the Great Khan was at Vochan [Yung-Chang] he said to himself that it behoved him to go against them with so great a force as would insure his cutting off the whole of them. So this King prepared a great force and ammunition of war, and he had 2,000 great elephants, on each of which was set a tower of timber, well bound and strong, and carrying twelve to sixteen fighting men. When the King had completed these great preparations to fight the Tartars, he tarried not, but marched straight against them. And after marching without meeting with anything worth mentioning, they arrived within three days of the Great Khan's host, which was then at Vochan in Zardandan, so there he pitched his camp. And when the Captain of the Tartar host,

Masaradin, had certain news of the aforesaid King, he waxed uneasy, as he had with him but 12,000 horsemen. However, he advanced to receive the enemy in the plain of Vochan, and when the King's army had arrived on the plain, and was within a mile of the enemy, he caused all the elephants to be ordered for battle, and began to advance. The horses of the Tartars took so much fright at the sight of the elephants that they would not face the foe. And when the Tartars perceived how the case stood, they were in great wrath. But their Captain acted like a wise leader, for he ordered every man to dismount, and to tie his horse to a tree, and then to take their bows. They did as he bade them, and plied their bows so stoutly on the advancing elephants, that in a short space they had wounded or slew the greatest part of them. So when the elephants felt the smart of the arrows that pelted them like rain, they turned and fled into the woods, dashing their castles against the trees and bruising the warriors. So when the Tartars saw that the elephants had turned tail, they got to horse and at once charged the enemy, and then the battle raged furiously, and when they had continued fighting till mid-day the King's troops would stand against the Tartars no longer, but felt they were defeated, and turned and fled.'

Perhaps some allowance is to be made for exaggeration on the part of the Tartars, and for credulity on the part of Ser Marco, but it must have been a stirring fight.

Yung-Chang was the theatre of war for three years during the rebellion, the Mahommedans occupying the right and the Imperialists the left bank of the river.

CHAPTER XL

YUNG-CHANG TO HUNG-MU SU

Ta-Shu O—Nay-Sui Ching—Loong-Sui Ching—Po-Paio—Fang-Ma Chang—Foreign trade—Ta-Ban Tsu—An early start—The magic pill—The Fever Valley—Bridge over the Salwen River—Plague—Ma-Ma Chih—Hung-Mu Shu.

WE left Yung-Chang on October 8, and after five miles to the south, along the western edge of the plain, entered the hill-country at Ta-Shu O, which must be the same as the A-Li Tse of the map. From this village we ran up a gully (west 10° south) for two miles to the little village of Ha-Tsu Pu (locally pronounced How-Tsu Pua). A mile further (just beyond a tea-house) we observed the outcrop of a seam of poor coal, about 2 feet in thickness, beneath a bed of limestone. Three miles further were Nay-Sui Ching (Warm Water Village) and Loong-Sui Ching (Cold Water Village), at an elevation of 6,920 feet. Half a mile from these villages we reached a pass (7,070 feet). From this pass the road to Po-Paio trends a little to the north of west, but we left it in two miles and turning off to the south-west, scrambled down for a mile to near the edge of the Po-Paio Plain to visit a newly-discovered tin-mine, of which we had heard at Yung-Chang. It proved to be a very small vein of antimonial lead ore.

Three miles to the north-west, across 'downs' country, we reached Po-Paio (4,840 feet), a village on the right bank of a small stream which flows to the north, where we camped for the night. Po-Paio has a 'likin' station for the levy of duties on articles imported from Burma. We met long trains of mules carrying piece-goods and raw cotton ; one bale of the latter was stencilled 'E. W. S.'

We crossed to the left bank of the stream at the lower end of the village by an arcade-bridge. A short distance below the village the stream enters on limestone downs, and its course is hardly distinguishable from the road which keeps well up on the left wall of the valley (north-north-west) for five miles, after which it turns westward into the range on the left, and in one mile enters Fang-Ma Chang. In this little village a market was going on, and we observed on the stalls German-made needles, Japanese matches, and salt from Chow Ho.

Half a mile further (south-west) was the divide between the Po-Paio Valley and the valley of the Salwen. After following a gully from its head in the pass, for a mile and a half to south-south-west, we reached Ta-Ban Tsu, a small village, with a 'likin' station.

The weather was fine, and, as it was still only a little after mid-day, we thought it a favourable time for crossing the 'Fever Valley.' Our followers, however, made such a to-do about it, and insisted so strongly on the advantage of starting fresh in the morning, so as to 'rush it' before the malarious 'steam' came up, that we had to consent to camp in Ta-Ban Tsu.

For once there was no occasion to 'bustle the East,' and our followers surpassed our most sanguine anticipations regarding an early start. They got us up shortly after midnight, and breakfast had been prepared and everything had been packed less than an hour afterwards. I solemnly gave every man the promised malaria pill. It was a good pill, compound of phosphate of iron, quinine, and strychnine; but it is needless to say that; even more than on its medicinal virtues, I relied on it as a 'faith cure,' valuable for keeping up the courage of the men.

About three o'clock, some moonlight-and-cloud effects having deceived us into the belief that the dawn was at hand, and tired of waiting, we started on our journey. Little could be seen under the circumstances; indeed, it was hard enough, in the semi-darkness, to keep on the paved road and flights of stairs which led down the valley. In about seven miles, daylight having come at last, we found ourselves emerging from the lateral valley into that of the Salwen.

The rather narrow cultivable 'bottom' of the Salwen is, as usual, occupied by rice-fields. Gill observed in 1877 that the flats, which had gone out of cultivation, were beginning to be cultivated once more. The re-occupation appears to be now complete. We failed to detect any of the conditions which might have tended to make this a specially malarious valley. The rice-fields were not more swampy than such places usually are, and the walls of the valley had been denuded of the jungle-growth which, no doubt, once covered them. The adjoining grassy slopes were favourably disposed for drainage. My belief is that some outbreak of plague or malarial fever, before Marco Polo's day, perhaps a thousand years ago, or when the soil was first turned up for cultivation, gave the valley a bad name, and that exaggeration and fear have done the rest. The evil reputation has been added to by the fact that plague has broken out in the valley several times, the last time only a few years ago; but where in China has plague not broken out some time or other?

The malaria is said to be at its worst during the summer, when, especially after rain, 'a lurid copper-coloured vapour fills the valley.' Marco Polo says it would be death to a foreigner to cross the valley in summer. Till the Mahommedan rebellion (which disorganized many Chinese arrangements), a guard was placed on each side of the valley to stop the traffic during the worst of the season.

Gill evidently believed the tales of malaria which he heard, but, then, his followers were weak with fever when they arrived. So did Colquhoun; but both he and his companion were very ill. Perhaps our own views, leading to a diametrically opposite conclusion, were biassed by the rude health of the party.

The Salwen (2,650 feet) is crossed by a fine suspension-bridge carried on sixteen iron chains. The bridge is in two spans. The eastern, 220 feet in length, cleared all the water there was at the time of our visit, the river being low. The western span, 170 feet in length, is thrown across a dry, stony channel. The eastern span had to be rebuilt after the Mahommedan rebellion. In 'Across Chrysê' Colquhoun gives a photograph of the bridge.

There are a few houses on the bank of the river west of the bridge, and a little further there are the ruins of a village, which was burned down a few years ago in consequence of an outbreak of plague. After rising over successive terraces of alluvium for a mile and a half (south 15° west), we passed a house surrounded by rice cultivation. Here we crossed a creek by a pretty 'hog-backed' stone bridge, and sidled up the right wall of the Salwen Valley, first south and then west 10° south.

The village of Ma-Ma Chih lay below us on the upper margin of the rice-fields. This village is occupied by the former inhabitants of the one which was burned down to stamp out the plague. Another village, which we had not previously seen, lies on the left bank of the creek which we had just crossed. It appears, therefore, that people actually live in considerable numbers in the dreaded 'Fever Valley.' The valley of this creek, it may be mentioned, has a little of the primeval jungle left—the first real jungle which we have seen, and the shriek of the cicala is heard for the first time.

Two and a half miles from the creek, we had climbed, most of the way by stone stairs, to the village of Hung-Mu Shu (5,680 feet), where we camped for the night (October 10). We were heartily glad to have crossed the 'Fever Valley' without losing a man—indeed, without 'turning a hair.' We knew that the impenetrable conceit of the Chinese, and some new theory, would prevent our soldiers from feeling ashamed of themselves. They no doubt attributed their safety to the magic pill. May their faith in 'foreign medicine' be increased !*

* On my return to Shanghai I learned that Wu Si Tang, my corporal, died of fever at Tali Fu on the return journey, and that two coolies, whose names I could not ascertain, died some distance short of Chengtu. I am not aware if the fever was contracted in the Salwen Valley. The corporal was a highly respectable man, and I deeply regret his untimely end.

CHAPTER XLI

HUNG-MU SHU TO TENG-YUEH

Shang-Po Tsu—Divide between Salwen and Irrawadi—Fung-Sui Ling—Monkeys—Tai-Ping Pu—The Loong Kiang—Yan-Tan Chai—Khan-Oo Tsu—Chin-Chai Pu—Yeh-Peh—Teng-Yueh Plain and City—The jade industry—Items of news—Kindness of the Deputy-Prefect—Wrath of the Chun-T'ai—Through the Chinese lines—A safe-conduct arranged.

AT Hung-Mu Shu the road got on the crown of the ridge dividing the creek which we had crossed at the 'hog-backed' bridge from another tributary of the Salwen lying to the south. In three miles to the west we had attained an altitude of 7,220 feet (the Salwen bridge bearing north-east by east), and a mile further had dropped down to the village of Shang-Po Tsu. In three miles west, over granite and gneiss, we attained a gateway on a summit at 8,020 feet. We were indeed nearing 'home,' for looking to the west we could see waters which we knew flowed into the Irrawadi.

A few hundred yards beyond the summit we passed a temple, called Fung-Sui Ling, between two gates. Here our attention was arrested by a noise in the adjoining woods, like the barking of a pack of dogs, and we were told that it was made by monkeys, which, however, we could not see.

Two miles south-west we reached the village of Tai-Ping Pu (7,370 feet), whose bamboo walls and straw roofs were a departure from the style of architecture prevailing to the east.

From Tai-Ping Pu to the Loong Kiang the descent is steep, although the road does not follow any valley,

HUNG-MU SHU TO TENG-YUEH

but goes into and out of one gully after another. Six miles from Tai-Ping Pu we reached the Loong Kiang (4,570 feet), a tributary of the Irrawadi, which enters Burma south of Bhamo. The hills are clothed with jungle down to the cultivated borders of the river. The village called Loong-Kiang Chow is at the eastern end of a good suspension-bridge, 145 feet in length (Plate XVI.).

Having crossed the river, we erred among terraced rice-fields for two miles (west) to the village of Yan-Tan Chai (5,120 feet), where we camped for the night (*cf.* Plate XV.)

For four miles (west 10° north) over grassy and fern-covered hills the road led up to a summit (6,720 feet). At five miles we passed a temple between two gates, a watch-tower, and three beehive-shaped erections of wrought stone (6,570 feet). Whether these were tombs, altars, or monuments, we could not divine, and no one was at hand who could enlighten us.

Half a mile further is the village of Khan-Oo Tsu, and four and a half miles further the village of Chin-Chai Pu (7,070 feet). Thence to the village of Yeh-Peh, on the edge of the Teng-Yueh Plain, is a steep descent of four miles.

This plain, as seen from the hills, presents one of the fairest views in China. On the plain itself the rice-fields are either just reaped or clad in the golden tints of harvest. It is dotted with grassy or wooded 'islands,' every one crowned with a village. The walls of the valley are of a vivid green.

It is about three miles across the plain to Teng-Yueh. At the lowest point, between Yeh-Peh and

Tsi-Cha Pu, the aneroid showed 5,570 feet. Here there was a watercourse which was little more than a ditch, the bulk of the drainage of the valley having been diverted for irrigation. The creek falls to the north, but after circling round the city of Teng-Yueh it empties into a much larger watercourse coming from the north.

In the suburbs, where our arrival appeared to excite a good deal of attention, we were met by a runner who brought a message that we were to go to the yamen of the Ur-Fu (Deputy-Prefect), where that official thought we would be safer from molestation than in an hotel. The people certainly ran after us and peeped into the windows, and generally were more noisy and curious than in any other town in Yünnan which we had come through, though certainly we had met with the same sort of manners in a worse form in several Szechuanese towns.

The city wall encloses a very large space, but only a small proportion of it is built upon. The population is probably less than that of Yung-Chang. Within the grounds of the yamen itself is a lake or swamp given up to the cultivation of the lotus. A fine gilded pagoda ornaments the market-place.

The principal industries of the place are jade-cutting and jade speculation. Almost every shop in the main-street has a lapidary's wheel of copper. The jade is said to come from places from one to two days' journey from the city. The market has all the fascination of gambling. The purchaser buys at a sporting price a piece of stone, a few pounds or hundreds of pounds in weight, and takes his chance of its turning out well or ill when cut up after coming into his possession. According to the quality and size of the pieces, they are manufactured into rings, snuff-bottles, seals, pipe mouthpieces, etc.

Here we heard some news or gossip: it is hard to say under which head it should be classed. The French had imported firearms wholesale into Tali Fu under the disguise of railway material, and it was owing to the popular tumult which resulted that all foreigners had to leave the city. We have not yet heard the story as told by the French. Another tale was that the English had advanced from Sin Kai with the avowed intention of pacifying a turbulent tribe of 'wild men,' and had murdered 112 inoffensive and unarmed Chinese. Later we heard the other side, at Bhamo, which was that the simple pastoral people had repeatedly 'sniped' the Gourkas, who had put an end to the annoyance by surprising the Chinese camp at daybreak with fixed bayonets.

The last European in Teng-Yueh was Mr. H. M. Hobson, who left after waiting for some months to establish a Customs station, having satisfied himself that nothing could be done in the then state of the country, and in the absence of a British Consul. He reached Burma on August 14, four days after we left Maha.

Chang Sung Ling, the Chun-T'ai, or General-in-Chief in command at Teng-Yueh, was said to be very wroth over the border 'massacre,' and to be anxiously waiting for permission from headquarters to lead his army against the English forces.

The Ur-Fu, Li Liang Yen, called and did everything possible for our comfort and protection. Probably owing to his good offices, the Chun-T'ai must have been mollified, or at least persuaded that we were not responsible for the border affair, for he not only sent us the usual party of soldiers with an officer and an open letter for his subordinates along the road, but also paid us a visit, in great state—unfortunately, about an hour after we had left. He informed the interpreter, who had not yet left, and also received his visit, that he had intended to convoy us out of the city—an attention, it may be said which is always offered in such cases, and always declined with profuse thanks.

To Li Liang Yen we also owed the fact that there was no nonsense about our getting a muleteer and fresh mules, although we had been led to anticipate renewed opposition on the part of the Carriers' Union. The muleteer who had served us so well from Li Kiang returned rejoicing with a suitable 'kumshaw' in addition to his stipulated earnings, and a treasure which he had long coveted—a Worcester Sauce bottle from which the last dregs had by this time been squeezed! Poor fellow! we parted from him with genuine regret. He said that, if we had needed him, he would have gone with us all the way, but if he went further his mules would not be worth taking back.

It is well for the traveller in China to endeavour to see through Chinese spectacles—in a word, not to oppose too obstinately Chinese prejudices, which, however absurd they may appear, have a comprehensible foundation. For this reason we had reconciled ourselves to a delay in Yung-Chang and Teng-Yueh, in deference to the popular argument that it looked very suspicious when strangers arrived in a town late one day, and left early the next without allowing time for the ceremony due to officials—and, no doubt, for inquiry into the strangers' antecedents. 'Raw haste'

Terraced Rice Cultivation, Shun-Ning Fu Valley, Yung-Chang.

PLATE XV.

is ever 'half-sister to delay,' especially in the Far East, and we should probably have had reason to repent if our anxiety to push on had led us into a course of action which might have been construed as rudeness.

CHAPTER XLII

TENG-YUEH TO JU CH'ENN

A vast necropolis—A Phlegræan Field—The 'Rumbling Bridge'—Ho Ti—Roads turned into reservoirs—Lang-Sung Kwan—Large stone bridge—The deadly banana—Corporal Lion-in-the-Path again—Cheap fuel—Nan T'ien—A Shan village—Chi-Tai Kai—Diversion of the road—N'yow Kan—High-level gravels—Landslip—Shan village of Tang Fang—Man Pu—Lever-reservoir rice-hammers—Shan village of Pah-Yi Tang—Ju Ch'enn—A threatened boycott—The Toussa's 'shintai' yamen.

For some miles after leaving Teng-Yueh, the low hills traversed by the road and telegraph-line were simply a necropolis, the dead far outnumbering the living citizens. Of course, in a country where graves are never molested and rarely neglected, the tombs represent many generations; but here they were so very numerous that the conclusion was irresistible that the city must have been, not very long ago, much more populous than it is now.

Four miles south-west of the city we attained a low hill-top from which we could see that the small Teng-Yueh Creek comes through a gap and joins a much larger watercourse coming from the north. A village lies a little to the east of the road, near the hill-top.

A mile and a half west of the summit we crossed

to the right bank of the creek (5,120 feet) by a stone bridge. Here the creek has cut down to the granite foundation, our course to this point from the city having been over basalt, forming a red soil, and low grassy hills. Beyond the creek we crossed about a mile of a veritable Phlegræan Field, formed of immense boulders of vesicular basalt—a newer flow than that which forms the smooth, grassy hills. After another mile over the smooth basaltic soil, we recrossed to the left bank of the creek by a boldly-arched stone bridge thrown across a narrow gorge. The bridge and its surroundings strongly reminded me of the 'Rumbling Bridge' near Stirling. Below it the creek falls into the left bank of a much larger creek or river.

Three miles down the left wall of the valley (south-south-west) we dropped down to the bank of the river at the village of Ho Ti (4,170 feet).

Four and a half miles down the left bank we passed a hamlet where the basaltic country came to an end, and the granite emerged from beneath it. As our road descended to lower levels the granite gradually rose above us until it formed the entire mass of the hills. For the next three miles down the left bank of the river, to Lang-Sung Kwan, the road proved tedious and unpleasant, as the industry of the farmers had utilized the greater part of it for watercourses or reservoirs. We camped for the night at Lang- (or Nan-) Sung Kwan.

Half a mile below this village a very large tributary falls into the left bank of the river. An unfinished bridge across the delta of this tributary promises, if it ever is completed on the present plan, to be a great work. It is supported on pairs of stone posts mortised into beams or girders of squared stone, which are covered by a deck of solid masonry.

A mile and a half from Lang-Sung Kwan, at a village of sun-dried bricks and straw roofs, we saw for the first time groves of bananas. At the earliest opportunity we sampled this delicious and wholesome fruit, which had the additional charm of being fragrant with reminiscences. Is not Queensland nicknamed Bananaland? And does she ever feel the nickname a reproach? Our soldiers lost no opportunity of bringing us supplies, and, no doubt, expected to see us drop down dead, for of course the well-informed Corporal Lion-in-the-Path had heard and told them all about the fatal effects of eating ripe fruit. It was not till we had repeatedly demonstrated the harmlessness of the banana, or, at any rate, the strength of the foreign 'inside,' that the soldiers and mafus (always excepting the wise corporal) risked their lives in a similar manner.

Three miles further, a good part of the way between well-grown hedges of cactus, we passed another village, also straw-roofed, where the female population was employed in plastering the walls of the houses with clods of cow-dung to be dried for fuel. Here the alluvial terraces reach an elevation of at least 200 feet above the river.

Three miles further we passed through Nan- (or Lan-) T'ien, a small town containing many shops and surrounded by a mud wall. Here we were received by a guard armed with guns and tridents. We changed some silver sycee for rupees, and were pleased to think that we were about to enter a country where the medium of exchange was a coin of a definite value.

Just beyond the town a large tributary falls into the left bank of the river, which, below the confluence, has a west-south-west course. On the other side of the tributary is a village different in its architecture from the Chinese, and peopled by Shans. All the women wear high black turbans, widening upwards, somewhat after the style of a Greek Patriarch's hat. Whether the turban is moulded on the hair, or is a hat pure and simple, I am unable to say. They also wear garters, perhaps solely for ornament, as they have no stockings to support, and perhaps, as one account had it, as a charm against rheumatism. Many of the Shan (as well as Kachin) men adopt the Chinese custom and method of hair-dressing, and are in consequence less distinguishable from Chinese than the women are (Plate XVI.). I regret that my notes on the interesting non-Chinese races which we encountered must lack ethnological value. We could not speak their languages, and to evince curiosity was simply to frighten them. Our Chinese followers did not, and, indeed, could not, help us much, as to them the alien races are merely 'wild men,' whose language is unintelligible, or, rather, to use the significant Chinese idiom, who 'cannot speak.'

A little beyond this place is Chi-Tai Kai, the residence of the Toussa Toa Wha Lan.

Three miles below Nan-T'ien the cultivable alluvial plain comes to an end, and the river, on entering a granite gorge, is spanned by a suspension-bridge. The road followed by all previous travellers from Nan-T'ien to Manwyn, or *vice versâ*, whose writings I have met with, was that on the north, or right, bank of the river. It crosses the river here and passes by Kau-N'Gi (Muang-la) and Santa, but I learned from the Chinese that it has been abandoned to the 'wild men.' My impression is that the country is more broken on the north side than on the south. Colquhoun, in ' Across Chrysê,' refers to the Toussa of Kau-N'Gi as a powerful chief.

The road now in use by the Chinese, and followed by us, is that on the southern, or left, bank of the valley. From the bridge it leads for three miles (west-south-west) to the village of N'yow Kan (3,820 feet), over the wreck of high-level alluvial terraces which have been extensively denuded.

Leaving N'yow Kan, we travelled at first among the ruined alluvial terraces (which at times were at least 300 feet above the present level of the river, and then climbed down to the partially dry bed. Three miles from the village a landslip up a gully to the left, followed by a flood, has brought down to the river the material for a ' cone of dejection,' which must at one time have almost dammed it up and reduced the channel to a narrow passage on the north side. Two miles beyond this cone the road, which, from the suspension-bridge downward, has wound in and out and up and down among the denuded high-level terraces of the river, emerges on a low alluvial plain, much cultivated, at the Shan village of Tang Fang. Aloes were seen here for the first time, and the village street was barricaded with them so as to force the traffic round the outside.

Three miles further, at the village of Man Pu, we saw some rice-hammer mills of the lever-reservoir type. These mills have often been described before, and are only mentioned here because they seem to be getting scarce. We saw a good many out of commission, but in a journey across China these were the only ones we saw in use. A lever, balanced on an axle, has a hammer at one end, and is hollowed into a trough at the other. As the trough fills with water from the stream, the hammer end is raised, and at the moment when the balance is destroyed the water is spilt and the hammer descends. It comes very near perpetual motion.

A mile further and we were opposite a large village on the right bank of the river, in all probability Muangla, which, according to Colquhoun, is the seat of the powerful Toussa of Kau-N'Gi. Below this point the river takes a course of about 10° to the south of west, and the road keeps close to the bank, or in its dry bed. In a mile more we were in the Shan village of Pah-Yi Tang. We had an opportunity of examining the garters which are here worn by the men as well as by the women. They are composed of from six to fifty rings of bamboo wire.

We had congratulated ourselves that having been honourably conducted past the lines of the Chinese army (of which we saw little) at Teng-Yueh, our last difficulty had been surmounted. There was, however, still one remaining. Starvation stared us in the face! On arriving at the large village of Ju Ch'enn (3,170 feet), where a market was being held, we were informed that the Toussa across the river—at Muangla (?)—had sent his brother to see that the inhabitants gave us neither food nor lodging. He had probably heard of the approach of a party of foreigners, and did not know whether to look on them as friends or enemies. Happily, soon after our arrival the soldier who bore the Chun-T'ai's letter turned up, and, instead of being beheaded, boycotted, or drummed out of the town as vagrants, we were conducted to the Toussa's 'shintai' yamen, the most comfortable quarters we had occupied for many a day.

The Toussa, we were informed, was a very powerful chief, very rich, very old, with a wonderful white beard, and Lord of Two Elephants. The quarters in which we were lodged were on such a scale as to prove his wealth and importance. The yamen is enclosed in a loopholed wall, and the buildings are well designed and in good repair. The stables are the best I have seen in China. Outside the city wall a similar yamen is occupied by the military officer of the district—the 'fight-official,' in our interpreter's language.

After we had settled down, the usual presents arrived on the part of the Toussa, and a message was brought that he would call if we wished to see him. Much as we should have liked to meet him, we had to say that we could not think of giving him the trouble, as it was now dark and his residence was some distance on the opposite side of the river.

A feature of this day's march was the interminable string of coolies carrying sucking-pigs. Each pig was enclosed in a bamboo cylinder, and two of them balanced on the ends of a pole formed a load. We could only conjecture that some approaching feast in Teng-Yueh had made a market for young pork.

CHAPTER XLIII

JU CH'ENN TO MANWYN

Shan customs—Kachin merchants—Man-Chang Kai—Peepul-trees—The Toussa's elephants and their function—Betel-chewing—The Tai Ping Ferry—Shan villages—Manwyn—We discover Sin Kai.

The escort provided by the Toussa was armed with Hotchkiss rifles.

We could not distinguish the junction of the river which we had followed down from Teng-Yueh with the Tai Ping River, although we kept a sharp lookout for it. It must have been about Ju Ch'enn, as the first time we saw the river below that village its volume had enormously increased, and it was turbid, whereas the Teng-Yueh River was clear.

From Ju Ch'enn our course down the left bank of the river lay south-west. At three, three and a half, five, five and a half, and six and a half miles we passed villages, which were generally in pairs, and each was enclosed in a fine clump of bamboos and surrounded by a mud wall. The Shan inhabitants evidently do not appreciate the advantage of a 'business stand,' as they do everything they can to keep the traffic out of their villages. The road is taken round the outside, and by way of further 'hints to travellers,' barricades or hurdles are thrown across the ends of the streets. Owing to these circumstances we saw little of the Shan people. They are great workers in steel, and are renowned for their sword-blades.

Eight miles from Ju Ch'enn, on a low ridge which runs down to the river, is the large village of Man-Chang Kai. Here a busy market was being carried

SHAN GIRL, YÜNNAN.

SUSPENSION BRIDGE OVER LOONG KIANG.

PLATE XVI.

on, and we had our first opportunity of seeing the Kachin people, who are darker than the Chinese, and wear their hair in thick locks hanging all round the head. Women greatly predominated. The Chinese say that the Kachin women do all the work, while the men walk about with gun and knife. A Kachin missionary whom I afterwards conversed with says this is a calumny, and that the men work in the fields and hunt. The women certainly do all the trading among the Kachin tribes, as among the Burmese. In the market the women wore their gala dresses, and were to be seen at their best. Silver ornaments were profusely employed, as tubes piercing the ears, as necklaces, as bracelets, as brooches, and as rings. The clothing is generally a dark navy-blue serge (?) with red stripes, and consists of a tunic and a petticoat, not long enough to prevent the display of garters like those worn by the Shans. In this village we saw for the first time a few Burmese priests with shaven heads and yellow robes.

The Toussa's 'lordship of two elephants' proved to be no mere figure of speech, as it often is, for there were the two elephants in the flesh—and a great deal of it. We argued from their presence that the roads ahead of us promised to be better than those we had become familiar with. How the King of Burma ever got his 2,000 elephants to Yung-Ch'ang (as related by Marco Polo) passes comprehension.

A mile and a half below Man-Chang Kai we came down to the riverside at a fortified gate on the end of a granite promontory (2,970 feet). From this point the course of the river is 10° west of south. Here for the first time we saw a boat. The river is distinctly navigable (for boats) between Ju Ch'enn and Manwyn, but there must be impassable rapids below the latter town.

Four miles below the gate we observed a dark carbonaceous shale, almost a lignite, in the second alluvial terrace. A mile further was the market village of Hsiao Sin Kai. Three miles beyond this we camped in the village of Lung-Chang Kai (3,030 feet). Our lodging here was in a Shintai yamen belonging to the Toussa of Ju Ch'enn—a poor building which could not have been distinguished from the common hostelry of the country but for the combined temple and school-house which occupies one side of its quadrangle.

The Tai Ping River is now very large. The road for the whole of this day's stage has meandered between rice-fields, the cultivated flats averaging two miles in width. From Hsiao Sin Kai to Lung-Chang Kai it is shaded with fine peepul and other trees, and is often wide enough for wheel traffic, although narrowed in places so as to make wheel traffic impossible. That any portion of cultivable land should be devoted to merely ornamental or shade trees evinces the intrusion from the West of ideas which are foreign to Chinese economics.

The two elephants arrived in the village at night, in anticipation of next day's market, and we learned some interesting particulars regarding their functions. It appears that they and their riders, or 'mahouts,' attend every market in the Toussaship, and the riders collect and the elephants carry in huge baskets the tax levied on the traders by the Toussa, amounting, it is said, to 140,000 copper cash per market. As every day is market-day in one village or other, the Toussa's annual revenue from this source alone must amount to something like £7,000. It need not, however, be supposed that this is personal income, as in all probability the fund is drawn upon for public works and the expenses of government. For example, we learned from an inscription which was translated for our benefit that the Toussa had erected the school-house and temple at Lung-Chang Kai.

Betel-nut-chewing, first seen on the right bank of the Mekong, had been gradually on the increase westward, and was now almost universal among the Chinese, as well as among the Shans and Kachins.

One mile west brought us to the river, and five miles south, 35° west, down the left bank brought us to the ferry. On this reach there were great herds of fine water-buffaloes (steers). The river was very wide at the ferry; the water was slack and shallow, as the boats could be poled across. The latter were long, narrow 'dug-outs' with a thick bamboo lashed along each side. When loaded the gunwale was not 3 inches above the water.

The hills which form the right and left walls of the valley have dwindled considerably, and are probably not more than 2,000 feet above the level of the river.

Half a mile below the ferry there are Shan villages on both banks. I was unable to learn their names, as the Chinese of our followers was of no use. It was rather amusing to observe the mortification suffered by the Chinese when they found that they them-selves were the foreigners who 'could not speak.'

Three miles below the ferry is Manwyn (Man Gin) (2,830 feet), a large village or small town of a superior style of architecture, and wearing a general air of prosperity. A busy market was going on, and among the merchants were numerous Kachins, women, as usual, greatly predominating. They were in their gala costumes, covered all over with silver hemispheres, and had silver tubes in their ears. We camped in an upper chamber of the headman's house. The room was over a stable, but was scrupulously clean. On panels on the walls were spirited drawings representing (so said the Chinese legends) well-known Chinese stories and fables. Some had Burmese as well as Chinese inscriptions.

On calling at the telegraph-office, we were informed by the operator that our goal, Sin Kai, instead of being, as we had supposed, some place on the Tai Ping River, near the head of boat navigation, was Bhamo itself. The question, 'Where is Sin Kai?' had tormented us for a long time, as it had tormented Colquhoun before us. The Chinese know the place by no other name than Sin Kai, and the English officials only knew the Burmese name of Bhamo. Very circumstantial tales related by the Chinese had prepared us to find the two places some distance apart. For example, one account said that at Sin Kai there was a bridge, one end of which was watched by Chinese soldiers, while at the other end black Englishmen walked to and fro day and night carrying guns—clearly pointing to a town on the border, and consequently some distance from Bhamo. Another tale related how a misguided foreigner, who would not listen to good advice, had, with the object of saving steamer freight, started with his caravan of 100 mules for Bhamo instead of shipping them at Sin Kai, and, in crossing a mountain range inhabited by 'wild men,' had lost more than half his mules.

JU CH'ENN TO MANWYN

Our interpreter, in the course of conversation with the Chinese inhabitants, learned that the question of the day in Manwyn was : ' Why didn't the Chun-Tai kill these foreigners in Teng-Yueh, as he is so anxious to kill foreigners ? He sends them here with soldiers to protect them instead. What does it mean ?'

From some merchants in the town we heard of very good gold-mines, both 'stone' and alluvial, on the Loong Kiang, two stages from Manwyn, and the property of the Toussa of Ju Ch'enn.

Manwyn has a military yamen surrounded by a loophooled wall with flanking towers. In the town itself is an elegant new temple, with gilded finials, and some more than usually elaborate bamboo masts, with several crowns and long streamers inscribed with prayers in the llama fashion. The place owes its importance to the fact that it is at the ' inland ' end of the hill-road connecting the navigable tributaries of the Irrawadi with the plains along the Teng-Yueh road. From its geographical position it enjoys the advantages resulting from the establishment of a reloading station. It is said that the Kachins of the mountains were very ' bad ' until three or four years ago, when military stations were established all along the road. It was the custom of carriers to wait at Manwyn or the other end of the stage till they were 200 strong before venturing on the journey.

CHAPTER XLIV

MANWYN TO BHAMO

Margary's monument—The last mountain range—Kachin villages and tribal dwellings—A military cantonment—Pongsi—Hill fortalices—Across the frontier into Burma—Nampoung telegraph-office—In touch with the world—Myothet—By boat to Bhamo.

Two miles west-south of Manwyn a large tributary falls into the right bank of the Tai Ping River near the lower end of the alluvial plain which extends to Tang Fang. Below this creek the river plunges into gorges, and must be far too full of cascades to be navigable. The fall must amount to 2,300 feet in thirty-five miles.

On the right bank of this tributary, a short distance above the road, is a monument to Margary, who was killed in 1875. Unfortunately, I did not see it, and other members of the party who did were not made aware of its character till they were overtaken by the interpreter.

Two miles from the creek the road has given up the attempt to follow the valley, and the ascent of the mountain begins at two huts. Two miles up the jungle-clad valley of a little creek we reached a house (4,160 feet) on the top of a pass. After crossing another creek we attained, in half a mile, an elevation of 4,480 feet. In two and a half miles we came to a point (5,070 feet) from which Manwyn bore east 30° north, and in half a mile to a village (5,040 feet). Just beyond this village was a summit (5,070 feet), on which were numerous elevated cane couches and chairs, in which on festal days images are seated. The gods are invited to partake of the cattle which are slaughtered on the occasion. On both sides of the road are stockades of heavy posts, called 'wild-devil gates,' designed to keep out the Yüren, or wild men. A bar across the road might be more effective.

Half a mile further was a cantonment, or village, called Sui-Li, where an officer named Wong was in charge of 200 men. The bicenturion was very hospitable, and pressed us to stay with him for the night instead of going on to Pongsi. It turned out that he was the father of the young man who had guided us from Ju Ch'enn, and who must have reported favourably on us. We could not, however, accept the proferred hospitality, as our mules had gone on.

In two miles more we reached Pongsi, locally known as Poong-Si Ah (5,170 feet). There is no part of the road which is not commanded by the Sui-Li station. The village of Poong-Si consists of only a couple of houses, and owes its existence to the necessity for a camp for the carriers and their mules. There are two fortalices, surrounded by double trenches and *chevaux de frise* of pointed bamboos, on the summits of little hills.

The prospects of being on 'England side' the following day excited our Chinese friends almost as much as it did ourselves, and many and strange were the tales they told one another. Nee Sui Ching, better informed than the rest, invited anybody who had a grudge against him to strike him there and then, as, if he waited till to-morrow, a policeman would lock him up. The well-informed Corporal Lion-in-the-Path 'went one better,' with the news that in England a man who expectorates on the pavement is condemned to a long term of penal servitude.

Three miles west-south-west of Pongsi is a hill-fortalice with a small Kachin village just beyond. Two miles further there is another hill-fortalice, named Shi-Ti, with huts of bamboo and straw for the accommodation of 100 soldiers. We were invited in, and were given tea by the officer in charge. From a point just above this fortalice the junction of the Tai Ping with the Irrawadi was visible.

At six miles we entered a Kachin village (3,770 feet). These villages generally consist of only a few houses, but every house is practically a street, a long—sometimes enormously long—straw-roofed shed with a wooden floor. Each house is practically a common tribal dwelling as well as a guest-hall.

During our stay in Manwyn, I had provided myself with the supposed Kachin equivalent of the question most useful to us, ' What is the name of this place ?' It was given me by a Chinese resident as ' Ho naga he lee ?' but, alas ! it always missed fire.

At seven and nine miles there were two hill-fortalices, both neglected and in disrepair. At ten miles there was one in repair, and from this point we could see some buildings which, from their trim appearance and glittering iron roofs, were unmistakably English.

The whole of the day's march (October 20) had been down a ridge forming the left wall of the valley which heads at Pongsi. Eleven miles from Pongsi we dropped down into the creek at Hung-Ma Ho (1,370 feet), and having forded it, found ourselves on British soil at last, and at home among the 'kindly dark faces' of the native sentinels. The building occupied by an outpost of the Burman Police had been till recently the telegraph-office. The telegraph-office, of which the official name is Nampoung, is now beside the police barracks on a rising ground (1,700 feet) on the right bank of the creek a mile below Hung-Ma Ho.

The telegraph-manager, Mr. A. H. Bastien, made our short stay at Nampoung full of interest and pleasure. He could give us news of the world. The war in South Africa was still dragging on; there was trouble still in Pekin, but that darkest tragedy of all, the massacre of the foreign residents, which had been reported and believed for a time, had not taken place; there was still a perplexing uncertainty as to who was at war with whom; the King of Italy had been assassinated; the Federation of Australia was an accomplished fact. Such were a few of the items of news which we obtained after the first greetings were over. For details and for news of minor importance we could turn to Mr. Bastien's newspapers and magazines. What if some of them were a month or two old? They were new enough for us.

Then we could, and did, place ourselves in communication with friends in Britain, India, and Australia, and confidently anticipate an answer in a few hours. It was a treat to foresee one's movements with some degree of certainty, and make appointments for a given time; to telegraph to London or Brisbane saying, 'Expect to reach Bhamo to-morrow. Telegraph news about . . .'

We left Nampoung early on the morning of October 21, and by a, comparatively speaking, well-graded track over the mountains and through the jungle, reached Myothet (known to the Chinese as Ma-Mo Ho), near the head of navigation on the Tai Ping River (480 feet), about 11 a.m. Here we took a boat for Bhamo, which we reached about 6 p.m., the mafus and soldiers going round by the road and making two days of the journey. Our land travel from Maha to Myothet had taken seventy-three days, and covered 874 miles.

We had an excellent training in pedestrianism, for although we had ponies, it was necessary to spare them as much as possible, and the nature of the roads made riding so much of a cruelty to both man and beast that, as a rule, the men only crossed the ponies' backs occasionally for a change, or to present an imposing 'face' in deference to Chinese susceptibilities. Morris and Lockhart must have walked four-fifths of the distance. Mr. Way, having been so unfortunate as to be crippled by the accident already mentioned early in the journey, was obliged to ride on horseback or in a chair as much as possible.

A chair was procured at Yen Ching (August 24), and used wherever it was possible (often, indeed, where the state of the roads made it seem impossible). The sore had only healed sufficiently by the time we reached Chow Ho (September 25) to enable Mr. Way to take much walking exercise. From that town, the roads having become somewhat better, and chair-traffic beginning to be the regular thing, I took turns with him in his chair, and at Yung Chang I hired one for my own use.

In Bhamo, for the few days we remained there, it was amusing to see what things struck our Chinese following most. The form of indulgence the soldiers delighted in, after having got over their first feeling that they were being run away with—for they had never before seen a carriage or a road fit to bear one—was driving about in the luxurious 'gharry.' Another thing that struck them with surprise was that sentries should actually take the trouble to walk about and carry their guns all day, as it would have been so much simpler, they said, to sit down and smoke, and rest the guns in a corner, or hire coolies to hold them.

CHAPTER XLV

THE LAST CHINESE CAPTURE OF BHAMO

A sort of a hero.

IN Bhamo we met, among others, Mr. H. M. Hobson, of the Chinese Imperial Customs, who had left Teng-Yueh in August, and the Rev. W. H. Roberts, of the American Baptist Mission to the Kachins. To the last-named gentlemen I am indebted for the following tale, which may be given in illustration of the border relations a few years ago before the British occupation of Burma. It is only because of my inability to write a 'Ballad of East and West' that I use the humbler medium of prose.

Sin Kai, or Bhamo, has long seemed desirable in Chinese eyes, as it gives access, by a navigable river, to the Indian Ocean. It has, in fact, been occupied by the Chinese several times, the last time of all under circumstances which bring out a quaintly heroic side of the Chinese character.

'If you want Sin Kai,' said King to the Viceroy of Yünnan in the year 1884, 'I can get it for you.'

'Get it, then,' said the Viceroy, 'and if you hold it

for two months I shall send reinforcements and appoint a Governor who will rule the place for China.'

King surprised the town, and held it with 300 men, from December to March, occupying the Chinese temple.

Now it came to pass that, when the Viceroy had considered the matter, he reasoned with himself, saying :

'I have done rashly in this thing, and my Imperial master, fearing the envy of the nations of the earth, will not sanction the annexation of Burmese territory. It were better that the head of King should fall than he should give me away.'

The result of the Viceroy's deliberations was the despatch of a young officer with 200 men, nominally to reinforce King, but under secret orders to assassinate him or bring him back a prisoner to Yünnan. This officer saw no reason why he should not make a profit out of the transaction, while at the same time conscientiously obeying orders; so he sold the head, still on King's shoulders, to the Burmese General for 3,000 taels of silver, payable on delivery.

It soon became clear to King that the newcomer and the so-called reinforcements had added no strength to his hand, but that, on the contrary, his own authority was being secretly undermined. King, who was a man prompt in action as well as quick in apprehension, invited his coadjutor to his room, and, confronting him with a loaded pistol, extorted a confession. Then sadly he addressed the traitor :

'I knew that to go back to Yünnan would only be to lose my head. The Burman leader has some right to it if anybody has, and is willing to pay for it. He is frankly my enemy. I have nothing against him.

THE LAST CHINESE CAPTURE OF BHAMO 239

I will never be taken alive, but you, you dog, may carry my head to the Burmese camp. What does it matter to me if you get your blood-money?'

King then sat down, and made a deliberate attempt to commit suicide by smoking opium. Perhaps he was a healthy subject, or perhaps a too well-seasoned smoker; but for one or the other reason the opium had produced no effect whatever, though he smoked hard till the cock crew. With an expression of impatience, he threw away the pipe and called for a rope, with which he strangled himself.

This story has the disadvantage of being true; otherwise it would have been easy to bring the hero's logic more into accordance with Western ideas. But if King's logic was open to exception, his action was worthy of ' the noblest Roman of them all.'

CHAPTER XLVI

THE RETURN JOURNEY

Precautions which miscarried—Inaction of British Consul—Good faith of Chinese officials—Return of our Chinese party—Our return to Shanghai.

BEFORE leaving Maha, I had taken great pains to make certain that the authorities on the Burmese side of the border should be made aware of our intentions. I wrote first to the ' Officer Commanding the British Forces at Bhamo, Burma,' giving the names of the party and details of the proposed route, and suggesting that a small party should be sent across the border to meet us, or at least that a messenger should be sent with instructions for our guidance. Next, I asked the Consul-General at Shanghai, through the Company's manager, to make a similar request of the authorities in Burma. I found, on arrival at Bhamo, that my letter had not been received. This was, perhaps, not very surprising, as the letter had to be entrusted to a Chinese messenger, who had been paid half in advance, the other half to be paid, on his arrival, out of the proceeds of a cheque which was enclosed. Perhaps he thought it easier to pocket half of the fee and stay at home than to earn the whole by making the long journey viâ Ning-Yuan and Tali Fu; perhaps he had as much difficulty in identifying Bhamo as I had in identifying Sin Kai.

It was much more astonishing to find that neither Major Mannering, the officer in command, nor Mr. Chumley, the Deputy Commissioner at Bhamo, had heard from the Consulate at Shanghai. If a telegram had failed, there had been ample time for the usual 'confirmation' to arrive by post. Considering that we had left our business at the request of the nearest British Consul, and undertaken a long journey across a presumably hostile country, it was not too much to ask the Consul-General to do what lay in his power to facilitate our escape.

On my return to Shanghai, I made inquiries. Mr. A. M. A. Evans (the agent of our company), to whom I had telegraphed, informed me that on August 18 he had written, as requested, to Consul-General Pelham Warren, and had also seen Mr. Warren and Consul Bourne, and had been assured by them that everything possible would be done. On December 13 he wrote to Consul-General Brennan, asking what action had been taken, and repeated the inquiry on January 7. The answer (January 8) evaded the question at issue,

THE RETURN JOURNEY

and consisted of the snub: 'I do not know what sort of reception Doctor Jack anticipated, but am sure that the British authorities at Bhamo were quite willing to render him any assistance of which he stood in need.' It would appear as if I had asked for a brass band or for alms! Mr. Evans was informed verbally (I understand by Mr. Bourne) that no communication had been made to the authorities in Burma, and that it was none of the Consul's business to make such a communication. I am strongly of opinion that it is precisely for such purposes that Consuls exist, and that the Shanghai Consulate culpably neglected a plain duty.

In strong contrast to the apathy of the consulate, to which we had an undoubted right to appeal, was the good faith with which the Chinese officials acted throughout. We had to pass through a population in the last degree ignorant of the ways of foreigners, of whom they only know that they steal their lands, prevent the rains from falling in due season, feast on children's eyes, and violate ancestral tombs. Seeing that China was at the time at war with 'the foreigner' (distinctions matter little in China!), what would have been easier than for an official to court popular favour by handing us over to the fury of the mob? Yet I will say that in no civilized country could the terms of a 'safe-conduct' have been more honourably observed than they were by the Chinese officials. We had, of course, on the other hand, to be careful and tactful in our dealings with them, and the trip cost a great deal of money. The consideration with which we were entertained was due, no doubt, in a large measure, to the show of having money enough. Escorts, messengers, presents of ceremony, and the like, although nominally gratuitous, always cost their value in hard cash. I cannot help concluding that we should not have fared so well had we not been under the special protection of Kwei Chun, the Viceroy of Szechuan, or even if, with such protection, we had been missionaries or 'Consuls,' under which latter head Chinese officials class the representatives of foreign nations of whatever degree.

My impression is that the Chinese peasantry are not impulsive or quick to act. It is likely enough—nay, it is certain—that Boxers were plentiful in the districts through which we passed; but, failing distinct orders from the head centre, or a conflagration lighted by a spark, however small or accidental, the character of the people lends colour to the belief that it would take them some days (and a world of talking) to nerve themselves for an attack in cold blood.

I am, further, greatly impressed with the power of the officials, and believe that (at least, in the west) it is always possible for them to prevent the 'hustling' of foreigners if they choose to exert their authority. I fully realize that in our case the problem set before the officials was a delicate one, on the proper solution of which they must have felt that the safety of their own heads depended. The edict circulated in every province in the name of the Empress-Regent commanded them to 'exterminate' all foreigners at sight, and yet, with a better grasp of the meaning of foreign relations than was held by the isolated and conceited Court, they dared to disobey.

Our party was broken up, while we waited for the steamer, by the return of our followers, with the exception of the interpreter, Nee Sui Ching, the cook, and the 'boy.' The others had the option of return-

THE RETURN JOURNEY

ing by steamer to Shanghai and up the Yangtse, but could not trust themselves among foreigners after our departure, and deliberately elected to trudge back on foot to their homes at Li Kiang, Wei-Si, Maha, Chengtu, and Chung King, distances varying from 200 to 1,500 miles. Poor fellows! their adventures, I feared, were about to begin. They demanded, and, of course, obtained, enough of the malaria pills to see them across a dozen 'fever valleys.'

A few days in Bhamo among the good-natured brown men with skin-tight (because tattooed) lace pantaloons; a quick passage in a well-appointed steamer of the Irrawadi Flotilla Company through pretty but (after what we had come through) somewhat tame scenery; a few days among the lovely foliage and gimcrack palaces of Mandalay; a day-and-night journey by mail-train; a few days in Rangoon, rejoicing in the possession of one of the fairest of earth's shrines, the Shway Dagohn Pagoda;[*] a fine passage by a British India steamer; a few days in Singapore; a crowded steamer of the Messageries Maritimes; Saigon, a revelation with its great opera-house, costing £300,000, its cafés, its boulevards—wider than those of Paris, or even than those of Marseilles, and shaded by infinitely greener trees—and its 'Tour d'Inspection,' six miles of what must be the best-kept road in the world; four more days of the sea, and half a day at Hong Kong; three more, and our destination, Shanghai. These rounded off a 'circular tour' which had been full of interest because it was far from the beaten tracks.

[*] Mr. Way left Rangoon at once for London.

CHAPTER XLVII

INDIA TO CHINA

Railway projects.

THE question of trade routes to the interior of China has been before the world for the last fifty years. France has never for a moment lost sight of the importance of a commercial advance from Indo-China by way of Yünnan. England, with India extending to the western gate of China, has concerned herself only with the question, 'Will the necessary railways pay working expenses and yield dividends?'

The protrusion of railways into the west of China has suffered a temporary check from recent emphatic pronouncements of Lord Curzon. I met on the Irrawadi (October, 1900) an elderly gentleman, who claimed, or, rather, boasted, that it was he who had advised Lord Curzon to take up his present attitude towards the opening of commercial relations between India and China. His argument was that the country was unprecedentedly difficult, and the traffic would be insignificant. 'Why,' he wanted to know, 'should British credit be compromised to put money in the pockets of English speculators and company promoters?'

Encouraged to talk, he made it clear that he had never been beyond the Indian frontier; that he was neither an engineer nor a railway specialist; that he knew nothing of the country except from his reading; that his reading had not been exhaustive or even extensive; and that it had never occurred to him to take any steps to learn the views of intelligent Chinese on the subject.

To me, who have seen some of them, it is doubtful if the approaches from the Indian side offer insuperable difficulties to the advance of railways into China.* The French line viâ Lao Kai is being steadily pushed on in the face of engineering difficulties as great as those which confront the British line, and if it gets to the Yangtse first will interpose a barrier of French 'influence' between India and China.

I see no reason why China should not, in the near future, learn to exchange her products for those of her Eastern neighbours. That China and India, when China begins to feel the pulse of a new life, will derive mutual benefit from railway communication is as certain as that the sun shines, fertilizing and rejuvenating, above them both. It is even possible that twenty years hence, if British India has not been wise enough to build railways to China, China will have learned to build railways to India. The sun will not stand still in these days, even at the bidding of a Joshua.

CHAPTER XLVIII

THE DECLINE OF CHINA

Its causes—Virtues run to seed—The written language—Ancestor worship—Ignorance—Traffic in public offices—Opium—Coinage—Hair-dressing—Foot-binding—Status of women—Breeding of animals—Degenerate Buddhism—Bad roads.

THE fact that China is in a condition of decay must be obvious, not only to the traveller, but to all who

* In a paper read before the Royal Geographical Society, Nov. 23, 1903, Lieut.-Col. Manifold announced that a practicable route for a railway was surveyed in the course of his expedition.

come into diplomatic relations with her. It must be evident to the most superficial observer that the systematic isolation of the Chinese has brought about a degree of ignorance which places them at a disadvantage, and leaves them far behind in the race with other nations. It is difficult to distinguish in this case between cause and effect, the isolation resulting in ignorance and arrogance, which in their turn increase the isolation.

Many of the troubles of China result directly from actions and qualities which in themselves are meritorious. For instance, the early adoption of written characters might have been supposed to give China a leading place among enlightened nations, and she certainly did take and keep such a place for centuries. But the system of writing which she adopted was, unfortunately, not the best. With a separate character for each thing or idea, instead of a combination of characters designed to represent the sounds of speech, the written language was powerless to serve the important end of fixing and unifying the speech of the land. Hence it offered no bar to that confusion of tongues for which the old story of the tower of Babel has endeavoured to account. The ideograph has undoubtedly its conveniences, inasmuch as, no matter how widely provincial dialects may have drifted apart, the inhabitants of provinces speaking practically different languages can read from the same writing straight into their own tongue. On the other hand, a character more or less phonetic, such as is employed by nations which have risen into importance in modern times, would have tended to unification and de-provincialization.

Of the nation-building which may be brought about

by the spread of a common language and literature, European history furnishes many examples. China has, indeed, the semblance of a national literature, and persuades herself that she holds the monopoly of all literature worthy of study. In this she deceives herself grossly. She accords the highest academic distinctions to gentlemen who have learned to repeat a number of the standard works of antiquity by rote, or who have acquired a degree of proficiency in penmanship which would in other countries only lead to the modest remuneration of an engraver or signwriter.

Another virtue which has 'run to seed' with the most disastrous results is the respect due to parents. There probably never was a more harmless injunction than that given in the fifth Mosaic commandment to 'Honour thy father and thy mother,' and Jews as well as Christians have profited by it through having grasped its spirit. A similar injunction was laid on the Chinese by their early law-givers, and was most strongly insisted upon by Confucius, but has, unfortunately, been taken literally, with the result that respect for parents has degenerated into ancestor worship. The Chinaman has arrived at what he takes to be the logical conclusion that he dishonours his parents by doing anything which they did not. Hence we must not even know what was not revealed to them, and all innovation is profanity. For this reason no good Chinaman will condescend to learn anything new, and the nation sinks deeper and deeper into the mire of ignorance.

It is invariably the case that ignorance is closely allied to conceit. No one who has not been in the country can possibly realise the Chinaman's exalted opinion of himself and his contempt for the outer barbarian. Every traveller has noted the contemptuous smile on the faces of the inhabitants as he passes through villages or towns, and it requires much patience to endure some of the other forms in which this contempt is manifested. A European visitor probably does not enjoy his promenade through a crowd where every ragged coolie holds his nose as a precaution against the supposed offensive odour of the foreigner.

Chinese ignorance is equal to the feat of not recognising the existence of any language but their own. The Chinese do not say of a person speaking a foreign language, ' I do not understand him,' or ' He does not speak Chinese,' but use the significant expression, ' He cannot speak.' Chinese maps are too well known to require more than a passing reference. Their central idea is to represent the Celestial Empire as occupying all but the margin of the paper, with such few foreign countries as are known by repute to the topographer depicted as insignificant islands near the Continent of China.

Ignorance of foreign affairs is by no means confined to the lower classes. I have known officials of exalted rank, qualified for their positions by high literary degrees, who believed that all foreign nations were tributary to China. The most ludicrous versions of the Japanese war and its outcome are held as gospel truths by educated men, and equally absurd accounts of the recent war are already in circulation.

I can recall the case of a gentleman with whom I was on intimate terms, and who was on the staff of one of the Shanghai newspapers, who asked me, in confidence, if it was really true that the French (he was too polite to say the English) eat babies' eyes. I was glad of the opportunity of clearing the French of the imputation, but was conscious that I had lifted only an infinitesimally small corner of the veil of Chinese ignorance.

A fertile source of corruption is the sale of public offices. The idea prevails, and theoretically is correct, that all posts are open to successful competitors in the literary examinations, but it is a fact that lucrative offices are, in practice, conferred on the highest bidders. The official who has paid, say, 100,000 taels for his billet as Magistrate reckons that he must exact that amount, and something of a margin, from the district to which he has been appointed, and as the tenure of office is always precarious, he generally contrives to repay himself in a very few years.

It is said that, after an official has enjoyed the emoluments of office for a longer period than usual, he is invited to Pekin to give an account of his stewardship. There is no refusing the invitation, and knowing what it means, the official takes care to go provided with generous presents for those who have the bestowal of promotions or of dignities in the form of buttons or other insignia of rank.

A great deal has been said and written about the effects of opium on the Chinese. From my own observation I am inclined to think that the physical effects have been somewhat exaggerated, while the moral effects have been more or less overlooked. Habitual drunkenness, it has been observed by specialists, is apt to undermine the will-power, and to produce an absolute inability, in confirmed cases, for telling the truth. The same is true and even truer, I believe, of the besotted opium-smoker, who becomes incapable of even thinking on straight lines, and the prevalence of the habit must tend to national deterioration. Besides, the opium-smoker spends in stupor a great deal of time which might otherwise be profitably employed. The millions of acres of the best agricultural land which are gay with poppy blossoms would, no doubt, be better employed in growing rice or beans. On the other hand, my observation goes to show that the stupor produced by opium smoking is succeeded by a period of intense brain-stimulation.

The want of a standard medium of exchange, and the general debasement of the copper coinage, tend to retard commerce in a marked degree.

The popular mode of shaving the head and dressing the back hair in a queue may be thought too insignificant to mention; and yet I cannot help thinking that a frivolous custom which occupies an hour or two of a man's time every day must be an appreciable drain on the resources of the nation.

Of much greater importance is the pernicious fashion of cramping the female foot. It is a mistake to suppose that this custom is confined to the wealthy and leisured classes; on the contrary, in certain provinces which I have visited it is almost universal. Granting that the æsthetic result is all that could be desired from a Chinese point of view, I must say that I never could behold, without compassion, the poor deformed creatures tottering about for all the world like goats learning to walk on their hind legs. The suffering involved in the process has obviously a very bad effect on the general health of the victims, as the pale and waxy faces of the women testify, and it must be that, in the long-run, unhealthy mothers will produce a weak progeny. I am inclined to believe that small feet are becoming hereditary, as I had the greatest difficulty in finding ready-made boots in the city of Chengtu large enough for my own wear.

A common standard by which in modern times the civilization of a people is gauged, is the degree of respect paid to its womenkind, and, to a certain extent, the Chinese may claim to stand high when measured by this standard. From all that I have seen, a woman in China is just as safe from injury or insult as she is from flattery or compliment, or even courtesy. I suspect, however, that the feeling is rather toleration than respect, and that woman is merely regarded as a domestic animal too useful and valuable to be ill-treated. Polygamy may possibly be numbered among the causes which make for China's decay, but on that subject I have no observations to offer. Only a woman could possibly penetrate the mysteries of the Chinese household. Men may be very intimate for years without knowing anything of each other's family affairs. As for kindly inquiries about the health of a neighbour's wife—'Oh no, we never mention her; her name is never heard!' I am inclined, however, to believe that polygamy is less seriously prevalent in China than in many other countries, as every man, no matter how poor, must have at least one wife, otherwise he would have no descendants to honour his bones, and superfluous women cannot therefore be very numerous. In European and other countries it is gradually becoming more and more the case that only successful men can afford to marry; but in China, with its dead-level of poverty, a wife costs little, and is often self-supporting. In Yünnan I was the guest of the headman of a village, who, as I incidentally learned, had five wives; but he was unusually well-to-do, and was, moreover, of Sifan rather than of Chinese blood, and I believe such instances are rare.

The precept that no animal must be allowed to die without having had the opportunity of reproducing its species is based on religious convictions; but it works out, notably among horses, in a very unpleasant manner. The intelligent breeder knows that a race of 'weeds' will be created by permitting every horse to become a sire. The fact that all Chinese riding-ponies are stallions makes it imperative that the rider should always be attended by a groom to manage, if not to lead, the animal. The deterioration of the race of riders follows as a matter of course, and the grooms are diverted from more useful employment to the service of luxury.

That Christianity is a higher form of religion than Buddhism, I believe, and the proposition will be readily admitted by Christians. At the same time, the conceptions and precepts of Buddhism are lofty, and well calculated to elevate the condition of an Eastern people. Had China adhered to the true Buddhist faith there is little doubt that she would have attained a much higher position than she holds at present. But the Chinese have interpreted their Buddhism, as they have most other things, by the letter while ignoring the spirit. A rank growth of formalities and superstitions has almost choked the life out of their religion, which is now merely a system of cast-iron observances and expedients to propitiate the gods, who, by the way, have mostly degenerated into malignant demons. This state of things has, naturally, brought about a desire to propitiate the gods at the lowest possible cost. Under the pretence that the gods are content with the spirits of things, sacrifices of no value are offered to them, such as a smear of blood, a tuft of feathers, or a lick of opium, while the substance goes to the crafty priests, and the Chinaman only too readily falls into the spirit of the fun when he finds that the gods can be tricked by the use of sacrifices in effigy or the burning of paper-money. It is not good for any nation to despise its gods. It would be well if those esoteric Buddhists who try to convert Christians would preach pure Buddhism to the Chinese Buddhists. I fully appreciate the devotion and self-sacrifice of the Christian missionaries, who carry on their work in China amid surroundings which must be distasteful in the extreme, but my impression is that many centuries must elapse before Christianity makes the slightest impression on China. In the meantime, the Chinese might, perhaps, be brought back to a purer form of Buddhism and the other 'isms' which they cultivate. It is possible to conceive that even Christianity might become a nuisance and a grave public danger should it ever degenerate into mere ritual and superstitious reverence for the letter of the law.

The roadways of China are paved with the best of good intentions. In China the construction of a road, a bridge, or other useful public work, is a common method of 'accumulating merit,' as the Chinese say, or 'laying up for one's self treasures in heaven,' as the Christians phrase it; but, judging by results, there is no merit to be acquired by keeping anything in repair. The material pavement of a road, consisting of solid flagstones, must in many instances have been laid down centuries ago. The flagged roads are not graded, and ascents are always negotiated by flights of steps. The zigzag ascent is in use, but the idea of a long zigzag, forming an easy grade, has not met with favour. The wear of shod hoofs, continued for generations, has rounded the flagstones into smooth boulders and widened the joints between them, until it becomes a mere chance whether one steps on a boulder or in the mud; or, where it happens that the centre of a flagstone offers the only foothold, the successive impact of hoofs in the same spot has drilled a hole right through the stone into the mud beneath. Men and animals stagger, slide, and flounder over these incredibly bad roads, which are frequently left, or partially left, by the progress of denudation, standing on ridges.

Again, the worst available position is invariably assigned to the public road wherever the land is of any value for agriculture, and a road is never regarded as a means of communication between two given localities, but is only a grudging concession made by the farmer to the public convenience. The farmer does not scruple to acquire soil for his fields by paring away or even undermining the roads, and converts them, when he pleases, into reservoirs for the irrigation of his rice-fields. The road must, perforce, be carried between the boundaries of rice-fields, often going round three sides of a square. The intolerable condition of the roads, of course, adds to the cost of carriage, and, consequently, to the expense of living, and erects a formidable barrier in the way of intercourse with the outside world—if, indeed, the Chinese desired such intercourse.

I was amused to read lately that the flight of the

Empress-Regent from Pekin had been delayed for some time owing to the condition of the roads, which had not been repaired since 1780—a modern instance of being hoist with one's own petard. Whoever undertakes the rejuvenation of China must commence with a radical improvement of the means of communication.

Much has been said lately of the Indianizing or Egyptianizing of China, and I for one believe that it would be the best thing that could happen. I doubt, however, whether the resources of any European, Japanese, or American Power are equal to the task. Russia, indeed, may be willing to take the burden—in a general way she seems inclined to take anything she can get—but it would beggar her and paralyze even her magnificent organization.

One result of the late war is pretty sure to be the snipping off of corners of China for foreign settlements, sooner or later. Such settlements, it may be contended, will provide the Chinese with object-lessons in the art of good government. Judging from past experiences, they will do nothing of the sort. The Chinaman near at hand comes to reside and trade in the foreign settlements, and enjoys his share of the resulting prosperity and security; but the Chinaman of the interior knows nothing of the lesson, and would not learn it even if he did. The conclusion I have arrived at is that the rejuvenation of China must be left to reformers of Chinese birth, who have seen the world and profited by their travels.

CHAPTER XLIX

A REJUVENATED CHINA

Speculations on the future of the Empire.

THE right to exist may be conceded to China without hesitation and without reserve. The manner of her existence is a question which, in the near future, will concern all the kingdoms of the earth.

Some will say, without thought: 'Let China live on as she lives now, and as she wishes to live. She asks nothing better than to be let alone. Let her alone!'

Such a solution is only the visionary Utopia of the indolent. In reality the imaginary Utopia, if it were ever realized, would prove a smouldering Inferno.

The time is at hand when civilization can no longer look with indifference on the spectacle of the fourth part of the population of the globe sunk in ignorance and selfishness, and of no use to the other three-fourths. It is the part of civilization to help the submerged fourth, and this part must be played whether the civilized nations will or not. Since it has to be done, it may as well be done with a good grace.

No one who has mixed with the Eastern races can doubt that the Chinese individual is, mentally and physically, at least the equal of the Japanese. Whatever the Japanese have achieved in the last quarter of a century, the Chinese are capable of achieving.

In presence of a future China, which shall have discarded the pernicious doctrine that it is impious for any man to know more than his father did, and which shall have assimilated the latest teachings of Western science, what will be the attitude of the nations?

After all, the elevation of Japan only adds one more to the Powers of the first rank, and has not seriously disturbed the balance. Many, indeed, are of opinion that, as regards the Far East, the balance has only been adjusted as by the interposition of a Providence.

But when it is not a Japan with her 40,000,000, but a China with her 300,000,000, which emerges from the darkness sane and fully equipped? She will contest the markets of the world; she may even possess herself of a great part of its soil. Assuming that China were not only rejuvenated, but also united and animated by a lust of conquest, many other nations would have to assert, under deadly disadvantages, *their* right to continue to exist. The expression 'the balance of power' would acquire a meaning infinitely more pregnant than its formulators of the nineteenth century ever dreamed of attaching to it. Not Europe or Asia, but the whole world, would be involved in a struggle to the death before the question could be settled, even temporarily.

The advance of a united China in an aggressive mood would constitute a menace to the peace of the world which no enlightened nation can foresee without deep anxiety. Such a China would outweigh almost any conceivable alliance designed to oppose her ambition.

At the present day there is, happily, no such thing as a united China. The life of China is essentially provincial. A Cantonese in Shantung is almost as much a foreigner as a Frenchman. The man from Shansi has a dog's life in a city of Yünnan until he associates himself, for his own protection, with the local guild of his exiled compatriots. Need there ever be a united China? China does not—at least, for the present—call for Chinese Unity: the rest of the world has no need for it.

The various provinces are, in population, extent, and resources, fairly comparable to European States of the first and second importance. Are they not, in all conscience, large enough for admission to the family of nations? Would they not, if reformed and united, be overpowerful for the world's peace?

To 'divide and command' is a political method which has been practised for many centuries. In the present case there is no question of 'command,' but simply one of 'live and let live.' A united China cannot be created except by the aid of the civilized world. The lifting of a hand to assist in its creation would be suicidal.

There is no cohesion in the Chinese Empire. The Empire itself is little more than a name. It is only held together by the feeble strength of use and wont and the ancestral indolence of the East. To these may be added the ideographic written character, which is the only thing common to districts differing in dialect, and even in language. The ideograph itself must vanish (as it is vanishing in Japan) as soon as the Chinese have the opportunity of comparing it with more modern orthography. The province is the only real unit of national life, and the provinces will find that, whenever they will, they can be just as independent as they choose to proclaim themselves of the Central Government, which they do not know, and therefore cannot love.

A REJUVENATED CHINA

It may be objected that the provincial officials pay tribute to Pekin, and derive their dignities from the Imperial centre. This is certainly the case at present, but this condition of things will cease at a moment's notice, whenever the provincial democracy takes the trouble to abolish it.

If ever the provinces of China should assert the independence which they have practically achieved without knowing it, every nation which has an interest in progress, commerce, civilization, and peace, will do well to recognise them. Enlightened and independent, these provinces would be good neighbours for the rest of the world, for whom they would perform services and with whom they would exchange products, and the world would, in its turn, be compelled to respect their right to continue to exist.

The latter-day condition of China is one which periodically calls for armed intervention. It is as if a householder in a crowded city from time to time went mad and set his house afire. Neighbours will and must step in to extinguish the conflagration, and to punish the man who fondly imagines that he may do what he likes with his own.

In the event of the independence of the Chinese provinces being brought about by the process of evolution, it may be asked whether the existing dynasty has no right to be respected.

The present dynasty has hardly existed long enough to acquire vested rights. It was founded only two and a half centuries ago by a foreign (Manchu) chieftain who was a leader of men. His successors and their friends have not followed in his steps, but have learned to surround themselves with luxury and to live on exaction. With the possible exception of the present Emperor, who is understood to have been at one time favourable to reform, but who is now a prisoner in the hands of the Reaction, and physically weak, the dynasty is not worth considering for a moment in comparison with the well-being of the people. While we may be ever so sorry for the Emperor, the idea of forcing him to reform and unite the Empire may as well be abandoned. Personally, from all that is known of him, it may be surmised that he would be happy if he were only freed from the malign influences which surround him, and if the tributes of the emancipated provinces were commuted for a generous pension. The life interests of a number of officials who depend on the present state of things might also be considered. There is no room for doubt that the provinces themselves would be better off if left to work out their own salvation independent of Pekin.

INDEX

A-Li Tse, 209
Ah-Lung, 192
Ah Mow, 3
Ah Kow, 4
Aloes, 223
Amundsen, E., 127, 146, 180
Ancestor-worship, 247
An Hsien, 74
An-Ning River, 98
Appian Way, 73
Architecture, 149, 214, 122
Arms, 61, 90, 122, 128, 130, 150, 165, 194, 226
Arrows, poisoned, 175
Arsenal, 61, 65
Art, 94, 149, 159, 166, 230
Atuntze, 149, 168, 174

Bamboo bridges, 76, 77
Bananas, 221
Banking, 45, 104
Barley, 120
Batang, 174
Beach, Mr., 75
Bears, 112, 123
Beef, 194
Bei-to Pu, 196
Belgian engineers, murder of, 89
Bellows Gorge, 20
Bells, 69, 94
Betel-chewing, 229
Bhamo (Burma), viii, 175, 184, 202, 230, 236, 237, 239
Bianconi's map of China, 180
Bigham, Captain, 43
Birch, J. G., 43, 65, 84
Bishop, Mrs., 10, 31, 33, 75
Blast-furnaces, 72
Bonin, M., 111
Bonsdanty, Consul, 43
Book, Tibetan, 131
Boring (salt wells), 52
Boxers, vii, 42, 87, 103, 172, 242
Boycott threatened, 204, 224

Boys, 4, 105
Breeding of animals, 252
Bretschneider, 226, 140
Bridges, 31, 35, 36, 47, 51, 56, 60, 69, 76-78, 80, 87, 91, 93, 117, 132, 136, 137, 148, 151, 152, 163, 171, 180, 183, 186, 187, 195, 199-201, 210, 212, 215, 220, 222
Brine wells, 48, 51, 134, 138, 189
Brooks, Miss, 65
Buckwheat, 120
Buddhism, degenerate, 252
Buffaloes, 49, 51, 73, 159, 229
Bullocks, pack, 46, 199
Burma, 209, 235
Burniston, Dr., 34, 43
Bush, J. Holton, 40, 43, 89

Cactus, 221
Cady, H., 65
Cain-du, 99
Cantonese Club, 74
Capons, 119
Carriers' Union, 204
Cartridges, 191
Cave-dwellings, 48, 116
Ceremonial, 2, 7, 8, 21, 24, 59, 62, 85, 241
Cha-Ergh-N'gai, 86
Chamutong, 169
Chang-Chow Hsien, 40
Chang-Lou Kio, 13
Chang Sung Ling (Chun-tai), 217
Chang Ye, 40
Cha Ning, 87
Chao-Ting Shan, 55
Charcoal-burning, 127
Cha-Tien Dza, 53
Chen Chuen Ta, 10
Chengtu City and Plain, 53, 54, 60, 73, 89, 94, 100, 104
Chevalier, 10, 12, 27, 29
Chian Kiang, 69
Chi Chow, 49

261

262 THE BACK BLOCKS OF CHINA

Chi-Chuen, 76
China Inland Mission map, 126, 140, 146, 160
Chin-Chai Pu, 215
Ching-Chai Hsien, 94
Ching-Kow Chow, 93
Ching Kwan, 151
Chin Kiang, 2
Chin Shan, 171
Chi-Tai Kai, 222
Chi-T'ien, 163
Chiu Chow, 78
Chiung, 169
Chiung Chow, 58, 60
Chi-Yang Hsien, 50
Choh, Tartar General, 65, 66
Chow Ho, 187, 188
Chow-Tang, 163
Chow Yen Tsi, 21
Christians, 199
Chü, General, 65, 196
Chü Hung Chi (Wai-Yuan), 90, 156
Chun Kwan Pit, 64
Chu-Kwo Lia, 163
Chu Ling Kwan, 64
Chun-Chan Shan, 70
Chung-Chow, 35
Chung Chui Lin (interpreter), 2, 35, 63, 105
Chung Kiang, 55, 73
Chung-King, 41, 43, 45, 89, 96, 100, 103
Chung T'ien, 127, 150, 155, 174, 178
Chun-tai at Teng-Yueh, 217, 224, 231
Chu Shan, 76, 77
Chü Tang, 197
Chu Yuen Hse, 21
Club-houses, 61, 74
Coal, 17, 36, 40, 41, 44, 46, 48, 50, 51, 59, 77, 88, 98, 138, 139, 148, 209
Coffins, 18, 162
Coldré, Father, 52
Colquhoun, A. R., 150, 193, 200, 202, 212, 223, 224, 230
Conceit, 247
Consecration, a llama, 166
Consuls, British, viii, 43, 44, 96, 104, 240
Consul, French, 43, 172
Consul, U.S.A., 43
Cook, 3, 47
Corliss, Dr., 92
Cormorants, fishing with, 75

Court, a Lolo (Kwapit), 124
Court, a Sifan, 143
Court, a wayside, 91
Cooper, T. T., 145, 170, 175, 189
Copper, 20, 23, 69, 71, 152, 167, 168, 182, 183
Cotton, 50, 51, 195, 198, 199, 201, 210
Crier, 203
Crossbows, 165, 167
Cultivation, 57, 87, 120, 146, 181, 192, 211, 228

Dancing, Sifan, 144
David, Abbé, 78
Davidson, J., ix, 38, 43
Davies, Major H. R., 127, 173
Deaths in the party, 82, 213
Decline of China, 245
Deer, 184
Depopulation, 190, 219
Desertion threatened, 205
Dogs, 142
Domato, Mr., 65
Downs, 129, 132
'Dragon festival,' 89
Drill, 176
Dry valleys, 53, 116, 181
Duclos, Paul, 43, 47
Dwen Ying Shang, 108
Dyeing, 58, 201
Dysentery, 47
Dzo Hai Ching, 183

Eastern Pioneer Company, viii
Edelweiss, 142
Egrets, 151, 182, 201
Elephants, 207, 225, 227, 228
Er-Lang Kwan, 46
Escorts, 59, 65, 76, 90, 128, 156, 167, 176, 191, 226, 241
Esk, H.M.S., 10
Evans, A. M. A., 240
Ewen, Dr., 65
Examination halls, 47, 59, 61
Extermination of foreigners ordered, 242

Faith cure, 211
Family names, 3
Famine at Yueh Sui, 96
Fang-Ma Chang, 210
Fan-Sui Ki, 39
Female carriers, 87, 98, 135, 151, 185
Ferguson, Mr., 65

INDEX

Fever Valley, 205, 210
Finger-nails, 23
Fire on house-boat, 30
Fire-setting (mining), 81
Flint and steel, 170
Flogging, 125, 204
Foot-binding, 151, 203, 250
Foreign Office, British, 108
Foreign trade, 41, 43, 61, 160, 163, 170, 190, 202, 210
Fortifications, 40, 44, 49, 80, 81, 83, 86, 131, 134, 139, 177, 210, 227, 233, 234
Fossils, 20, 25, 78
Fraser, Consul, 43, 96, 104
French, the, at Tali Fu, 189, 217
Fu Chow, 36
Fu Kiang, 75, 77, 80
Fu-Lin, 95
Fu-Li Tsi, 18
Fung-Hoang Tse, 35
Fung Shui, 18, 51, 67
Fung-Sui Ling, 214
Fung-Tu Hsien, 34, 35
Fu Ting Shing, Admiral, 6

Gallay, Père, 95
Game, 113, 182
Geese, 197
German Minister murdered, 100
German steamer *Sui Hsiang*, 42
Gill, Captain W., 33, 49, 55, 78, 86, 157, 160, 162, 180, 184, 197, 205, 211
Goitre, 87, 113, 118, 165
Gold, 6, 30, 35, 37, 39, 40, 50, 69, 74, 78, 81, 87, 102, 121, 134, 163, 171, 175, 179, 231
Golden Sand River (Yangtse), 162
Gordon, General, 65
Gorges of the Yangtse, 9, 41
Gourkas, 217
Grant, Mr., 43
Graphic, ix
'Great Gold and Silver Road,' 194
Guides, 108, 141, 191, 233
Gunboat (Chinese), 23

Hair-dressing, 250
Hamilton, Mr., 75
Hancock, Mr., 43
Han Kow, 6
Han Shing, 64
Hao-Kan, 25
Hartwell, Miss, 65
Ha-Tsu Pu, 209

Hawking, 76
Hay Lü Tzu, 126
He-Ien Tse, 14
Henri, Prince, d'Orléans, 140, 172
Hero, a Chinese, 237
Hia-Ma, 20
Hillman, Captain, 23, 34, 43
Hislop, Mr., 43
Hoang-Ki Sha, 47
Hoang-Lien Pu, 195
Hoang Ling, 13
Hoang N'gai Kwan, 82
Hoang-Pei-Ki Chang, 30
Hoang Shaa Ba, 137
Hoang-Tsao Hia, 40
Hobson, H. M., 13, 217, 237
Ho Chiu Shun, Admiral, 10
Hong Kong, 243
Hoong Sui Ho, 98
Ho-Show Pu, 135
Hoo Tung Sung, 4
Hosie, A., 53, 60, 126, 134
Hospitals, 40
Ho-Ti, 220
House-boats, 1, 9
How Chang, 185
Hsia-Kwan Tse, 81
Hsiang-N'gai Pa, 78
Hsiao-Ho Ying, 81
Hsiao-K'ong Ling, 14
Hsiao-Pa Chow, 17
Hsiao Shao Ling, 98
Hsiao Sin-Kai, 228
Hsiao Wei-Si, 172, 175
Hsiao-Yui Toong, 72
Hsin-Chin Hsien, 55
Hso-Pa Kwan, 81
Hsueh Shan, 82
Hui-Li Chow, 174
Hung-Ma Ho, 234
Hung-Mu Shu, 213, 214
Huntingdon Mill, 102
Hupeh, 18
Hwa Chai, 198
Hwa Hwa, 4

I-Chang, 12, 42
Ideographic writing, 246, 258
Ignorance, 247
Inns, 49, 58, 60, 79, 87, 110, 133, 157, 162, 169, 183, 185, 187, 197
Interpreters, 2, 105, 106, 198, 242
Iron mines and works, 36, 41, 69, 93, 99, 138
Irrawadi River, 214, 234, 243
Irrigation, 50, 54, 69, 151, 216

Isolation, 245
I-Tan Rapid, 17

Jack, R. Lockhart, ix, 2, 30, 38, 70, 95, 236
Jade, 87, 155, 216
Jang-Ki Kow, 21
Jansen, Mr., 194
Ju-Ch'enn, 224

Kachins, 222, 227, 229-231, 234, 237
Ka-Ga, 168, 170, 175
Kai-Ja Pu-dza, 120
Kai Tsa, 162
Ka-La Ba, 129
Kampti (Burma), 140, 172
Kau-N'gi, 223
Kerr, Mr., 65
Khan-Oo Tsu, 215
Kia-Ling River, 41
Kiang-Yu Hsien, 77
Kien-Chang Valley, 99
Kien Chow, 50
Kien-Ch'uan, 183, 184, 193
Kien Kiang, 36
Kilham, Dr., 65
Kin-Ing Ho, 20
King, 237
Kin Sha River (Yangtse), 162
Kiu Kiang, 5
Kiu-Tui Tse, 30
Knight, Miss, 76
Knipe, Mr. and Mrs., 75
Ko-Lo Lo, 101, 102
K'ong Ling Chow, 14
Ko-Ta Pa, 80
Kreitner, Lieutenant, 91
Ku-Ah Tse, 191
Ku-Ah Tsin, 191
Kung-Ling Island, 14
Ku-Tu Wah, 163, 179
Kwa-Chow, 191
Kwang-Ni Pu, 93
Kwan Hsien, 54, 56
Kwan-Ki Chang, 35
Kwan Kow, 69
Kwan Pu, 201
Kwan Shan, 182
Kwan-Tao Hia, 25
Kwan Ti, 74
Kwa Pit, 114, 120, 122
Kwei-Chow, 17, 21
Kwei Chun, Viceroy of Szechuan, 61, 65, 66, 242
Kwo-Feng Yeh, 81

Kwo-Tu, 162, 179
Kwo-Tung, 182

La-Che Chu, 142
Lai-Feng Yi, 46
Lakes, 121, 159, 181, 184, 185
Lan-Chow, 168, 190
Lan-Chu Island, 35
Landslips, 27, 110, 223
Lang-Sung Kwan, 220
Lang-T'iung, 190
Lan T'Sang, 200
Lan-Tzu Ko, 139
Lao-Kwan Tsi, 32
Lao-Shu Chu, 18
Lapidaries, 88, 216
La-P'si Ku, 164
La Soh Toong, 137
La-Sü Ba Llamaserai, 159
La-Tzu Yi, 190
Lead, 209
Lei Su tribe, 170
Leopards, 97, 123
Leprosy, 93
Li Cheng Yung (Commissioner for Mines), 23, 64-66, 100
Li-Chi Yuen, 36
Li-Chow, 105, 108
Li-Chu River, 146
Lien-Ti, 190
Lifeboat service, 6, 16, 19, 26
Lignite, 135, 228
Li Kiang, 155, 167
'Likin,' 209, 210
Li Liang Yen, 217
Ling-Chang Shih, 50
Lion-in-the-Path, 206, 221, 233
Li Ping, 56
Li Show Tin, 62-64
Li Shi Cheng, 36
Li Sieh's insurrection, 124
Li Tae Shing, 108
Li Tang, 174
Literature, 247
Little, Archibald, 6, 10, 41-33, 53, 65
Litton, Consul, 78
Li-Tu Cheng, 36
Liu Chuan Liu (ex - Viceroy of Szechuan), 92
Liu Chung Yu, 63, 65
Llamas, 83, 86, 132, 165, 231
Llamaserais, 159, 164, 165, 178, 179
Lo-Chi Pu, 171
Lo-Kiang Hsien, 74
Lo-Ko Ti, 110, 111

INDEX 265

Lolos, 44, 61, 97, 100, 101, 110, 116, 118, 128, 129, 142
Long Shan, 2
Loong Kiang, 214, 231
Loong Kiang Chow, 214
Loong-Sui Ching, 209
Loong-Sui Valley, 181
Loong-Yu Tsun, 182
Lotus, 201, 216
Low Luan, 207
Lu-Kiang Ba (Salwen Valley), 102, 108
Lu-Ku, 98
Lung-An, 78
Lung-Chang Hsien, 46, 47, 183
Lung-Chang Kai, 228
Lung-Chuen Yih, 53
Lung Si Tang, 206
Lu-T'ien Llamaserai, 164, 178
Lu-Tzu Chiang, 175
Lyons Mission, 43, 181

Machinery, transport of, 102
Ma-Feng Chiao, 47
Mafus, 153, 205, 236
Maha, viii, 101
Mai-Tsa, 162
Mai-Tzu Ping, 118, 120
Maize, 120
Ma-Jong Tzu gold-mine, 121
Ma-Ma Chih, 213
Ma-Mo Ho, 236
Man-Chang Kai, 226
Mandalay, 243
Manifold, Colonel, 174
Man Pu, 223
Mantzü, 44, 48, 61, 82, 83
Manwyn, 229
Mao Chow, 87
Ma-Pi Ku, 13
Marble mountains, 115, 118, 121
Margary's monument, 232
Mathieson, Mr., 43
Ma-Ti, 182
May-Hwa Pu, 196
May-To, 192
May-Tsu Show, 183
May-Tze Sha, 182
Medicine, 72, 213
Mekong River, 171, 200
Mengtze, 99
Merit, accumulation of, 253
Miao-Ho, 14
Miao-Ki Tse, 25
Mien-Chu Hsien, 55, 58, 59, 73
Mien Ning, 127

Mili, 127, 174
Mining Bureau, Szechuan, 64, 99, 100
Min River, 54, 55, 86
Missions and missionaries, 2, 5, 18, 43, 65, 75, 76, 79, 92, 95, 99, 103, 104, 155, 169, 173, 183, 193, 227, 237
Mitchell, Miss, 75
Mi-T'sang Gorge, 15, 17
Mahommedan rebellion, 164, 167, 190, 193, 197, 207
Monasteries, 5, 33, 69, 117
Money, 105, 250
Monkeys, 214
Monuments, 73, 232
Moon's birthday, 163
Mo-Pan Tan, 39
Moo-Chi Ti, 161
Moo-Li Chang, 109
Mooquooi tribe, 175
Morehead, Mr., 43
Morgan, W. Pritchard, viii
Morris, J. F., 3, 35, 70, 82, 236
Moso tribe, 124
Mountain sickness, 82, 94
Muang-la, 223, 224
Mules and muleteers, 108, 109, 169, 176, 183, 204, 218
Murray, Mr., 42
Mu-Tung Tse, 40
Music, Sifan, 144
Myitkyina (Burma), 173
Myothet (Burma), 236

Nampoung (Burma), 235
Nan-Ching Yi, 50
Nan King, 5
Nan Mien K'eng, 12
Nan T'ien, 221
Navigation of rivers, 6, 42, 49, 78, 164, 227, 236
Nay-Sui Ching, 209
Nee Sui Ching (interpreter), 106, 187, 233, 242
Nei-Kiang Hsien, 48
New Year (Chinese), 19, 23
N'gan Kai, 5
N'gan Pin, 25
Nicholson, Mr., 43
Ning-Yuan Fu, 103
Niu-Kow-Ma Fei, 14
Niu-Kow Tan, 17
Nui-Shih Tse, 36
Nuns, 159

Oats, 120, 152
Officials, Chinese, good faith of, 240
Officials, Chinese, power of, 242
Oil, 39
Om Mani Pami Hum, 166
Opium, 36, 41, 50, 82, 249
Orphan Rock, 5
Ottewell, Mr., 65

Pack-saddles, 109
Pagodas, 5, 33, 48, 79, 163, 165, 182, 190, 216, 243
Pah-Yi Tang, 224
Pai Fungs, 51
Palmistry, 203
Pa-Mu Tse, 25
Pan Chiao, 201
Paper, 59
Parker, J. H., 37, 47
Pa-Tong Hsien, 18
Pay-Chi Sui, 171
Pay-Chow Hy, 78
Pay-Fin Chang, 163
Pay-Han Chang, 182
Pears, 143
Peat, J. F., 65
Pediculi, 176
Peepul-trees, 228
Peh-Yang Tsun, 142
Pei-Chung Cheng, 91
Pei-Ma Tsin, 48
Pei Shih, 18
Pei-Shung Shi, 19
Pei Sui Ho, 132, 137
Pekin, 93, 103
Pen Hsien, 58, 69
Phlegræan Field, 220
Photographs, ix
Pidgin English, 106
Pien-Nao, 13
Pien Ta San, 152
Pigs, 134, 225
Pi Hsien, 58
Ping-i Pu, 78
Ping K'io Ki, 13
Ping-Yi Pu, 96, 104
Pioneer (Yangtse River steamer), 42, 96
Plague, 211
Ploughing, 73, 159
Poi Yang Lake, 5
Po-Lo, 143, 146
Polo, Sér Marco, 55, 99, 145, 205, 207, 211
Po-Lo Ti, 201
Polyandry, 171

Polygamy, 111, 251
Pongsi, 233
Pong-Sha Tsi, 30
Pontoon-bridge, 78
Poo Ta, 123
Po-Paio, 209
Poppy cultivation, 50, 56
Potanin, 111
Potatoes, 87, 95, 97, 149
Prayer-mill, 79
Prayer-poles, 83, 86, 165, 231
Presents, 24
Prisoners, 73, 120
Proclamations, 66, 156, 183, 203
Pu-Ah, 170
Pu-Tai Kow, 18
P'yin Pu, 200
Pyrites carvings, 7

Quicksilver, 65, 178

Rafts, 78, 88, 179
Railways and surveys, 6, 53, 89, 186, 190, 195, 244
Rangoon, 173, 243
Rapids, 9, 25, 28, 35, 39, 76
'Red Basin,' 45, 52
Red Rivers, 98, 197
Reduction (Gold) Works, Chinese, 101
Rejuvenated China, 256
Rice, 5, 41, 97, 182, 185, 192, 211, 215, 228
Rice-mills, 223
Richthofen, Baron, 60, 98
Roads, 20, 53, 69, 77, 88, 109, 111, 133, 147, 193, 200, 201, 253
Robbers, 50, 75, 119, 167, 175
Roberts, Rev. W. H., 237
Roe, Mr., 43
Rope bridges, 77, 80, 87, 171, 179
Royal Geographical Society, ix
Rupees, 143, 221
Ryder, Captain, 92, 141, 174

Sa-Chi, 185
Saigon, 243
Sale of offices, 249
Salt, 21, 36, 41, 51, 53, 61, 97, 134, 138, 187, 190
Salt-smuggling, 173
Salwen River, 205, 211
San-Cha Tung, 190, 193
Sang Shan, 46
San-Pa Ki, 26

INDEX 267

San-Pei Tu, 40
San-Shien Ku, 162, 179
Santa, 223
Sa-Sung Sae, 196
Schools, 192, 228, 229
Seals, 3
Seaward, Mr., 75
Seh-Da Kwan, 87
Shaa Ba, 99, 100, 132
Shaa Ba Shan, 108, 113, 141, 149, 158
Sha-Ma Ho, 199
Shanghai, 1, 243
Shang-Po Tsu, 214
Shan tribes, 222, 223, 226, 229
Shantung troubles, 89
Sha-Yang, 199
Sheep, 83
Shih-Foong Hsien, 58, 59
Shih Chiao, 50, 51
Shih-Chuen, 75
Shih-Why Chi, 32
Shi-Ku, 160, 179, 180
Shi-Pao Shih, 33
Shoh-Sui Ho, 73
Show Ping, 146
Shuang-Liu Hsien, 58, 60
Shu-Pa Pu-dza, 113, 117
Shu Ye, 146
Shwan-Pi Chow, 195
Shwang-Nang Pu-dza, 118
Shway Dagohn Pagoda, 243
Si-An Ji, 48, 52
Sifans, 83, 110, 113, 126, 143, 155, 165, 167
Signatures, 2, 45
Silk, 61
Silver-mines, 110, 114, 150
Silver work, 50, 61, 87, 100, 105, 110, 200, 227, 230
Sin-Chin Hsien, 58
Sin Fan, 58
Singapore, 243
Sin Kai (Bhamo), 149, 155, 196, 202, 230, 237
'Sinks,' 121, 142, 160, 182
Sin Tan, 15, 26
Sin-Tu Hsien, 58, 59
Small-pox, 95
Smith, Dr., 65
Smithers, Consul, 43
Snowy Mountains, 70, 74, 81, 82, 160, 173, 174, 177, 182, 184
Song Chao Yuen, 73
Song-Si Pu, 49
Spelling, x

Springs, 154
Squeezes, 4
Stallions, 129
Standard Oil Company, 43
Stoned, 25, 38, 136
Suction-pumps, 138
Sugar, 50
Sui Chai, 200
Sui Chang, 89
Sui-Chin Kwan, 81
Sui-Fan Hsien, 58
Sui-Li, 233
Sui-Wen Ping, 88
Sung Chi Fung, 44
Sung Pan, 83
Sycee, 105, 221
Széchenyi, Count, viii, 74, 91, 127, 141, 157, 162, 181, 197
Szechuan, province of, 18, 139
Sze-Tang Tse, 132
Sze-Te Chow, 73

Ta-Ban Tsu, 210
Ta-Chien Lu, 92, 172, 174
Taels, 105
Ta Er Doh, 108, 110, 141, 158
Ta-Fu Tse, 41
Ta Hong Ki, 13
Ta Hsien, 55
Tai Ping Canal, 6
Tai Ping Pu, 183, 195, 214
Tai Ping River, 226, 228, 234, 236
Tai-Ye Fang, 139
Taku Forts, 93
Ta Kwan, 88
Ta-Liang Shan, 98
Ta-Li Chow, 201
Tali Fu, 99, 141, 184, 189, 194, 196, 217
Ta Mo, 41
Ta-Niu P'ien, 195
Tang Fang, 223, 232
Tang-Tung Island, 35
Ta-Pa Chow, 17
Ta-P'ien Ta, 164, 178
Ta Pu-Dza, 117
Tartar General, 64–66
Ta-Shu O, 209
Ta-Tang, 162, 179
Ta-Tong Tan, 13
Tang-Tung, 35
Ta-Tu River, 95
Ta-Whan, 152
Tea-houses, 94, 133, 195, 196, 199, 201
Tea trade, 95

Telegraph-lines and communication, 31, 49, 63, 65, 89, 92, 95, 96, 100, 103, 108, 183, 184, 194-196, 202, 230, 235
Temples, 13, 18, 19, 49, 61, 74, 76, 79, 84, 94, 123, 131, 132, 154, 185, 187, 190, 191, 195, 214, 215, 228, 231
Teng-Yueh, 194, 196, 215, 231
Theatres, 77, 151
Thompson, Miss, 76
Tibetan book, 131
Tibetans, 61, 73, 84, 155, 164, 169, 173, 174
Tien-Ching Pu, 196, 199
Tientsin, 86, 89, 104
Tigers, 131, 173
Tintet, Abbé, 172
Toa Wha Lan (Toussa), 222
Tobacco, 59
Tombs, 68, 95, 190, 201, 219
Tong Sing Kow, 63, 64, 102, 108
Toong-Choo Kaija, 151
Toong-Show Ah, 171
Torrance, Mr., 65
Toussa of Ju-Ch'enn, 225, 228, 231
Toussa of Kau-N'Gi, 223, 224
Toussa of Kwa Pit, 114, 120, 122, 132
Toussa of Toong-Su, 136, 137, 139
Toussa Toa Wha Lan, 222
Tower, natural, 117
Tracking, 9, 12, 14, 19, 28, 29
Transport companies, 45
Treasurer, Provincial, 64, 65
Tribal dwellings, 129, 234
Tsi-Cha Pu, 216
Tsu-Kwo Tang, 162
Tsü-Li Chang, 52, 152
Tsü-Liu Ching, 52
Tsung Ho Chung, 118
Tu Ho, 182
Tui-Na Ko, 154
Tung Kow, 77
Tung Ling Tse, 68
Tung-Yang Rapid, 26
Turbines, 55, 71, 72

Upcraft, Mrs., 92
Upper Yangtse Syndicate, viii, 65, 90

Valleys without outlet, 53, 128
Viceroy of Szechuan, 61, 65, 66, 90, 156, 242

Viceroy of Yünnan, 183, 237
Village war, 119

Wai-Yuan, 65, 67, 70, 90, 103, 156, 203
Walnuts, 149
Wan Hsien, 31
Water-wheels, 50, 55, 74, 78, 186
Watson, Captain, 23, 34, 43
Watts-Jones, Captain, 43, 65, 84
Wax, white, 61
Way, H. W. L., 65, 90, 106, 157, 175, 176, 243
Wei-Si, 157, 167, 168, 175
Wheel traffic, 50, 128, 132
Whistling a crime, 131
Wilson, Mr., 43
Win-Tsen Lu, 82
Wolfendale, Dr., 43
Woman, status of, 251
Wong Lien Sing, 38
Wong Su, 23
Woodcock, H.M.S., 10, 23, 42
Woodlark, H.M.S., 10, 23, 42
Wool, 77, 84
Wrecks, 14, 15, 25, 29, 33, 42
Wrench, Mr., 7, 9
Wu Hu, 5
Wu-Liang River, 127, 146
Wu-Lu Pu, 163, 179
Wu-Lu T'ien, 163
Wu-Shan Hsien, 18
Wu Si Tang (Corporal), 213
Wu Sung, 1

Ya-Chow, 92, 103
Yaks, 83, 112
Ya-Lung River, 109, 127
Yang-Pi, 193
Yangtse River, 1-42, 152, 160, 180
Yan-Tan Chai, 215
Ya-Show Ping, 142
Yeh-Peh, 215
Yeh Tan (rapid), 25
Yeh Tang, 81
Ye-Luo Tse, 40
Yen-Ching, 133
Yen-Hung Ping, 88
Yen-Tang, 138
Yen Yuan, 120, 134
Yerkolo, 174
Yueh-Sui, 96, 104
Yung-Chia Chong, 55
Yun-Chwan Hsien, 47

INDEX

Yung-Chang Hsien, 46, 47, 194, 201, 202, 207
Yung-King Hsien, 93
Yung-Ning, 127, 141, 178
Yung-Peh, 147, 149, 150
Yung-Ping, 197
Yünnan Company, ix

Yünnan Fu, 103, 149, 155
Yünnan, province of, 139
Yünnan Syndicate, 65
Yün-Shan Tsin, 49
Yün-Yang Hsien, 26

Zing King, 171

THE END